The Remarkable Effect

The Essential Book for Tech-Entrepreneurs-on-a-Mission

Why your software business isn't as good as it could be, and what you can do about it

Ton Dobbe

THE CHOIR PRESS

First published in the United Kingdom in 2020 by
The Choir Press

ISBN 978-1-78963-097-8

Contents

Remarkable

adj. notably or conspicuously unusual; extraordinary. Worthy of notice or attention.

Remarkable is more than just a word. It's a vision. It's the art to create meaningful impact to prospects and customers. Being remarkable is something that I believe every company can achieve.

My Story

It was Tuesday, 11 October 2005. The world was just starting to recuperate from the effect of the bursting of the internet tech stocks bubble. Technology companies everywhere were still reeling. It was a time of survival of the fittest.

That day, I was at the Unit4 corporate HQ in Sliedrecht, the Netherlands. If you realize I grew up as the son of a tulip farmer, my desk at the ERP software company was a bit of a strange place to be. How I ended up there was the same way most of us develop our careers; I was invited by Chris Ouwinga, founder and CEO of Unit4, to run a strategic project before I had even graduated. From there I landed my first job leads, which grew into the next opportunity and the opportunity after that, and almost before I knew it, I was sitting in an office trying to solve problems that no school, university (or tulip farm) can ever really prepare you for.

I had gone from working all my spare time in the famous colored tulip and hyacinth fields in one of the flattest countries in Europe, to being globally responsible for product marketing, product management and analyst relationships for an international enterprise software firm. And I loved it.

That day, I was at my desk preparing for an analyst call. These calls could have a massive effect on the business. What well-respected analysts said about us was often much more important than what we said about ourselves. My call was with Predrag Jakovljevic from Technology Evaluation Centers (TEC), nicknamed PJ for short. He is a man who holds a great deal of power in our industry. It was my job to impress PJ with the architectural concepts of our flagship ERP solution, Agresso Business World.

I couldn't leave anything to chance. It was an important call. I was prepared when the phone rang.

One by one I ran through the areas of differentiation and talked PJ through all the important elements. I thought that the call had gone well, but I hadn't read the interaction as well as I thought ... Before we ended the call, PJ had something to share. He is a direct and honest man. Presumably that's why over half a million people care about what he has to say.

I was a little taken aback when he told me, "There's something that truly differentiates your solution, you just have a very odd way of communicating it,

Ton. You need to do some work on that. I think your product deserves to really stand out in your market but right now, it's not doing that."

I was shocked, but knew PJ was right. He goes through vendor pitches every single day and is therefore able to distinguish what resonates and what does not. And the problem is – too often people are too polite to tell you the truth. They just glaze over, and move on. Not PJ – and that's what's so valuable about him.

Luckily, I thrive on feedback and I love to take on a challenge. It's in my nature to explore the possibilities. It was clear that I had some more work to do. I was about to open up a whole new world of knowledge and applications.

PJ did me a huge favor with his honesty that day; it turned out to be a pivotal moment in my career that led to the discoveries that I'm going to share with you in this book.

He introduced me to Judith Rothrock, President of JRocket Marketing, a disruptor, innovative thinker, and mentor. She's been fundamental in turning my own thinking upside down and working out ways of seeing new perspectives. I was about to learn how to really position a company and a product. I was about to find out that it was possible to create a brand new category in what was a highly competitive and crowded marketplace (ERP software).

That one phone call turned out to be a catalyst that would teach me about hypertargeting, storytelling, and about selling and outcome rather than a product. The power of this shift helped us to stand out. We got great at hypertargeting. We got great at storytelling in a way that really resonated with business owners.

At Unit4 this enabled teams to deliver win rates of +80%. It enabled teams to increase the deal size of every order, often far above the second vendor on the shortlist.

Seeing the impact first-hand helped me to really understand how to apply the true power of product marketing and how a few small changes can make a business software company become remarkable – remarkable in the way you communicate, remarkable in the way you strategize your product, remarkable in the way you approach selling.

This book is all about helping you to make that journey from being one of the pack, to being 'the one' by having and being something truly remarkable that excites your customers.

I wrote this book to help tech-entrepreneurs-on-a-mission shape the software business they've always aspired to run: Remarkable and Impactful.

However, maybe you aren't the CEO (yet!) and are still selling products day to day with prospects, or maybe you are at the strategic helm of your company, you are looking for solutions to uniquely position the value you have to offer, or potentially you are looking for fresh product strategy perspectives to keep you stay one step ahead. If your goal is to further the business you own, run or work for, then I wrote this book for you.

This book is not about running your business, i.e. how you structure it, your processes and procedures – that's the 80% under the water. This book is about the 20% that will separate you from the rest. It's about becoming the business you always wanted to run: Remarkable and Impactful.

I believe that the key lessons I learned throughout my career to date, working with dozens of software companies, have some common threads that every business can learn from in these highly competitive and fast-moving times. Throughout this book I quote many business books. What struck me was this: Isn't it remarkable that all this knowledge is already out there and still many software businesses don't know how to adapt it? That's why I wanted to provide a simple 10-step model to apply it in such a way it becomes second nature.

The ideas and strategies in this book have been proven to be highly effective for start-ups, underdogs, established market leaders (who are often in danger of losing their edge), small companies, large companies and everything in between. There's an art and a science to being remarkable, and it hasn't got anything to do with where you are on your journey.

I have undertaken this journey many times, and I can confidently say that it's easier with a guide. Sometimes a good guide supports you. Sometimes a guide will challenge you. Sometimes a guide will be a little bit irritating because they make you uncomfortable, like a piece of sand inside an oyster.

Just remember, without a little discomfort, no pearls exist. Are you ready to take the journey to being remarkable?

Great! Let's get started.

Introduction:
The Journey Starts

It was Friday, 9 February 2018, the day before I decided to go on a trip to Nazare, Portugal to experience one of the three events in the World Surf League (WSL) Big Wave Tour.

On Thursday the news came in that 'it was on', meaning that on Saturday twenty-four of the best big wave surfers in the world would compete in this one-day event, where the forces of nature would come together to build massive waves of 35–40ft.

Surfing has always been my passion. All my life I've been fascinated by the sea. I used to live about fifteen minutes away from the sea and was an early adopter of the new sport of windsurfing in the early 1980s. I'm captivated by the power, rhythm, and the often unexpected behavior of the water. It's never the same.

That's particularly true for big wave surfing – the Champions League of all surfing. Big wave surfing separates the 'men from the boys'. It has everything that defines 'remarkable'; it's earth shaking (literally), it's full of surprises, emotion, it's about urgency (all forces join together), it's desirable (you want to be there as it's a one-of-a-kind-experience for everyone involved – contenders and spectators), and it's all about getting in the flow and exceeding expectations.

So that's where I was headed on that Friday afternoon. I'm so crazy about the sport, I was about to surrender comfort and convenience to get there. It was going to be a ten-hour journey, and I live in Spain, so if you look at a map you would think it would be an easy journey. But very few things worthwhile are an easy journey. The trip to Nazare was going to be no different.

The plan was to drive my car from my hometown of Javea to Valencia, where I'd take the train to Barcelona, get on a Ryanair flight to Porto, where I'd pick up a rental car and drive to Nazare, which is about two hours away from the airport, right in between Porto and Lisbon.

I parked my car in the city center of Valencia, walked to the train station, grabbed an espresso and waited for my train to arrive. At 17:00, the train arrived, I went through security, boarded the train, searched for my seat and sat down.

I greeted the man next to me. He was dressed like someone going on a business trip. He introduced himself: "Hi, I'm Rob. Where are you off to?"

I told him I was just starting a crazy trip to hopefully experience and see some of the biggest waves in the world. He instantly replied, "Nazare!"

I was surprised. He must be an insider, because Nazare is not a place many people know about.

"How do know?" I asked him.

"I'm from Portugal," he replied. "I live close to Nazare, as a matter of fact, and am on my way back home."

"Now I understand. So what brings you here?" I asked him.

"I run a company, a business software company, and I have been in meetings with some of our partners here in Valencia today. Since there were no direct flights back to Porto and I wanted to get back tonight, it's a train to Barca, the 9.30 p.m. Ryanair flight, and I'm home before midnight."

"That's funny – same for me. It was my only option to get to the event on time," I replied. "Tell me about your business software firm. I've been in this space for over twenty-five years myself."

That's where Rob started talking. "The business I run is creating solutions for the financial sector – for banks. We have created a digital banking platform to enable our customers to provide a digital experience for their customers."

"Interesting," I replied. "A completely new category, I assume?"

"Yes," Rob replied, "it's a category that's at the top of the hype cycle. It's booming. Every bank in the world is struggling with digital transformation, and this is a platform that enables them to do just that."

"So how's business for you?" I asked. "You must be growing rapidly, have a line-up of banks knocking on your door screaming for your help?"

"I wish that was true," Rob replied. "It's a tough world out there. The competition is fierce, solutions are overhyped, and as a relatively small player – we're only fifty people – we have to work hard to even get invited to the tender process. And once we are in, we're fighting a tough battle to win trust and, finally, the business. Then we are too small, then we are not known, then we lack this, then we lack that. Honestly, it often feels like we're in a flipper machine being thrown around and squeezed out of a deal. And it's not that we're not credible. Our solution does everything you can possibly think of – Facebook banking, watch banking, internet banking, augmented reality, video banking, you name it."

I started laughing. "Such a common story. I can tell you that you are not the only one. I see business software companies – small, midsized, large, start-ups or established – every single week. Often, companies just haven't found their identity yet, even though they don't realize it. When that happens, the prospects have to figure it out for you – and they don't want to work that hard! Therefore, you end up in the wrong deals more often than you can bare – and this is very ineffective on the utilization of your people, your commercial position in key deals, and makes it impossible to make the right choices for your business. It's the flavor of the month you are chasing. Correct?"

Rob replied: "You read my mind. That's the perfect summary of how I, no we, feel. But what can we do? We started this business coming from of a system integrator background. The product is a meltdown of all the cool things we had built for individual customers. We decided to move away from the one-to-one projects, productize what we had created and create scale to grow a software business."

"That's how many of your colleagues start," I replied. "And that's also why many fail. Let me give three simple questions to help you challenge everything you do:

1. Is what you offer valuable (not just interesting)?
2. Is it urgent (i.e. high on the priority list for your ideal customer)?
3. Are you exceeding expectations in delivering it?

"These three simple questions are critical in every step you take with your business – from the way you start it – the creation of your value proposition, the decisions you make around product strategy – all the way to how you sell."

"If any of the three questions arrives at a 'no', simply start again – challenge your approach and ensure you arrive at three times a yes in everything you do. If you do this then first, you'll stand out towards your ideal customer with regards to your value proposition; second, you'll stay fresh as a business from a product strategy perspective, resulting in an ability to drive continuous value for that same customer, and third, it will grow your ability to continue to win new business. And last but not least, you'll win more, and win bigger. But since I am going to the Big Wave event in Nazare, let me explain this by linking it to the essence of big wave surfing."

What's your big wave?

"There's something really interesting to learn from big wave surfing. As you can imagine, big wave surfing is a league of its own. The contenders in big wave surfing compete there – and nowhere else. Fact is, they made the deliberate choice that's what they want to be known for. This is their bold vision, their big idea.

"They could have played it 'easy' and choose to compete in the traditional surf competitions, but decided not to. There's a two of reasons for that:

- Big wave surfing to them is like a 'blue ocean' – it's less crowded with competitors.
- Big wave surfing is remarkable in its own right simply because of the size and the power of the wave itself, and the uniqueness of the event. It's unusual.

"So how does this relate to business? Well, these reasons are all about the art of segmentation. It's all starts with defining who your ideal customer is, and what you bring to the table to stand out and deliver unique value. It's about finding and defining your edge. It's about understanding your strengths and where they are going to be valued most."

"Yes, I understand," interrupted Rob, "but big wave surfing is not something everyone in the world can do, it's reserved for the elite, for the best athletes."

"Exactly, I hoped you would respond in this way," I replied. "That's exactly what it is – and that's why I made to point. That's why the metaphor is so strong: it forces you to define what are the big waves you can ride in your market, where you can be the elite. That starts with clarifying two things. First, your big idea about the change you want to bring to the world, and second, in relation to that, defining very specifically who the audience is that will benefit from this the most. That's your ideal customer.

"To do this you need to understand their 'why', what drives them, what do they want to achieve, and what stops them from achieving that. It's strategic segmentation at its best. It's these two forces together that build your massive wave.

"You're not delivering a generic solution to everyone in the banking world, correct?"

"Correct," Rob replied. "We have our best results with consumer banks that have to fight every single day to remain relevant for their customers in a world where the FinTechs are moving in rapidly, and top-tier banks overpower them with their brands and budgets."

"Well, that's a different league," I replied. "You know it, they know it. That's your big wave in a market full of smaller, very crowded waves. Surfers that commit to riding big waves answer exactly the same three questions as I raised earlier:

1. Is what I offer valuable (not just interesting)? Yes, their biggest fans are waiting for this – a subsegment of the market, their ideal customers.
2. Is it urgent? Yes, one moment, one location, it's about having your act together for your ideal customers when it really matters, no second chance.
3. Are you exceeding expectations in delivering it? Yes, with all the preparation you do just for this 'segment' you can be the go-to specialist, and surprise every single time.

"It all starts with the question: What's the big wave you'll surf one day, i.e. picking your big idea – your definition of what it is the world is waiting for, and then go all in. Big wave surfers commit to that – nothing else is more important. Once you are in that league, all other leagues are downgraded – i.e. you're making your competition irrelevant.

"Your big idea needs to be something highly valued, urgent, and take the best of you to exceed expectations when it's shared with the world."

The opportunity of transforming service experience

"Let me give you an example from a a CEO I recently interviewed for my weekly podcast: Ryan Falkenberg,[1] co-founder and co-CEO of CLEVVA, a business software company that's delivering solutions to improve the performance of call-centers. This in itself is a very crowded place. There are hundreds of vendors out there that automate the process of managing tickets and supporting customers to get answers to their questions.

"What CLEVVA did differently was to define their big idea and focus the execution of it towards the segment of the market that's most receptive to it: organizations that want to grow their brand value by building a more human

---

[1]   https://www.valueinspiration.com/augmenting-sales-support-experts-to-exponentially-scale-the-value-they-deliver/,

relationship with their customers. What CLEVVA realized was that many call-centers struggled with exactly that, simply because of the complexity of the solutions they offer and the regulations they have to comply with.

"As Ryan rightfully said:

> *Human beings are currently trapped in the role of robots. Human beings are not differentiators. They're actually a scale problem. In most companies, we give them flashy interfaces, but we ask them to be robots. We ask them to ask certain questions, based on certain answers. They need to do certain outcomes, based on compliance, based on rules.*

"So CLEVVA broke the pattern by asking this simple question:

> *What if we freed people from all these rules through the smart use of technology? How many people are effectively held hostage in their job because we still force them to do things they shouldn't do in the first place?*

"This anecdote from Ryan illustrates this perfectly:

> *When our executives were interviewing sales consultants at one of our customers, one sales consultant actually started to cry in the interview, and we were all sitting there. It was a bit awkward. The executives were apologizing and saying, 'We're sorry, we didn't mean to intimidate you, we're just trying to understand.' This lady stopped them and said, 'Actually, I'm not crying because I'm feeling intimidated. I'm crying because I'm feeling emotional. The reason I'm feeling emotional is because I'm a single mother. I've got two children and I actually really need this job. I've worked for your branch for the last three years and every day I come in terrified that I'm going to make a mistake that you're going to penalize me for, and I'm going to lose my job. What this does for me is it's taken the weight off my shoulders. I no longer worry that I'm going to make a mistake. I can now do what I actually love and that is serving customers because that's really what I joined your business to do. To have customer conversations that I can add value to.*

"As you see, they raised a question that was all about value creation. It was urgent as it really is about creating competitive advantage for their ideal customers in a world that's rapidly transforming. It was about creating a solution where they could exceed expectations in a crowded market of customer experience solutions. They found their big wave – and they've been riding it successfully since delivering performance improvements of over 50%."

Are you in the comfort zone, or where the magic happens?

"This brings me to a question I believe every entrepreneur should ask themselves on a regular basis, especially in the technology industry: *Are we operating in our comfort zone, or where the magic is happening?*

"CLEVVA is definitely doing the latter – not only for their customers, but also as a company. They are pushing the limits of what's possible. They haven't taken the obvious path. They've stepped back and raised the question: 'What is fundamentally broken, and how can we use the art of today's technology in a relevant way to solve it?'

"Why am I making this point? In my day-to-day work with ISV's around the world I continuously see a willingness to be 'on the cutting edge' and 'innovative', but as we know, only a few come up with truly transformative concepts and ideas. That doesn't matter – to be remarkable isn't necessarily about being transformative.

"What it is about is being different and delivering value to both prospects and customers that's worth making a remark about. That's where the magic happens – at scale. And it's exactly in this space where many business software companies neglect a big opportunity. There are three examples I regularly see – often all together in the same company:

The big idea is missing – the foundation for value creation

"Many business software companies get stuck because they either haven't defined or they have lost their identity. They are in a category, following what everyone else is doing. It's stunning to see how roadmaps of different companies feel like they developed in the same building in two different rooms with paper walls. You can almost predict what's on each page. The reason? There's nothing to challenge their status quo because there's no North Star. This immediately leads to challenge number two.

The inability to make bets – the product strategy dilemma

"Because the big idea is missing, input to the roadmap cannot be challenged accordingly. Consequently, millions and millions are invested, keeping entire companies 'busy' without making a remarkable impact to their customers and prospects.

"What I constantly see when I interview CEOs like Ryan Falkenberg is that companies that thrive have a strong ability to focus and make an orchestrated impact to do one thing right. To the contrary, companies that are in their 'comfort zone' spread their R&D budget across many different things – often stuff so small it's not even worth publishing a press-release on. And this leads me to challenge number three.

The inability to turn their idea into value – the sales performance dilemma

"Value is only created if the bridge is built from the problem to the solution. To do that is pretty simple: it's about your ability to resonate with your ideal customer. That starts by raising awareness by bringing a unique perspective on an important problem they struggle with, or even by making them aware of a problem they didn't even realize they had. From there it's all about becoming their guide by convincing them how they will improve using your solution, what they will gain from it, and what sets you apart to make you the obvious choice. Lastly, show them the path to make this a reality for them. It's about relevance – nothing else. The more relevant you appear in the eyes of your ideal customer, the bigger your success. Very often this is where a lot of value is lost because messaging is too generic, impersonal, dull, and the same as every other player in the market. Besides that, sales are not equipped to sell value, hence they fall back to selling features.

"It's this trinity of product, marketing and sales where the magic happens. Question to you Rob – what CRM system are you using?"

Rob looked surprised: "Salesforce."

"Good," I responded. "That's exactly the example I wanted to make a point about. Salesforce is one of those brands that master the art of focus to make magic happen – they've done that for almost two decades now, and clearly lead their space. One example that opened my eyes years ago was my visit to Dreamforce in the year Salesforce introduced Chatter. That was the theme, that was the push, and that was the bet they made to drive remarkable impact in that particular year. And they did.

"Two years later I was at Dreamforce again, and guess what – Mobile was the central theme, and Chatter would only be spoken about in a few conference tracks, in hotels far from the main convention center. Not that it wasn't important, not at all, but Salesforce had moved on in its marketing, sales, and product strategy.

"Where 2010 Chatter had the bulk of the R&D, marketing and sales budget, the year after, they moved it to the next big thing. Undoubtedly, the Chatter team would have had many more ideas to take things to the next level – but enough was enough. It's not about more effort, it's about following their North Star, making the right bets, and turning their ideas into value – creating yet another market shift.

"So for me the big question is: where do you want to be – in the comfort zone, or where the magic happens? And may I remind you that 'the comfort zone' is only a reference to the mindset within your company, not a state of doing easy business. Being in the comfort zone quickly results in entering the 'not so comfortable zone' of declining business, high discounts and unwanted reorganization efforts to align the bottom-line with the top line.

"I really like the way Seth Godin recently summarized this: 'It's not our lack of talent, it's our self-talk and belief that comfort is a safer path.'"

Generic is risky

Rob was quiet for a moment, visibly thinking. And then he said: "I see what your mean, and I see how it's really about my ability to make the right choices for my company. But the question that arises now is 'What if I make the wrong bets? What if I explicitly segment my ideal customers – wouldn't that make my target market too narrow?'"

"Excellent question," I replied, "and the answer is a simple 'no'. Let me explain it from two angles: who you focus on, and what you focus on.

"Let's start with 'who' you focus on. By being generic, like most, if not all your competitors, you'll resonate with nobody. You'll use a shotgun approach trying to hit anything, where in reality you'll hit nothing. By being too generic, aiming at every organization in the banking sector, with as wide as possible a solution, you'll become average in all you do – resulting exactly in the challenges you just told be about. Let's face it, if you have a good year, how many new customers could you handle?"

"Thirty to forty customers," Rob replied instantly.

"And what is the territory you're aiming at?"

"Europe, North America, and the Middle East," Rob replied.

"Well, I don't even have to guess that in this enormous territory you can find a hundred different niches that would be large enough for you to deliver double that amount, with less effort and less cost than you're experiencing today. If I may ask, what is your current win-rate?"

"No problem," Rob replied. "It's around 20 to 25%."

"So one in five or one in four at best. That's a number that I see a lot – and it's a magnifier of the issue you have at hand. Since you are 'shooting at every-body' you'll appeal to nobody. This means most deals in the sector you won't even be invited to. And if you are, you are kicked out four out of five times, simply because your prospect goes for safe – selecting the established brands that might not be as good as you, but no one has ever been fired by betting on them. Sound familiar?"

Rob nodded.

"To quote Seth Godin again, 'The riskiest thing to do is to be safe', and there-fore, by not making specific choices, by blending in what everybody else is doing, you are increasing your risk of winning nothing.

"In a podcast interview with Tim Ferris[2] he added something that's very relevant to this:

> Your problem isn't greed. Your problem isn't that you are trying for more and more and more. Your problem is fear. The fear of someone saying you're not as good as you say you are. The fear of once you've narrowed it down to the 500 people (that you are actually targeting), to be rejected by those people. That's really hurtful, because there's no one left. That's all there is. And living with that fear is the hard work of the professional. So the way we niche-it-down is by committing to want to niche-it-down. To not have false niches that are actually just excuses for reaching everyone, but to be really, really specific.

"Now let's address the issue from the other angle: 'what' you focus on.

"There's often an issue with the way business software companies define themselves. 'We are an ERP player', 'We are a CRM player', 'We are an

---

2.   https://tim.blog/2018/11/01/seth-godin-this-is-marketing/

omni-channel digital banking platform player'. And although that clarifies clearly 'what' you do, the risk is high that it will inhibit your success over time as it can direct you into a dead-end alley.

"Here's why: customers are not interested in 'what' you do, they are interested 'why' you do it. Let me give you an example. Let's assume the majority of organizations around the world are still struggling every single day to meet the rapidly evolving expectations of their customers – and in today's experience economy, that's an issue.

"Guess what? Companies in search of a solution are not interested in SAP, Oracle, or whatever vendor delivers Enterprise Resource Planning (ERP). They are interested in a solution that helps them achieve a big shift in operational excellence. They are interested in the outcome, not the output.

"However, that problem might now reside in the back office, but over time could easily shift towards the front office, from a siloed organization to the ecosystem, from the internal organization to the customers of your customers. That's exactly why defining it correctly matters.

"If you start with the big problem, i.e. clarify what fundamental change you want to deliver to your ideal customers, for example, 'excel in every aspect of your organization' and define your company around that, you could still end up delivering an ERP, a CRM, an omni-channel digital banking platform – you name it. However, it's the means to the solution. You'd be in the business of delivering a unique experience to your customers where what you do *today* makes a lot of sense. But as the market evolves – and it will – it won't handcuff you. Instead it will give you the creative freedom to innovate in different directions if that happens to deliver a larger shift in value for your ideal customers. And it won't impact your brand. Your ideal customers' perception about your brand will be around the problem you solve or the aspiration you help them become, not the product category you use to do so."

"Fascinating, I've never thought about this this way," Rob replied. "So is it as simple as defining my sweet-spot customers, and being clear about how they will transform by working with us?"

"That's a very good start – it's your foundation – but if you stop there then you're not doing yourself any favors. From here the leverage opportunity starts – here's where it gets really interesting."

The Remarkable Effect

"Now why I am I saying that? From all the work I have been doing in the business software space I have identified a pattern of what defines a remarkable software company across three distinct layers. And within those layers there are ten traits that, by stacking them up behind each other, will not only help you stand out in your category, but also create clear leverage of value; that is exponential value, not just incremental."

"Tell me," Rob answered with a smile.

That's when we were interrupted by the service team of the train. Coffee service. Being a coffee fan, I couldn't resist getting a café solo. Rob copied me on that.

"So where did we leave off? Ah, yes, the ten traits of a remarkable software company. Let's review them quickly:

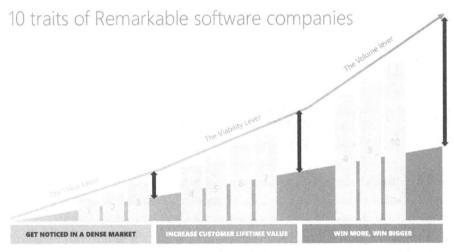

10 traits of Remarkable software companies

"If I look at the ten traits, they stack up in three core groups. These are your levers to become a remarkable business software company:

1 – The Value Lever: get noticed in a dense market

Within this first step three traits are fundamental:

1. **They realize they can't please everyone.** Remarkable software companies know they're not for everyone. They understand there will always be naysayers, and that's fine.
2. **They offer something valuable and desirable.** They focus on valuable problems, not just the interesting ones. They also don't jump on new technologies for the sake of the latest technology, but instead apply them in a way that transforms, not just improves how we work.
3. **They strive to be different; not just better.** They are the businesses you hear about and cannot get out of your mind. They stand out from the pack, even if they are in a highly commoditized segment of the market.

2 – The Viability Lever – increase customer life-time value

4. **They master the art of curiosity.** They never lose their sense of why they got started in the first place. This defines their 'why', their North Star. This helps to stay curious, and avoid complacency.
5. **They create new value possibilities.** They take things further, they're aim is to always be one step ahead. Challenge the status quo. They don't simply improve inefficiencies, they remove them and instead create new opportunities.
6. **They create fans, not just customers.** Remarkable software companies understand the art of meeting their customers at their point of the journey and work with them to solve significant challenges and achieve their lofty ambitions.
7. **They focus on the essence.** They make their bets, and challenge everything that doesn't move the needle. With that they become extremely resourceful.

3 – The Volume Lever: win more, win bigger

In this last step three traits are fundamental

8. **They create momentum.** They create customers wanting more. They are not just lucky once but design their success to build momentum and exceed expectations in every step of their customers' journey.
9. **They sell the idea, not the product.** They understand the art of inviting their customers into their story. They understand their business is about solving customer challenges in achieving new ambitions.
10. **They surprise and hit the right nerve.** They understand buyers purchase based on emotions first, and logic second. They don't buy 1,000 transactions per second; they buy 'confidence'. They don't buy a streamlined sales process; they buy 'advantage'.

"All of this results in them receiving value because they provide value. Remarkable software companies take an outside-in approach, focusing on customer value first. They don't have to explain why a customer needs their product, their customers already get that and is prepared to pay a premium.

"These are not just ten traits. They are used by remarkable software businesses as an infinite loop, not a one-off linear process. It's routine, a habit if you want, part of their business DNA to help them challenge the status quo and ensure they keep improving on all levers all the time. They create the forces, the ground swell if you like, that build the massive wave behind you. They build on each other like dominos, and by doing so they create leverage in terms of their impact on customers and impact on your business in terms of both top and bottom line"

"Fascinating," Rob replied. "I can't wait to hear more! So how do I start?"

At that point the train stopped. We had arrived at the Castellón train station. People around us started moving, and new passengers entered the train compartment we were sitting in. I saw Rob's eyes were staring, looking out of the train window without visibly looking at something. You could see the entrepreneur waking up inside of him – dreaming about what could be for his company.

After five minutes the train started moving again.

Part 1

The Value Lever: get noticed in a dense market

Trait 1
You can't please everyone

What business are you really in?

"How do you start? Great question. Let's take the analogy of big wave surfing again. Imagine you were such a surfer and you could choose one spot in the world to show what you're worth. One location – one shot. What would you do? Well, given the importance to get it right, given the disastrous results of failure, i.e. a wipeout, and given the fact you have to still beat a range of other big wave contenders, you'd probably make an assessment of where you'd have the highest chance of winning hands-down. Where would your competence and strengths come to fruition best – is it Peahi, Hawaii? The nerve-wrecking reef-break of Teahupoo, Tahiti, or the 'box' at Margaret Rivers, Australia? Or the largest wave in the world at Nazare, Portugal?

"What you're doing is smart segmentation – so in 'the market of big waves' you're making a sub-selection where local conditions, special requirements and your unique skills blend towards the ideal cocktail to win. Knowing where your powers come to bear best is half the work. So, taking this back to business – why wouldn't you do the same there?

"To answer your question 'How do I start?' – it all starts with this simple question: what business are you really in? Tell me, how would you respond?"

Rob instantly replied: "We're in the business of automating the omni-channel communication of banks with their customers."

"Exactly what I expected you would say," I responded. "It's the way 90% of business software companies would respond. The challenge here is that you respond with 'what' you do, not 'why' you do it. Let me ask you a different question: what is the biggest challenge banks have to cope with these days?"

Rob pondered the question. "It's the challenge of keeping up with the raised expectations of their customers around how to do business with them. Expectations around speed of answering questions, convenience of getting basic things done, like opening new accounts, making payments, making enquiries. Helping their customers to better understand their financial position and what this means."

"Now why is that important?" I asked.

"Well," Rob started, "if they don't meet those expectations their customer churn will go up. It's easier than ever for a customer to switch banks. Loyalty is typically low, and the alternatives are plenty."

"Understood, and is this a challenge every bank has?" I questioned back.

"One bank more than the other. At the end size and budget matters. Large tier 1 banks have the budgets and resources to address this with more force than tier 2 or even tier 3 banks," Rob answered.

"And who do you believe you add more value to?"

"It's tier 2 and 3 banks, simply because we can bring in a solution at a fraction of the cost and effort compared to our competitors in the market."

"So the real business you are in is enabling 2-tier banks to help their customers to be one step ahead at a fraction of the cost," I concluded.

Rob went quiet. "Gosh! Yes, that sums it up perfectly."

"So do you see the difference?" I replied. "Here's where you lead with your 'why'. Just compare the two responses:

"'We're in the business of automating the omni-channel communication of banks with their customers'" versus this one "'We're in the business of enabling 2-tier banks to help their customers to be one step ahead at a fraction of the cost'.

"If you were a prospect, which vendor would you call?

"Let's analyze this approach with the three fundamental questions I told you about when we left Valencia:

1. Is it valuable? Yes it is! It's about the life-blood of your ideal customers.
2. Is it urgent? Absolutely! It's a matter of survival, if they don't act now, their competitors will. Case closed.
3. Are you exceeding expectations in delivering it? Yes you are! In the eyes of 2-tier banks you absolutely are. Unlike tier 1 banks they don't have the budget, resources and time to address this issue. Hence what you offer is beyond what they could ask for.

Rob interrupted me there. "You just opened my eyes. But what frustrates me is how on earth is it possible we didn't come up with this? This is so obvious – and so simple."

"Agreed," I replied. "It's the problem of being too close to the problem. You get solution blind. Happens to the best. We love to talk about ourselves – how big we are, the products we offer, the number of clients we have, the growth we are enjoying – it's all about us. So when we or any of our colleagues get asked the question, what do you do? We answer the way we do – and the conversation is dead.

"As you have seen, a very simple way to get this right is to start with the 'beginning' or the 'end'. It's simple: we're not in the business of selling a product – we're in the business of solving a problem and/or creating a desired state, i.e. a desirable outcome.

"If you start this way you create a hook – you get people to pay attention and to think 'is this for me or not.' It qualifies them in our out. That's what you want for your business – not only in Marketing and Sales. The sooner your prospect decides 'not for me' the less time you both waste on something that wasn't mean to be in the first place. The opposite is very true as well: The sooner he/she decides 'That's what I need!', the higher you'll rank on their 'want' list.

"So not having this clarity at the very core of your business will be the prime reason challenges start to grow. Because you start wrong, i.e. you're not clear, everything that follows from that point onwards – your product strategy decisions, your go to market approach, your sales approach – suffers from this unclarity.

"A way to get around this it to always take the outside-in approach. Simply ask your customers the very basic question: 'Why would you recommend us to your peers? What's the single word that sticks in your mind when you'd sum up the value we offer you?' Works 99% of the time – and if you are not happy yet, just keep asking 'why' till you get to the essence.

"One thing I can assure you is that it won't be about any feature you offer them. It will be about an aspiration you'll help them accomplish, something you take away that they fear or dislike, or a feeling of accomplishment, safety or convenience you give them."

What are the common pitfalls?

Rob smiled. "It sounds so simple – almost too simple to be true. There must be a trick here. Does this always work like this? Or are there more things to take into account?"

"Good question!" I replied. "And you are right, there are absolutely additional aspects to take into account that will determine the size of your success. Have you ever heard about Geoffrey Moore's book *Crossing the Chasm*?"

Rob looked at me and reacted: "Of course I have. Hasn't every tech entrepreneur?"

"You'd be amazed," I responded. "But that's a different discussion. A valuable lesson to learn is what I call Buyer Mindset. Geoffrey's book goes into full detail on this – but as you know, you can identify five different flavors: Innovators, Early Adopters, Early Majority, Late Majority and finally Laggards.

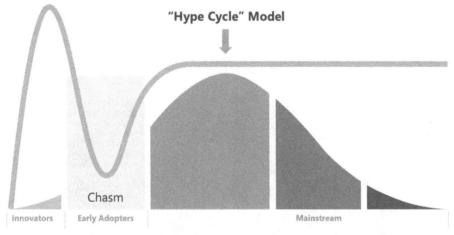

"It's the mindset of your ideal customer that's key to how you segment your market and who you aim your R&D, Marketing and Sales at. Many business software companies are not clear about that, and hence they end up confusing their buyers big time.

"Here's why it is so important. In every project I execute with my customers the three levers I just discussed become the center of focus of everything we do – whether it's crafting their value proposition, their product strategy or a pitch for a strategic prospect. Irrespective of the problem to solve, it's your ability to match the mindset of your ideal customer that determines whether your approach is successful or not.

"Here's why: Let's take a common problem that many organizations are struggling with: 'The inability to spot operational risk fast enough'."

Rob instantly reacted. "Big one for my customers – so excellent example."

I smiled. "Yes, this is a problem many vendors could offer a solution for, indeed. However, who wins is virtually always determined by how well a vendor can tune its actions to create a perfect blend to match its ideal customers' needs. It's where the trinity of Product Strategy, Marketing and Sales become a force – but more on that later.

"As you can imagine, mindset is a very big influencing factor – possibly the biggest. It's about what your ideal prospect is aiming for. Each organization might struggle with the common problem mentioned above, but the way they react and prioritize to it is heavily influenced by the mindset they have.

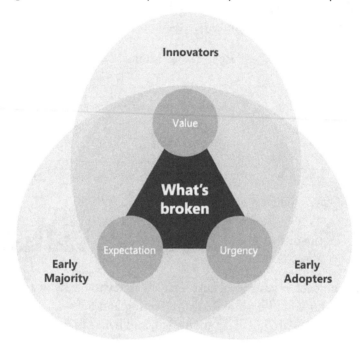

"An Innovator will judge your solution radically different than an organization that you'd categorize in the Early Majority group. Innovators are always on the lookout for something new; they are happy to take risks, it's part of who they are /who they want to be.

"Early Majority, however, are the opposite. They buy the cheapest, the safest, the lowest risk. They don't want to be first. They don't even want to be second.

What they invest in doesn't need to stand out, it just needs to do as promised. No more, no less. A segmentation challenge more than anything else.

"Many business software vendors think they are addressing innovators with their latest SaaS, big data, or mobile solution, but in essence, they are automating a problem that's been well solved for over a decade.

"It all comes back to the three questions we've discussed before:

1. Is it valuable?
2. Is it urgent?
3. Can you exceed expectations?

"The answers to this vary extremely between the five buyer mindsets, and, as such, the success you will have if you get it right. Let me illustrate this with another example around urgency. Urgency drives sales. If you can create tension between your prospects problem, your solution, and the fact that doing nothing is not an option, you've almost won. It's positioning at its best.

"That also provides the challenge. As you can imagine, an Innovator has a different vision of the world, different objectives to achieve it, and as such has a different concept of urgency. For them having your solution might give them an edge over their competition because now they can break the norm in their industry. That drives urgency behind the sale.

"The Early Majority, however, couldn't be bothered less. Their sense of urgency is not angled around creating competitive advantage; it's about avoiding waste and saving cost, being more efficient. It requires a different approach from you to stand out in their eyes.

"The same applies to question three: Expectation. Expectations always evolve and are very much influenced by what we believe is the norm of what 'good' looks like. Again, Innovators have different norms than the Early Majority – so one size fits all won't work. You have to be very articulate in who's your ideal customer, to the level where you can actually see that customer and in particular the key individuals that you serve as real people. Only then can you tune your solution to exceed the expectations of your ideal customer and gain an advantage over your competitors.

"But let me give you a real-life example from an interview I did with Timothy Willis,[1] Chief Operating Officer at Aerobotics, an AI company that's transforming the impact farmers can make in growing their yield."

The art of segmentation – a real-life example

"Let me shine the light a bit more on them. Aerobotics is a start-up from South Africa, a country with an enormous heritage in wine, but probably lesser known is the fact lots of farms specialize in citrus as well. It's the perfect climate to grow these fruits. However, it's not all sunshine. This is what Timothy shared with me:

Farmers have a real struggle in terms of managing their overall farm. You're looking at farms that are hundreds of hectares big, and some farmers can't get through their entire farm in three days. If they don't have technology, they have to basically walk around or drive around their farm trying to identify areas that could be potentially mismanaged, and employ large scouting teams to work in their farm.

If you look at the overall picture in the world, obviously food's going to be a scare resource, so we need even bigger farms, hence the inefficiency problem, and all the risks that come with missing critical early warnings will just grow.

"So this is the problem Aerobotics is addressing – it is both valuable and urgent to solve it. But Tim added some more to that:

Aerobotics effectively takes aerial images of mainly agricultural areas. We collect those images using drones and satellites and potentially even aeroplanes. With our technology, they're able to basically manage their farm from their office.

---

[1] https://www.valueinspiration.com/how-ai-is-intelligently-augmenting-farmers-to-expo-nentially-grow-yields-and-efficiency/

Now that's not all. The big idea behind our company is to predict what the yield of a specific farm will be based on our images. If we can do that, then we have a lot of forward-looking information which is extremely useful, not only to farmers, but also to people down the value chain.

"Can you see where this is going, Rob? The value is in thinking in outcomes, not in outputs. Aerobotics started around the idea that 'it was cool to fly a drone over a farm', but realized quickly that without the software to actually use, it was going to be difficult to commercialize.

"In other words, they started with the 'What', i.e. a more efficient way to spot yield issues via a photo taken by a drone, and realized it was answering the 'Why' question, i.e. the 'Value' question that would lead them to create remarkable impact, i.e. predict yield and help increase yield quality.

"This takes their value towards farmers from 10% impact to potentially ten times the impact – and more importantly, it gave them a by-product with which they – in the near future – can tap into other markets as well: providing qualitative insights to the retail-sector to help them anticipate issues in their supply chain planning weeks, if not months in advance, or providing key data to Insurance companies to help them create new disruptive business models to charge farmers based on adjusted risk-profiles, etc.

"What struck me was what came next in our interview – which is all about strategic segmentation; in other words, their acknowledgment that they can't please everyone. Timothy said this:

We made a strategic decision to focus specifically on tree crops. Although our software is useful for field crops, which is things like corn and wheat and sugarcane, we have taken a specific focus to really try and hone in specifically on tree crops: for example citrus, macadamia nuts, grapes, etcetera.

If I give you some overall stats, in the world there's about 1.35 billion harvested hectares every year. Of that, only 125 million of those hectares are actually tree crops. A lot of people who come into the space go for the 90 percent, which is field crops. However, there are very few providers in the tree crop space.

We've strategically chosen to play in that space, given that there's not a lot of people in this, it's an undeserved market and something that we can do exceptionally well. A combination of us being exceptional at it and, I suppose, a low competition in that particular space of the market really has allowed us to excel: we're growing 50% per quarter on average and revenues are up 4x from last year."

What you lose with too generic segmentation

"The hyper focus from Aerobotics brings me to something else. My experience tells me segmentation is a poorly understood topic, and as such an area where enormous value is lost and wasted. Most organizations think segmentation stops by identifying sector and size. I mean, go to any of your competitors' websites and you'll see they talk about 'mid-sized and large financial services organizations'. And obviously that's true, but it's both too generic, and too narrow. Besides that, it's very much the view of the vendor, rather than the customer. It's an inside-out perspective, something Aerobotics corrected in a timely matter, as you have seen.

"If you use segmentation as a strategic instrument, you can immediately hook your ideal customer by addressing them in a relevant way. Too often what they are looking for has very little to do with their size, and more with their mindset, goals and ambitions. You could possibly add more value to a small bank with a growth mindset, than a midsized bank with laggards mindset – just to give an example."

The power of micro-segmentation

"Now that I think of it, another form of 'micro-segmentation' is to hone in on a particular challenge that's common across many different organizations. Visualize it as a narrow band across different vertical markets. When I was still at Unit4 that's exactly the repositioning we did back in 2005 – we transitioned from software vendor that created ERP software for service intensive industries such as Professional Services, Not for Profit, Government and Education, to one that focused organizations within those verticals that were either driving or driven by radical business change, i.e. Businesses Living IN Change or short BLINC.

"I remember very well working on this project with Judith Rothrock of JRocket Marketing, the external consultant recommended to me by PJ from TEC. In was spring 2006 when she unfolded her findings and her recommended BLINC (Businesses Living IN Change) segmentation strategy and marketing plan for UNIT4 in our Victoria, BC office. This was an eye-opening moment that told me so much about the power of strategic segmentation. Long story short, when she did her well-proven marketing positioning exercise that includes talking to customers and partners, she kept hearing two conflicting things:

1. 'We like Agresso; however, we wished it was more out of the box. There are too many choices and it's too difficult'; and
2. 'We love Agresso, it's so flexible, we can do anything with it.'

"Same product, customers in the same segment of the market, two radically different reactions. We were informed where to focus, on which buyer, and given new messaging that would resonate with this better targeted group. From there win rates went up, deal value went up, and we made the life of a number of global ERP competitors pretty miserable."

Rob smiled and then said: "It's both odd and fascinating to see how sometimes things are right in your face, and you simply can't see the wood for the trees. I mean, you'd been working with these customers for years, they actually all bought your solution, so you did something pretty right, but still there was so much room for improvement!"

"Agreed," I responded. "That's exactly the case. You get blind to these type of signals, to the point where you start digging in and asking the right questions. Too often we're so busy that we don't allow ourselves the time to do this. We know very well 'what' we offer, and 'who' needs what. We don't pay attention to the question 'why' do they need it. And that's where you can reveal very interesting insight, that can fundamentally change the value proposition of your solution.

"In the case of Unit4 the idea was always 'We're selling an ERP to give you control over your business and financial situation'. All true, and customers bought it for that reason. However, a significant group bought with an extra motivation. They saw value in the architectural concepts that allowed them to address any level of business change in house, with a small group of business people, not IT people. This, for them, was essential to underpin their growth strategies and ambitions.

"As you can imagine, that's a totally different value proposition. Segmenting the market that way enabled us to make a lot of competitors irrelevant. And in the hands of the right sales people they'd be able to win four out of five leads, at list price, or higher. Often they'd win at twice the price of the second contender, who could match functional needs, but not live up to the business dynamics requirements of the prospect."

Rob nodded. "Very strong point. Worth doing some deep thinking on when I get together with my management team next week, and absolutely worth starting a strategic project around."

"Wise thinking! And now that you mention 'project' – this reminds me of another example," I continued. "John Heinz,[2] CEO of Aptage, an AI-powered start-up from Austin, Texas, also embarked on a micro-niche that's in essence sector independent. What they developed is a 'Project Manager Coach', an AI companion for project managers that's there with the single purpose to help them boost project success.

"When I asked him about the purpose of his business, he replied:

> 'We want to build software and products that help people work with more confidence, less drama, and no regret.'

"There's a lot of value in this. I think you and I both know from our own experience that we have all relied for too long on project management systems that gave us structure and helped us to work more process oriented. However, the choices we make on a day-to-day basis are, even today, most of the time based on 'gut-feeling', simply because we're creating things for the first time. Correct?"

"Agreed," Rob replied with a smile. "I could write a book about that."

"I can imagine," I copied. "Well, here's where it gets interesting. When I asked John about the solution to this, he rightly said:

> There's the old saying that if you have to deliver bad news, deliver it as soon as possible. And this is where Aptage really comes in – it's all about making a really old process smart by injecting the right technology to augment project managers with intelligent guidance. This gives them more confidence to deal with the now visible uncertainties and be able to make informed decisions way earlier. This avoids the 'drama' of bad news delivered too late. The result: more successful projects, more happy customers and teams, and higher margins.

---

[2]   https://www.valueinspiration.com/687-2/

"So, as you see, their focus is extremely narrow: projects/project managers, but since they go deep, rather than wide, they are highly relevant to this audience because they deliver remarkable impact. The problem they solve is universal though. It's not isolated to just management consultants, or engineers, or construction, or IT.

"Think about how much money is wasted on a day-to-day basis and across different industries, because we tend to be at ease that projects fail, overrun on budget, miss milestones, etc. We simply calculate with it. What would it mean for every project if intensive organization could increase that project's success rate by 10%, or even 1%?

"Think about the upside – that the 'OK is good enough' mantra could now turn towards a mantra that's about 'always going the extra mile to deliver a true experience – because we now we can'.

"Think about the competitive advantage this would create for a company or organization and the impact this could have on every one of us.

"Think about how much more value for money project intensive organizations could achieve. The economic outcome of that is significant – both for the service provider, it's customer, and even the customers' customers.

"So the valuable story to learn from this is that by micro-segmenting you can fundamentally lift the perceived value of your solution. You can address the market in a very specific way, targeting the exact problem that's highly valuable to solve. When you show your solution, you'll exceed the expectations of your ideal customer, and with that you have an ideal position to change perspectives. So if 'increasing project success rates' (or name your solution area) wasn't a high priority because of complacency or ignorance that this could be possible in the first place, it now becomes a high priority, because of the value it can unlock."

Here's where Rob interrupted me. "So let me rephrase to see if I get this right: you say that I should forget about the sector/size segmentation, and instead go one level deeper and articulate specific characteristics?"

"Correct," I replied. "Possibly even more levels – the more specific you get, the more likely you are to attract your ideal customer. Simply peel the onion till you get to the core of what your ideal customers are all about. We both know that a large range of banks around the world would never buy your solution – and for good reasons. And I bet you can identify customers that should never have bought your solution as well, because no matter how hard you try, they'd probably never be very happy with it. Correct?"

You could see the hesitation in Rob's eyes. "I guess you are right – now that I think about it, there's at least a handful that pop up."

"Exactly," I replied. "That's the waste I am talking about. And the implications are broader than you think. Let me illustrate this with three examples."

Change isn't happening

"The first issue that arises with poor segmentation is that the change you aim to make with your solution isn't happening. So we're all missing out on something big. That said, I know many vendors that have a brilliant idea behind their solution, giving them a solid competitive advantage, but because it's not coming across in the right way to the right customers, the impact gets lost in translation. I have actually seen that first-hand with the Enterprise Resource Planning (ERP) solutions I managed myself. Before 2005, we sold the features of the ERP but ignored selling the dream, the vision. Consequently, we didn't resonate with the C-suite and were downgraded to sell at the user level, selling a commodity, at a commodity price. Changing the market segmentation turned this model on its head. The rest is history. Same solution – different playing field – different impact."

Creating momentum is harder

"The second issue you could identify is that creating momentum is a more significant challenge because your marketing and salesforce are challenged persuading prospects and influencers of your point of view. This extra effort means you need a larger budget, to find more 'leads', to make up for a high loss rate. It's a simple calculation. If you sell your solution at an average of 100,000 (list price minus 60% discount) in a crowded commodity market, you need 500 leads to sell 10,000,000 in revenue, just because you are closing one in five at best (20% win-rate). Correct?"

"Yep," Rob replied.

"What if you'd sell at list price (250,000) because the value you communicate makes it a bargain, and because of this value you start winning four in five (80%). This difference means you suddenly only need fifty leads (to win forty). Factor ten difference. Easier on your marketing budget, more comfortable on your sales organization (and much more fun) – and very likely a model, where each of your customers brings you the next one because they become your biggest fan."

Bottom-line impact

"And lastly, issue number three, which is actually a consequence of the first two: your bottom line is impacted harder because you're forced to give more discount than necessary. Besides that, your sales pipeline is less reliable because of the extreme competitive pressure that makes it a roulette game. As such you're fighting a race to the bottom. No one can keep up with that for long.

"The example above I have experienced myself. It often felt like a cattle market, especially at the quarter end. Now, in the old days, where solutions where deployed on-premise, and we sold a one-off license, discounting that was still a choice, but in today's SaaS world, it's not. A 60% discount in the world of licenses would always give you a contribution to company results, a 60% discount on a subscription price often ends up in a loss forever. So the problem has just become more significant and more urgent to fix."

This got Rob thinking. "I never looked at this in the way you just described. We're so busy getting the leads in via our digital campaigns and via the numerous FinTech conferences we attend that we never challenge what's arriving on our desk. We just go after everything that moves and is called a bank. And I must say, we've had some interesting discussions already with our investors on the topic of profitability . . .

"I realize now that we can't please everyone – we shouldn't even dare to try. By focusing on less, we'll get more. That offers a lot of perspective!"

"Spot on!" I replied. "Just take this golden rule from Kevin Kelly[3] to hand: 'If you can gain one true fan, you can gain a hundred and then a thousand.'"

At that moment the train slowed down. We looked at each other. "Tarragona already? Surely not." The train speaker then explained the sudden stop. There was a technical issue with the control system on the next track so we had to stop for a few minutes. A good moment to walk together to the restaurant car to get a drink.

[3.] https://kk.org/thetechnium/1000-true-fans/

Ask yourself

STEP 1: Reflect critically how you score your own ability around this particular trait by rating your organization on a scale of 1 (poor) to 10 (remarkable).

How clear are you on 'who you are for', and 'who you are not for?' (i.e. How easy is it for the market to qualify themselves and say: 'That's for me!' or 'That's not for me'?)

0 |————————————————————————————————| 10

What's your ability to attract an audience that's prepared to pay a premium?

0 |————————————————————————————————| 10

What's your current average win-rate?

0% |————————————————————————————————| 100%

STEP 2: Take ten minutes to reflect on the next actions you could initiate to improve your score.

STEP 3: What's the single action from this list that would give you the biggest impact?

Take it to the next level

- Not only become remarkable, but ensure you'll stay remarkable as well by introducing the 'Remarkable Monday' habit within your organization. Download the three simple steps that will help you create and keep momentum: https://valueinspiration.com/RemarkableMonday
- Join the Remarkable Tribe Program to create accountability with other tech-entrepreneurs like you. Not only will you build traction to shape the business you aspire to be, but you will also obtain new ideas, create new contacts, and will be part of a movement that defines what it means to be remarkable as a business software vendor: https://movement.valueinspiration.com

Trait 2
Offer something valuable and desirable

'For them' and 'not for them'

As we arrived in the restaurant car I asked, "So, what can I order for you?" Rob smiled and replied, "It's 5 p.m. in Portugal, so let's go for a Chardonnay." I copied his idea, ordering two glasses of Chardonnay.

We sat down in the restaurant car, enjoying the view. The train at this point follows the coastline, so we had a fantastic view over the sea, and some secluded beaches surrounded by large rocks.

"Tomorrow will be a different view," Rob started. "The Mediterranean Sea is so different from the Atlantic Ocean – you'll see how in about twelve hours."

I smiled as a I stared out of the window, enjoying a sip of my Chardonnay. "Yes, it's been something I've longed to see – and within twelve hours it's going to be a reality. A strong groundswell building monster waves 10–12 meters tall, with the best of the best watermen surfing them. Can't wait!"

Rob looked at me. "I can see your eyes twinkle," he said.

"You are right," I responded. "There's something about that sport that hooks me. Something that makes me go above and beyond to be part of it. Look at me. Yesterday I decided to drop everything I was doing, buy last-minute tickets and throw away my rule that the only good flight is a direct flight. Instead I now take a detour of eight hours, just to be part of the experience."

"This is what happens to people when you have something valuable and desirable to offer – whether that's in your private life or in business. Do you see how powerful that is?

"Once you have carved out the segment that clearly identifies your ideal customer, that's where the next exercise start: identifying your 'why', i.e. spell out what's broken in the world of your ideal customer so that, if you can solve it, they'd be first to buy it from you.

"Remarkable software companies understand this like no one else – that's why I positioned it as their number two trait. And now that I think of it, there's a valuable lesson to learn from big wave surfing.

"As I told you earlier, it all starts with segmentation – and in big wave surfing that's about defining the exact spot/condition/location where your competence and strengths come to fruition best. But that's not enough. Here's why: imagine you are now are at that spot, the enormous waves are there. However, you'll realize soon that big waves by themselves are not enough. At some point even a 12-meter wave gets boring.

"So, let's look at what happens. Big waves come in sets, a new set is arriving, the athletes in the water are scanning the horizon, you see them paddling to the left, something is about to happen. You see the nervousness in the line-up, and suddenly one surfer starts paddling rapidly. A huge wave is rapidly building up behind him, 8 meters, 9 meters, 10 meters, 12 meters, and right before it's about to break, right in that spot, the surfer stands up and commits. The drop is frightening, almost vertical going down, the lip of the wave is crawling over the surfer, he's now inside the 12-meter monster, it seems to last forever, and then he's 'spit out' and scores a 10-point ride.

"It's exactly that moment where the monster wave meets the surfer, delivering the perfect ride. That's the moment everyone wants to see – that's what makes them surrender everything they are doing – that's what makes them travel twelve hours. It's something they value being a part of – it's a desire they are prepared to pay a premium for.

"This is what I call the art of positioning. True winners know exactly which wave to pick in a set, and where to position themselves in the water to actually have the perfect take-off point. They have the patience to decide to wait for 'that single' wave – leaving many smaller/lesser waves for their competition. Because they know that wave will give them the perfect score, they therefore decide to not waste their energy on mediocre opportunities."

Rob smiled. "The way you talk about it makes me want to be there. It makes the point so clear. I mean, I have learned about segmentation and positioning when I was still in High School. But then you forget, and you just do what feels OK. And I realize oh so well now that the segmentation we have used so far isn't of any help to us, nor the positioning of our product either."

I watched Rob reflect on his business and draw his own conclusions. "The fact you are taking a 30,000ft view on your business and are reflecting upon what's really going on is the first step required to become a remarkable business. It reminds me of something I'd experienced first-hand a good decade ago.

"I was presenting at 'Out of Chaos' in Rotterdam, back in 2006. My dear colleague and friend Roel Caers sat in the back of the room and during my twenty-minute presentation something magical was revealed to him: As I was speaking he realized that 50% of the audience was 'all in', while the other 50% had opted out. The result was a direct engagement with 50% of the audience – which appeared to be organizations right into the sweet-spot of our products differentiation.

"What happened during that presentation is what I'd call 'the power of instant qualification'. And although it might sound weird, the good thing was that 50% qualified out – all by themselves.

"Now why is that good? As Seth Godin[1] says:

> It doesn't matter if your solution is 'not for them'. You want to spend your time with prospects and customers that become your fans, and then help you spread the word. If it's 'not for them' you will never achieve that, and end up with a frustrating, often non-profitable, relationship.

"So the art of positioning is all about qualifying the wrong prospects out ... FAST.

"Roel shared his experience right after the presentation, insisted I send him my presentation, which he then made his default pitch directly after, resulting in transformative results for the business he led."

It's not about your company – it's about their company

Rob sipped his Chardonnay while watching out of the window as we passed a small characteristic Spanish seaside village. "This is more fundamental than I thought it would be," he said.

---

[1]   https://www.amazon.com/This-Marketing-Cant-Until-Learn/dp/0525540830

"Spot on," I replied. "I call it your value foundation. Without this foundation everything else goes 'off course'. It's like walking in the desert without a compass. I know over 500 business software companies, and every single one of them offers a solution to the market in one shape or another. However, many companies do so without understanding or clarifying why they do it. There's no purpose, no vision, no North Star. These companies have either forgotten or never really defined their purpose, and many of them see limited or no success as a result.

"It all starts with challenging the status quo. A very simple trick to do that is if you critically review the product positioning of your flagship solution with the point of view of your ideal target customer. If you do that, what do you conclude? What score would you give yourself for being Valuable and Desirable?

"Even easier. Just turn it around – if you were a bank looking for a new solution, what element in your messaging would trigger you instantly to call for an appointment?

"What you sell is not a product; you're selling an outcome, a change. You're helping banks to transform from 'something' to 'something more desirable'. So that's what you need to be very clear about. You have to describe the change you will deliver to your potential customers. Explain what will be the transformation they'll notice, and why that matters. If you are offering a replacement for what they have today, they won't move just because you say so. The saying is: if it ain't broken, don't fix it. So you have to bring something that's irresistible."

Rob nodded. "I realize now that my team and I run a pretty interesting business, we know all the ins and outs; we also know how our products and services benefit the lives of our customers. We've seen that first-hand by working with them. However, just because we are intimately in tune with these benefits doesn't mean our customers will understand them. That's where our dilemma starts."

"The fact you just realized that is a massive step in the right direction, Rob," I replied. "It's that realization that helps you to make tangible steps forward. Here's where a range of tools are available to help convince people to buy what you offer. It might sound like an open door, but the first 'tool' you should focus on is the creation of your value proposition."

"Many people misinterpret this. They use it the wrong way, and hence it falls flat. Let me explain the essence: A value proposition is a summary of the value your service or product will deliver to customers once they choose to buy from you. Your value proposition should summarize the benefits you offer, the problems you solve, and the things that differentiate you from your competitors/alternative offerings.

"When your potential customers read your value proposition, they should instantly understand why it's worth spending their money on what you're offering; how you help them achieve their ambitions or create remarkable impact; how you'll solve their problems; how you'll add to their lives and how they can experience something that no other business software company or product can give them.

"It's not about your company – it's about their company. Your value proposition explains what your customers need and want, and it is an important psychological device not only for getting leads to pick you over competitors/alternative offerings, but also for convincing them to actually spend their money, i.e. it's about creating desire.

"High performance coach Brendon Burchard[2] put it like this:

> *If people would spend the same time on thinking how they can make a difference as they do on how they can make money, they would truly have wealth beyond their imagination.*

"Just think about that. Done well, value propositions help companies increase sales. In fact, a study showed that value propositions can increase conversions[3] up to 90%. As you can imagine, that's huge. It can help make the difference between financial success and failure. In addition to increasing conversions, value propositions help you build a niche for your particular business software company brand and strengthen your reputation.

"Finally, you don't just create value propositions to just benefit potential customers. You also use them to help your organization internally. Value propositions are clear, easy-to-understand and easy-to-reference statements that your team can look at to familiarize themselves with your company's mission and unique offerings. This can help shape a strong organizational culture and make everyone feel like they're working together toward a common goal.

[2.] https://itunes.apple.com/es/podcast/004-how-to-go-viral-on-multiple-social-media-platforms/id910990031?i=1000317947964&l=en&mt=2

[3.] https://www.slideshare.net/invesp/how-one-company-increased-conversions-20-through-better-value-proposition

"So, I hope you can see that this becomes your foundation for everything. It's the most critical jumping-off point to explain the reasons why clients should consider creating a long-term professional connection with your organization. It serves the impact of your marketing as it underpins all your messaging – from your company website to your campaigns, blogs and social media approach. It serves the impact of your product strategy as it helps product management and development to constantly raise the bar with regards to strengthening the unique value you offer. And it serves your sales approach – how you qualify – and how you ultimately win more business, and higher value business."

"I hadn't realized how far reaching this part is to the success of my business. So thanks for taking the blind-shields off!" Rob replied. I laughed.

He continued: "But now the big question – how do I get it 100% right? I assume there are many pitfalls that I should avoid?"

"Good point," I answered. "There are a hundred ways to get it right, and a hundred ways to get it wrong. I recently conducted a review of messaging in a commodity market like Enterprise Resource Planning (ERP), but also assessed the messaging strength of vendors in a market that's at the top of its hype-cycle – BlockChain Development Platforms. I guess the latter represents a similar dynamic as the market you are in, correct?"

"Agreed," Rob replied.

"The issues I revealed fall into four categories:

1) It's all very predictable

"What I found while researching the messaging of ERP vendors is that most vendors seems to be focusing their value around old, generic principles. Principles that haven't changed over the past twenty years and include ideas like increased efficiency, better user experience, easier implementation, improved compliance, enhanced insight and TCO. To a potential buyer these 'benefits' don't do anything. They're almost like table stakes. It doesn't resonate – hence there's no action.

2) It tries to be impressive

"A very odd habit software vendors have is, when they are not secure about the real difference they make, they try to be impressive with jargon and superlatives, i.e. 'big words'. You know what I mean: 'We're leading, state of the art, next generation, etc'. You don't need to show off and make potential customers think you're an expert. In fact, it does the opposite of what you aim to achieve – it turns prospects off. Your focus needs to be on simple, concrete and credible. You need to be relevant. Remarkable companies master this. Brand studies from Interbrand[4] consistently stipulate that brands generating the most stable growth over the past ten years are those with the highest overall scores on **relevance.** What's more, the top ten fastest-growing brands over the last five years are those where relevance is their top-performing dimension.

3) The focus is on the product – not the problem

"When you look at the marketing and sales messaging of, for example, the biggest ERP vendors, you can see that it's mostly focused on the 'what' of the things they're selling, and not the 'why'. The communication describes features of programs and platforms, explaining what customers will get once they make a purchase.

"It would be much more effective if it focused on the 'why', i.e. explaining what's fundamentally broken and underserved in the world of your ideal customer, what this results in, and what unique value would be unlocked if it was solved. By tying these benefits to the core business goals of existing and potential customers, vendors can make it crystal clear why subscribing to their software is worth the investment and why doing nothing is not an option. It all comes back to the focus on creating desire based on the unique value you offer, not the nuts and bolts of your product.

4) Too much inside-out focus, instead of outside-in

"The focus is on the vendor, not the customer. The focus is on how big they are, how long they've been in business, how many awards they've won, that they are the number one, i.e. me, me, me, me.

"It's not that this isn't important; on the contrary; it's about how you package it.

"Remarkable companies turn it around – their messaging addresses the world of the customer, or even the world of their customers' customers. It's outside-in. They talk with their customers, not to their customers. They empathize, invite their customers into a story. They create a tension between

---

4. https://www.interbrand.com/wp-content/uploads/2018/10/Interbrand_Best_Global_Brands_2018.pdf

what is, and what could be. And with that they guide the prospects and customers from where they are to where they need to by, thereby translating the credentials and achievements of their company into benefits that resonate with their prospects and customers, and that builds trust. Far more effective.

"I'll give you some key questions to ensure you always start the right way – making it very hard to fall into the traps above, simply because it forces you to take a different mindset. Simply formulate:

1. What's really 'broken' in the world of your customer (or what value is being destroyed)?
2. Why it's key to resolve this once and forever (creating a sense of urgency), and finally
3. Envision what the ideal world would look like if it was resolved.

"Once you've answered these questions you can start to articulate 'how' you can uniquely resolve the expectation you've just set, i.e. what sets you apart. And lastly, at the very, very end is where you can talk about your product, i.e. the 'what' you bring to the table to deliver the promise."

Rob responded: "Three pretty simple questions. I can see how this creates a different story. Do you have any examples of companies that applied this in a remarkable way?"

"Sure I have," I replied. "I get plenty of inspiration from my weekly podcast. Let me share two stories from guests that impressed me. They're actually both in the sales arena."

It's not about the problem, it's about the size of the problem

"Paul Teshima[5] is the CEO of Nudge, an AI company from the West Coast that has a pretty simple value proposition: build relationships. When I spoke to Paul one of his quotes stuck with me. He said this:

Success is not so much about the problem you solve, but more about the size of the problem you solve. If you want to create big impact, tackle a big problem.

---

[5]. https://www.valueinspiration.com/how-intelligence-augmentation-helps-sales-professionals-to-build-relationships-and-grow-sales/

"As I've mentioned already, I continue to see too many vendors focus on too small problems – or worse, in many cases they don't even address problems at all, simply because their communication is about features, but let's not dive into that right now. The idea is: The more valuable the problem you solve, the more desirable (urgent) it becomes for your ideal customers.

"When I asked Paul for that big problem they saw, he gave this response: There are three major things happening:

> *Firstly: The fundamental issue today is that people have all these digital connections that follow them around, and they're growing. They may have a couple of thousand people connected on LinkedIn, several thousand followers on Twitter, and a bunch of digital contacts that stay in their Gmail account or Outlook.*

> *Secondly: The theory by Robin Dunbar is that the human mind can only really manage 150 strong relationships.*

> *Thirdly: As a sales professional, 84 percent of all buying processes start with referral. So if you don't nurture and manage the right relationships to get into a deal, you're only going for the remaining 16 percent. And that's a significant problem.*

> *There's a simple reason: CRM and LinkedIn have mostly focused on storing the record. It has never been about actively increasing the strength of the relationship, let alone leveraging it.*

> *That's exactly why Nudge was founded. Our big idea is 'your network is your net worth.' If you're going to be successful in sales moving forward, you have to value relationships. You have to build them and grow them over time. You have to use your network as a way to differentiate yourself against other sellers going for the same business.*

"And this is just one example. The other interview I'd like to highlight is Mike Schneider,[6] CEO of First – and his story takes this challenge one step further."

[6.] https://www.valueinspiration.com/product-innovation-how-human-ai-combos-creates-disruptive-competitive-advantage-in-real-estate-sales/

Offer something so valuable and desirable that it becomes 'anti-viral'

"Mike runs an AI-led company that's transforming the sales process in the real estate industry. So, clearly he's targeting the innovators in his space. When I asked Mike why he decided to choose the real estate market, his comment had everything to do with carving out a niche where he could solve a very valuable, urgent problem – and have the ability to exceed the expectations of everyone out there. Here's what he said:

> *Real estate is one of those industries that's thriving on events – people buying or selling a new house because certain parameters in their life changed. When this happens, the process accelerates, and they virtually always turn to someone they know and trust to help them. It's very hard to differentiate and it really comes down not to how good your marketing is, but whether or not you're connecting with people at the right time.*

"My immediate reaction was: so what's makes you believe there's a big issue? And this is how he responded:

> *Top agents are missing two thirds of the deals from people they already know.*

As you can imagine, that landed the size of the problem for me. Two thirds! Sixty-six per cent of missed opportunity that's within their range of power (not even considering the massive investments in marketing spend that was invested upfront to capture all these records).

So I asked: 'And the reason for missing out?'. Mike smiled and said:

> *Simply not having enough time. After over a decade of intense automation, there's still a very inefficient system that's simply missing the very essence of the problem: It's not the record (the lead) that's important, it's the relationship you have with those records. If you are not in conversation, it's extremely hard to differentiate and win business. That's true in many sectors, but particularly in sectors like real estate where the transaction has often a very high emotional value: your next dream house.*

"So Mike found a sector with a sizeable problem. What fascinated me is the approach he took to not build yet another slightly better marketing tool for real estate agents (what everybody is doing), but to approach the challenge from a 180-degree opposite direction: using technology like AI and Machine Learning to provide the answer to 'Who do you already have a relationship with that's coming to market right now?' This literally flips the effort from focusing on 'the masses' to focusing on 'the target', and this has proven to have a 10x impact on the productivity of real estate agents.

"This gives him a very valuable story that appeals to the innovators in that market – he's solving a 'lagging' problem that everyone seemingly has got used to living with. So a seemingly small change in approach can have a dramatic impact on the competitiveness of a broker. Telling his story introduces a welcome change that, suddenly, has extreme high urgency, i.e. it becomes highly desirable. So high, actually, that it's providing First with an anti-viral product since none of their customers wants to reveal their 'secret' with any of their peers. I would say that's a nice problem to have.

"That's what I mean with making deliberate choices: honing in on a big problem in a particular market, one that's urgent to solve (even if that's hidden), and making sure every choice you make is about your product and your business is focused on exceeding expectations in solving that big problem. The reason I have picked First as an example of a remarkable software company is that their focus is so strong that they even take the 'anti-viral' effect of their product for granted. They deliberately focus their time, effort and investment on creating something so meaningful that their customers want to keep it a secret because they fear to lose the value they have started to fall in love with. For First, that's the foundation of their value."

A constant source for inspiration

I looked at Rob and stated, "Makes you think, right? That's pure dedication, offering something so valuable that it becomes 'anti-viral'. The reason why that is so powerful is because then, and only then, can you really narrow down on what's valuable, urgent, and what you need to do to exceed expectations. It all becomes super clear."

"You've hit the nail on the head," Rob answered. "This is clearly missing in the company I run. We're too eager to please everyone; we're pushing out feature after feature, with the hope something sticks. And I now I realize that will not work – not now, not tomorrow, never. We have to get back to the core. We have to do the soul-searching again for the exact reason why we started the business if we want to change the course of our momentum."

Rob sipped his Chardonnay again, clearly energized.

"That's going to be an exercise of well spent time, Rob," I continued. "On your journey to increase the impact of your ideal customers there will be a constant need to stay ahead of other start-ups – especially in the FinTech madness you are in. You will need to constantly challenge your priorities and investments to cement the differentiation between you and the alternatives on the market.

"And that requires you to say 'no' to tempting opportunities that appear on your path. It reminds me of my conversation with Tomas Ratia,[7] CEO of Frase.io, an AI-powered content creation tool. To my question 'What did you say no to, to ensure that what you deliver is remarkable?' he answered:

> *I've been in a number of meetings with big companies that come to us because they experience a major challenge dealing with documents. This has resulted in tempting opportunities that would require building Frase on-premises and with custom features for these companies.*
>
> *Although the situation came up frequently, we realized that by doing that work, we're not living our core mission of helping the individual create content, which is where I see a transformative potential. And to unlock this we need to be very focused on 'the content creator'. By saying 'No' to these bigger opportunities, and choosing to focus on the individuals, we're seeing a really, really high engagement with users. We're transforming the way they're creating big impact.*

"Saying 'no' is hard. But doing this will consequently pay off big time. Let me tell you another story. The story of WeDo Technologies from Lisbon, which was founded around the big idea to 'help telcos win the fight against fraud and revenue leakage in an increasingly complex industry.' Rui Paiva,[8] their CEO, shared their simple, but very powerful company value:

> *I won't sell things that I won't buy.*

7. https://www.valueinspiration.com/how-ai-is-transforming-the-way-people-write-and-research/

8. https://www.valueinspiration.com/product-innovation-how-ai-helps-telcos-win-the-fight-against-fraud-and-revenue-leakage-while-boosting-their-bottom-line/

"Think about this. This is where the essence of all three key ingredients unite: offering something valuable, that's critical to your customer, and delivered in a way it exceeds expectations. It's about the customer, not you. And to firm that statement even further, Rui made it one of their core company values:

> *If we convince our customers to do this or that, it's because I'd do the same, because I was in their shoes.*

> *We had that in mind since day one, and this means we are aligning ourselves together with them around the same objective, and in doing so we become kind of 'brothers'.*

> *So, if we are selling to a customer this means they bet on us. And therefore, if something fails, no matter if it's going to affect us negatively in our accounting numbers, we will spend all the money needed to solve it.*

"That's commitment, and that brings trust, which is essential in todays' world. This value mindset was behind the founding of WeDo Technologies in 2001, and it's the mindset that's kept the company relevant since. It helped the company stay curious and evolve with its customers. The result: they haven't lost a single customer since its inception. That's testimony that offering something valuable pays off.

"Knowing what your business stands for and what value you aim to bring to the world allows you to freely shape your strategy without being constrained by the artificial boundaries that have defined and limited an industry for too long.

"There are so many software companies that suffer from this. Just image your mission was 'to be the leading provider of electronic banking tools for Banks'. Technically you could say, yes, that's what we do. And that's exactly the problem. In essence it's the same, but it's extremely limiting. What if electronic banking goes out of fashion? Then you are stuck. And if you're lucky it's not, then you don't have the internal friction to keep a fresh perspective on staying competitive. The very likely thing you'll do is to keep adding more features, and change your user interface – nothing that will be remarkable in the eyes of your ideal customers.

"Now, let's assume your software company was indeed founded on the purpose 'to help banks thrive, by enabling their customers to always be one step ahead in life and business'.

"Within that framework, you can focus your attention on increasing impact. What you are founded on will always remain valuable, but what you need to do in order to live up to that promise will constantly shift as technology evolves, as norms change. But that's fine – that's what innovation is all about. It's a stretched goal. And that will keep everyone on their toes. So, following this construct, your ground principle isn't fixed, i.e. it doesn't define what you do, it defines why you do it."

"I can see how this is going to create a completely different dynamic, Ton," Rob replied. "And I can also see how exactly this is going to help us to free up some scarce resources who are busy with 'stuff'. I can almost guarantee you that a big chunk of our committed resources are allocated to things we believe we should do, simply because that clarity is missing today. Can't wait to get to the office on Monday!"

At that point the train slowed down again. We were entering the train station of Tarragona.

Ask yourself

STEP 1: Reflect critically how you score your own ability around this particular trait by rating your organization on a scale of 1 (poor) to 10 (remarkable).

Would your customers care if … you'd cease to exist today i.e. do you offer something they'd truly miss if it was gone?

0 |————————————————————————————| 10

Your ability to offer a shift in value perspective for your ideal customers? (i.e. You exceed expectations on something that's highly valuable and critical to them.)

0 |————————————————————————————| 10

What's your ability to ignite curiosity and desire amongst your ideal customers?

0 |————————————————————————————| 10

STEP 2: Take ten minutes to reflect on the next actions you could initiate to improve your score.

STEP 3: What's the single action from this list that would give you the biggest impact?

Take it to the next level

- Not only become remarkable, but ensure you'll stay remarkable as well by introducing the 'Remarkable Monday' habit within your organization. Download the three simple steps that will help you create and keep momentum: https://valueinspiration.com/RemarkableMonday
- Join the Remarkable Tribe Program to create accountability with other tech-entrepreneurs like you. Not only will you build traction to shape the business you aspire to be, but you will also obtain new ideas, create new contacts and will be part of a movement that defines what it means to be remarkable as a business software vendor: https://movement.valueinspiration.com

Trait 3
Be different, not just better

As the train entered Tarragona station we walked back from the restaurant car to our seats in the other carriage. It was hectic, many people leaving the train, while at the same time new people entering it for the final leg to Barcelona Sants. As we sat down in our seats Rob spoke. "I get your point about sharply defining our ideal customers, I get your point about honing in on offering something valuable. All of that will help us to communicate in a much more relevant way, to optimize our investments in our product and our go-to-market, and be more desirable to our customers. But what can I do to get our win-rate up?"

"Excellent reflection, Rob," I answered. "The icing on the cake will be your differentiation. That's what I would highlight as the third trait of a remarkable software company. It's essential. Not only for growing your customer base, but also in the broader sense; for example, to collect funding. I recently read a blog where the question 'Why do companies exist?' was discussed. Here's how that was answered by Pat Grady, partner at Sequoia:[1]

> *Companies don't exist to make people rich, whether those are the founders, the investors, or anybody else. Companies exist to solve a problem. What is the problem you're solving? How do you do so in a unique and compelling way that has some inherent durability to it? For us, those are the first principles.*

---

[1] https://www.drift.com/blog/lessons-from-pat-grady/?utm_content=bufferf8665&utm_medium=social&utm_source=linkedin.com&utm_campaign=buffer

"So, the value of your company in the eyes of a venture capitalists is built around three key components: 1) The impact delivered to your customers, 2) The approach you take in doing so, and 3) How difficult it will be for any alternative to match you in doing this.

"It's not enough to offer something valuable. You also need to clearly proove that your way of delivering the value is the most desirable for the customer. And lastly, for sake of your own company's long-term success, you want your approach to be very hard to copy by anyone. That's the essence of true differentiation.

"Once you get this right, it really pays off. Let me quote Sally Hogshead,[2] author of the book *Fascinate*:

> *People are willing to pay more for different, than they are for better.*
> *Not single digit %, but up to 4x more.*

"This is exactly what Olin Hyde[3] saw as well. Olin is the CEO of LeadCrunch, a company that's applying AI to generate demand for businesses that sell to other businesses. When I asked him about his experience in introducing his solution to the market, this is what he told me:

> *The demand for lead generation that actually works is massive [...]*
> *venture capital firms poured hundreds of millions of dollars into the*
> *startups that promised to generate demand using artificial intelligence.*
> *The early winners were Facebook and Google, which collectively*
> *captured more than 65% of all online advertising for consumer*
> *marketing. Yet, there are no clear winners in the business-to-business*
> *category. Rather, there are many failures. Why?*
>
> *Because almost all venture-backed demand generation companies fell*
> *into one of two traps: First, they pursued a business model that*
> *investors loved. They sold subscriptions to gain insights and analytics.*
> *This approach promised high profit margins to investors but ignored*
> *what customers wanted to buy: Leads that converted. So these*
> *companies found themselves trying to sell services that customers did*
> *not want. They couldn't change because of the promises made to their*

[2.] https://creativewarriorsunite.com/my-premier-podcast-with-sally-hogshead/
[3.] https://www.valueinspiration.com/product-innovation-how-you-can-create-your-unfair-competitive-advantage-by-applying-ai-to-lead-targeting/

investors and the mandates from their venture-controlled boards of directors. Those that did not have SaaS (software-as-a-subscription) model, failed because they were looking at the problem of demand generation as a single-point solution. For example, one competitor focuses on personalizing messages while another focuses on finding intent data to predict a sale. The number of these point solutions is dizzying. And really expensive to build.

We set out to win by thinking differently about the problem and solution for generating demand for B2B sales. We knew we had to be capital efficient and get started without any outside capital. After we got early traction, we raised about 18 million dollars knowing that we had to beat companies that raised more than 100 million dollars. It's like David vs Goliath. So, how do we beat them? Well, we looked at their business model and found a way to get high revenue retention and profit margins by selling A.I. on a lead-by-lead basis.

We think that the strongest differentiator for companies is in business model innovation, not necessarily technology. In technology there's always going to be somebody smarter, someone that can throw more engineering resources at the problem, and someone that can come up with a better solution. It's very difficult to beat someone's business model though.

Our competitors almost all try to sell subscriptions. The problem with subscription is that they required the seller to know the value of what they're selling on an annual basis. And it requires the buyer to commit that they're getting a good deal at that price.

From our customers' perspective we're in the business of building relationships. The problem with relationships is: they're not a commodity, right? Do you want to buy relationships as a subscription? I don't think so. People don't sell you gasoline on a subscription, or food on a subscription. Just ask any drug dealer. When it comes to something like food, eating in a five-star restaurant is going to cost more than eating in a fast-food restaurant. The more you need something or the more it is differentiated, the less sense it makes to sell it as a subscription. The same is true for relationships.

So what we do is: We sell campaigns on a cost per lead basis. It's all about outcomes. This allows us to right fit the price, so that our customers get remarkable return on investment and that we can ensure that we're putting enough resources behind every lead to make that relationship meaningful. Our primary resource is artificial intelligence – which has a high cost of development, but once it is built, costs almost nothing to deliver to millions of customers once it is built. From our customer's perspective, we sell artificial intelligence on a cost-per-lead basis. The more A.I. that goes into the lead, the more likely it will convert into a customer, and the more our customers will pay for it.

"Just to give you some perspective on how this plays out for LeadCrunch: straight 20% per month growth for the last two and a half years in a row. That's remarkable impact.

"So, knowing this, you wonder why more companies do not pay more attention to this. It might all sound like an open door, but believe me, I've seen hundreds of websites, hundreds of sales presentations and pitches. Nine out of ten communicate primarily about how they are better: they're faster, cheaper, they have higher ranking, more revenue, they are bigger, they're 'leading', or even 'it's our people that set us apart because of their knowledge and dedication'. Hardly any are talking about how they are different.

"The majority of messaging and pitches I see are challenged with poor value propositions where the unique selling point (USP) is often completely absent. No, let me rephrase that, they 'seem' present, but they are not unique at all. That's even more worrying. If there's a USP, it's of such poor quality that virtually any competitor can easily catch up within their next product release, because a lot of vendors let the latest features in their product drive their story of differentiation.

"To succeed in any business, you need both a strong value proposition and clear differentiation, i.e. one or more unique selling points. Having a strong value proposition absent of a clear USP is going to give you challenges in the closing part of the *sales* phase since you have to work harder to gain an advantage over your competitors.

"I also see the opposite: a clear USP, without a value proposition. This reminds me of that moment in 2005 when I was told by PJ from Technology Evaluation Centers that we had something unique in our offering, but had a very strange way of talking about it. The problem he identified was that there was a clear USP, just a very poor value proposition. Hence, it was very ineffic-ient to *market* the solution.

"I believe a big part of the challenge is a poor understanding of what is what. So here's my definition:

1. Your value proposition is the simple explanation for why your prospect should consider buying your product or service and what value they get in return. It typically addresses what's 'broken' in their world, what prob-lems/challenges this results in, in terms of achieving their goals and ambitions, and how, by addressing the problem, it will unlock significant value.
2. Your unique selling point(s) defines what separates you from other players or alternative options in the market, i.e. your point of differentiation. It's articulating the secret on how you can deliver the unique value you promise.

"Your value proposition, therefore, incorporates your unique selling points. That said, the strength of your unique selling point determines the strength of your value proposition. So, in your product and marketing strategy, you should really pay a lot of attention to creating differentiation that a) creates a shift in perspective in terms of value creation, b) that addresses a significant problem a refreshing way, and c) that's hard to copy.

"As you can imagine, you need to dig deep to identify the unique value you can unlock by applying your USP(s) to your ideal customers' largest problems. However, with that ammunition you can create the strongest value proposition – one that makes your competitors irrelevant. That's where the fun begins."

The value of differentiation

I paused for a second. I could see that Rob was thinking deeply. "You're making me realize we've fallen exactly into that trap, Ton," he said. "If I picture our company decks, our website, or even the way I and my management talk about our company, it's very much a story that's based on our own self-talk about how good we think we are. It's very much driven by the shiny object syndrome – the contest with all our peers in the market to see who can push out the most features, hoping this will spark an interest. And I agree with you, that's a challenging race that I don't think we can continue for very long."

"I'm simply handing you a mirror, Rob," I responded. "In every market the competitive playing field is highly optimized. Most vendors have credibility. They all have the skills. They all can technically win the game."

At that moment we passed a very scenic part of the coastline again, with free view on the Mediterranean Sea, reminding me again what my journey was all about.

"Let's mirror your business with the athletes that will participate tomorrow in the Big Wave Tour in Nazare. The playing field there is comparable with the vendors you meet on a daily basis when competing for your next customer.

"Who's winning tomorrow is not about who's the fittest, the smoothest, or the fastest. They are all top athletes; the differences are very, very small. The winners are often the ones that make the most of the conditions, they see the opportunity faster, they maneuver smartly so they are in the right position, they know when to take the risk and when to hold back, they commit where others shy away. And in doing so, they can be the most creative, the most unusual, the most different.

"And as you can imagine, this is not about luck. It's something they train for – years of dedication and sharp focus. In other words, its engrained in their core. They are not going 'wide' to be all-round and capable of competing in every surf competition. Instead they go deep. They're the specialist in big wave surfing, they are the specialist in a specific type of location. They are the specialist for specific conditions like the current, the wind angle, the way the swell builds, the way the monster wave breaks. They invest all of that so that when it all comes together, that's where they master the playground. That's where they make the seemingly impossible look simple. That's where they exceed everyone's expectations – and write history.

"So, it's all about being different, not just better. Being an underdog in the market, it's essential to place your bets and ensure you're truly different from the rest. It not only helps your prospect to set their shortlist – it's also extremely valuable to the productivity and performance of a company, not only in sales, but in everything aspect of your software business: Product Development, Marketing, Sales, and even Services and Support. It drives everything. It makes decisions easier – initiatives that don't support the differentiation should not be done. This frees up resources, and allows you to win more, win bigger, and grow the value of your differentiation even stronger".

Rob smiled. "It inspires me to see how by narrowing things down to the essence helps to create leaps in value for both our ideal customers and consequently ourselves. Your examples about big wave surfing make me realize that all too well. Until now, for me there was no differentiation in waves – to me they seemed the same, no matter where you are in the world. One being a bit bigger than the other, but in essence all the same. So, if I had to select a wave, I wouldn't know or even care to pick one. That's exactly how the market works – to my customers the digital banking platforms all look alike, just like any wave around the world. It's our responsibility as a vendor to find out what are the big waves my customers need to ride to stand out in their business. It's our responsibility to make them see and believe how we, and only we, can help them ride that perfect wave together in a way that gives them the best results, most comfort, and the least risk. Fascinating!

"So tell me," he continued, "what makes the strongest differentiator?"

"Excellent question," I responded. "Let me share three different ingredients with you."

1. Create a shift in (value) perspective

"The difficult thing with value is that it's all about perspective. It all depends on what you have versus what you get. If we buy something, we want it to provide a value that's different from what we have today – if it's the same, we won't make the investment, correct?"

"Correct," Rob replied.

"Astro Teller, CEO of X,[4] summarized the essence of this perfectly when he said:

> *The perspective shift is what it's all about.*

"And although Astro talked about this in relation to the challenge of innovation, the concept applies perfectly in the overall discussion of communicating value that comes from your differentiation. Differentiation is most meaningful when it convinces your ideal customer that you can do the same thing as the alternative offerings he/she is assessing, just with a fundamentally different outcome. An outcome that becomes irresistible for the buyer. One that surprises – that creates a shift in perspective. It needs to be specific. It needs to be extremely clear what impact it has on the business of your customer.

[4.]   https://tim.blog/2018/04/18/how-to-think-10x-bigger/

"All too often I see vendors using vague terms when they talk about their difference: 'Superior Usability', 'Our Expertise', 'Our Embedded Analytics', or the typical hype talk like 'AI-powered'. They don't articulate 'how' that capability provides value that's irresistible. With that you just sound like all the other vendors, and the perspective shift that Astro Teller is talking about is not happening.

"Danny Saksenberg,[5] CEO of Emerge, made a critical comment:

> *People are spending a lot of time focusing on interesting problems and not so much on valuable problems.*

"Now this is a challenge that inhibits the impact of many software businesses, but it's actually the same on the customer side as well. Customers often become 'blind' to what they really need. As such, this is a massive opportunity for you as a vendor to create the perspective shift Astro Teller talked about.

"Danny illustrated this nicely with an anecdote from one of his clients, who had a team of people in India to summarize the company's lengthy financial documents. When the client asked him if he could do the same, Danny said this:

> *I could do that. Just tell me again, how much are you paying this team?*

> *The client responded '$400,000 a month' to which Danny responded: 'What you're asking is a relatively difficult project. I'm not convinced I could do it, but even if I could, I don't see it taking less than six months, and if I got it right, you got it 100 percent right now, that would save you $4.8 million a year.*

> *I read your annual report before I walked in here. Just looking at that, even if I identified three different problems, and got this half right, that's a billion dollars a year in savings, and I could probably do it by next week.' It's a much simpler problem.*

"Here, Saksenberg identified the most valuable problem and smartly pointed the differentiation of his solution to solve this in a way that made it irresistible for his customer. He provided new perspectives by deliberately *not* settling for the most obvious problem raised by the customer, which seemed interesting at the surface. That's the perspective shift Astro Teller refers to.

---

5. https://www.valueinspiration.com/product-strategy-whats-required-to-solve-the-worlds-biggest-problems-through-technology/

"Danny's advice (based on the famous Theory of Constraints (ToC) developed by Eli Goldratt) is to identify the bottlenecks in your ideal customers' business and focus on solving that in a way that separates you from the rest. Focusing on areas which aren't bottlenecks will not actually improve the value of their business. This is a lot about education as well, as often your customers are too close to their own problems – they can't see the wood for the trees. So this is your opportunity to differentiate.

"Danny illustrated that in the following way:

> *Unfortunately, I think a lot of the time people [customers] lose sight of that and focus on maintaining the existing business, whether or not it's serving the public. So it's your obligation to challenge the status quo for them and think more about the purpose of the business of your ideal customer. As long as you're adding value to people, you'll do well. I think it ultimately boils down to what can you do to serve the public better. The more value you add to them or to more people, the better your business will do.*

> *People don't really care about your accuracy, they don't care about your root mean square error or your Gini coefficient or your ROC curve. They couldn't care less until you can make the connection with a problem that is truly hurting their business. That's where it all clicks.*

> *I think it's worthwhile just taking a step back on a regular basis and work out what does the public actually need, and how does your solution add unique value in a way alternative options cannot?*

Rob interrupted me then. "So if I understand you correctly, it's about finding a unique spin towards our customers that provides them with a fresh perspective on how they could gain more value."

"Correct," I replied. "Too often your customers think they want X, and then they'll focus their entire buying process on getting that exact X. It's very rigid, since they want to compare apples with apples.

"You know best where you have the unique cards, and if you follow the customer process, you would not be able to play those cards to their full potential. You're not that 'apple'. Hence you have to 'move the box', as my colleague Roel Caers would often say. You bring in fresh perspectives that connect to their larger vision, and from there you can start to own the buyer's agenda.

Here's where you can play your strongest cards and create shifts in value perspective.

"It's the art of segmentation and positioning. It all starts with understanding what you do best, and then tying that to the biggest problems, challenges or ambitions of your customer. Doing that wrong (or not at all) is where the most brilliant differentiation gets lost in translation. It's not articulated well enough, and as such the customers' perspective is: 'all options are equal'. Hence they opt for the vendor with the biggest brand, or the one that provides the highest discount. Both situations you want to avoid at all cost."

2a. Play by your own rules

At that moment the train's service team entered our carriage with a trolley full of delicious-smelling coffee. "I can do with one, what about you, Rob?" I said. Rob confirmed, "Ditto, café solo for me please."

I ordered two espressos and continued the conversation.

"So one aspect of being different, not better, is to differentiate by creating a shift in value. The second thing to pay attention to is 'play by your own rules'. Let me explain the essence of this by sharing another story.

"Adam Martel,[6] CEO and co-founder of Gravyty, the first provider of AI-enabled fundraising software, said this:

> If we play the game according to someone else rules, it's difficult to
> catch up.

"That's a very common issue in the software business – everybody seems to be copying each other. If one vendor releases feature X in their Spring release, the other vendors will have it available in their Summer release. If you open up the website of vendor A, and replace the logo with vendor B, you won't notice the difference. You see this copy mentality everywhere – in the products they build, the marketing they do, and the sales approach they follow.

"Now if you have deep pockets and if you are the market leader, that might be all fine. But the fact is, that's not the case for most of us. Instead of fighting every single day to just get 'even', we have to stand out, and one way to do that is to play by our own rules.

---

6. https://www.valueinspiration.com/how-ai-redefines-the-impact-of-fundraising-in-not-for-profit/

"Following this rule helps in every stage of your product's lifecycle. Obviously when you can start fresh, like the examples I gave with Nudge and now with Gravyty, that's ideal, but even if your solution has been around for a decade, it still works like a charm. It takes courage, but believe me, it pays off.

"Gravyty has focused its business around frontline fundraisers, i.e. people that work for non-profit organizations, higher education institutions, hospitals, and healthcare organizations, and works with the sole purpose of finding donors to fund their projects around the world. This is another good example of micro-segmenting, by the way.

"The problem they identified was sizeable, just like the example I shared with Emerge and Nudge: Adam himself faced the problem in the work he did with his previous employer.

> We had 37,000 alumni. The top 10 percent of our alumni pool, around 3,700, made up about 90 percent of our donations. The challenge that we were really facing was that we were only managing around 1,200 of those donors. So there were 2,500 donors that could make transformational gifts and really needed a personal touch, but we weren't getting to them – simply because we didn't have the bandwidth.

"When you realize this problem is universal for every non-profit organization, then you can see the massive size of the problem. This is how Adam illustrated it:

> This isn't about Gravyty or other ISVs, it's about our customers. It's about the wonderful work that our customers are doing. If we can accelerate cancer research, if we can help eradicate HIV, if we help these organizations change the world, it's our job to do that. They don't need to fit into us, we need to accelerate them.

"This goes back to what I told you earlier: 'What business are you in, no, what business are you really in?' The bulk of the vendors out there think they are in the business of creating efficiency around managing customer data, and that leads to all kind of issues. As Adam rightly said:

> We're seeing a lot of ISVs that are doing a lot of things the old way. They're investing a lot of money in their products and getting a lot of customers, but these exact customers are still facing the exact same

challenges they faced 20 years ago. If the problem and challenges don't change, then is the solution really adequate?

Blackbaud, Salesforce, Ellucian, and Community Brands – they are all selling databases. They are all selling the cup that holds the water, but nobody's doing anything with the water itself. What we wanted it to be was the outlet of all of this data. We want to be using some of it like we use fuel. We need to start burning this data so we can get to the point where we're generating something that's useful. Data for data's sake is not good enough.

That thinking changed the course of our company. Instead of competing with Salesforce or Blackbaud, or any of these big CRMs, we're completely transformative and we're selling to a set of users that nobody has ever sold to before: the frontline fundraisers.

"Gravyty followed their own rules. Instead of just delivering a 'better version' of what's on the market already, they delivered something that transformed the way fundraising is done. Following their own rules allowed them to shift perspective at the buyer side.

"Of course, this provided challenges at the start. Creating an entire category where you are saying, 'Listen, the way the entire world is working right now is wrong' requires you to be persistent. The power is hidden in the balance between the three key questions we discussed earlier. As long as you can address a valuable problem head-on, and exceed expectations in delivering the solution, you'll win over the market because it becomes something highly desirable. I mean, wouldn't you be 'sold' if a single solution would allow you to scale your workforce and impact by two to three times, without making any additional hires? I know I would be."

2b. Play by your own rules – the Onsophic case

"As you can see, taking a contrarian approach is a great way to create a strong point of differentiation in the market. It's more fun as well. It gives you the advantage of setting the rules, rather than following the ones others have set: rules that will always give you the feeling you are catching up.

"This reminds me of another example of a company that created clear differentiation by playing by their own rules: Onsophic, an AI company from the Bay Area, led by a leader from Belgium. Their aim is to accelerate human potential by systematically resolving knowledge gaps.

"Tom Pennings, their founder and CEO, made the following point:

> *The way I challenged our differentiation was by asking the simple question: 'are we chasing the right objectives?' I mean, in our market there are 536 different Learning Management Solutions (LMS). When we looked at that market we realized they were all following the wrong objectives. All these LMS's are about content delivery. And if you analyse what's the real challenge, it is not with the delivery process of content, it's with guiding each and every individual in a personalized way.*

"Onsophic decided to play by their own rules, but took a different, 180-degree approach. Instead of building LMS number 537 and focus on the output, they decided to build an intelligent platform that guides each and every individual in a company by focusing on the outcome, i.e. what's the objective you are aiming at or responsible for, and what learning gaps do you have to bridge to achieve that in the shortest and most impactful way.

"With this approach they have created a clear differentiator in the market for Human Performance Management. Tom added this:

The opportunity that arises these days with the technology available is that we can create far greater value by going beyond 'just' the process. The process has always been there, but now the technology is there to give individual guidance. Hence, we should revisit every aspect of our solutions – not to optimize output (volume), but to increase outcome (impact) by acceleration of human potential.

3. Make it defensible, i.e. hard to copy

As Rob finished his last sip of coffee, he looked up and said: "There's work to do on my end if I listen to your examples. Currently the way we articulate how we are different is, in short: our people all have deep experience in the banking sector, the rich functionality of our suite, and the fact we are delivering state-of-the-art functionality like Facebook banking, watch banking and so on. I realize now that doesn't really communicate a shift in value for our customers, or something that's radically different from what our competitors do."

"Correct," I responded. "And another thing it doesn't do is what I'd highlight as the third key ingredient of creating unbeatable differentiation: it needs to be hard to copy.

"Peter Thiel, co-founder of PayPal, once said:

> *In the real world outside economic theory, every business is successful exactly to the extent that it does something others cannot.*

"Here's why: it could very well be that the points you mentioned are indeed your core differentiators. I can't judge upon that. I am not an expert in your space. What I do see is that it's all pretty easy to copy – and that's a very dangerous situation to be in.

"Your people could leave to take a better position at one of your competitors – meaning your expertise have left the building, and you're back at square one.

"Your rich functionality is not what a customer is looking for. They couldn't care less how much functionality you have, as long as you solve their problems. Some vendors create thirty screens, some use a simple bot with just a Natural Language Interface to solve the same problem. I can tell you, that approach is going to appeal far better with their users. Simple, no clutter, intelligent.

"Your latest and greatest Facebook banking and watch banking are only as fresh as 'the moment'. I bet that all your competitors could add this to their roadmap today, and deliver it in less than three months. It's a battle you'll never win.

"But as I said before, many vendors fail to stand out in their target market. The product differentiation is there, but they sound the same as all their 'competitors'. It often makes me smile to see the 'clever' ways to make an impression: 'We're the leading solution for X'; 'Our robust, state-of-the-art solution …'; 'Our artificial-led, machine-learning-infused, hybrid-Cloud solution …, etc.'

"Remember, just by saying you are a leader doesn't make you one. Just by claiming you are state-of-the-art doesn't mean you are. Just by using all the hype words doesn't give you differentiation at face value, nor does it build trust – in fact, it does the opposite; it spells out there's something to hide, and as such your potential buyers are very much on their marks – making your position even more compromized.

"Aim to spend time on highlighting the capabilities that define your DNA – the founding principles of your suite, or your business model, or your approach. What is the constant force of value delivery as your solution evolves, something your customers keep receiving value from? Sometimes it's hidden, not even visible to the end user, but it's the engine that drives the core of your value. Spelling out the value of that DNA makes it extremely hard for a competitor to beat.

"Let me give you an example of the previous company I worked for. I already told you about the exercise to reposition the solution back in 2005. What came out extremely clearly is that a specific segment of the market loved the solution for its extreme flexibility. We were always talking about a range of 'principles' that people needed to understand in order to make the best of the solution. We never really connected the dots though, to connect 'the principles' to value that no competitor could beat. Instead we were talking about the four cornerstones of the solution – attributes, relations, rules and views – all meaningless without any context. However, we spent endless amounts of time in demos to explain it. We had to because you could only move forward if you really understood those principles. That's why PJ from Technology Evaluation Centers told me in that call in November 2005 'You have something special, but you have a very odd way of talking about it (in over eighty busy slides)'.

"It was that project that led to clearly articulating the true power of the solution in meaningful terms that everyone could understand. This solution helps Businesses Living IN Change (BLINC™) to embrace change independently in the fastest, least disruptive and most cost-effective way. It's underpinned by the only architecture on the market that smartly couples three things: data, business process, and the delivery methodology (i.e. reporting and analytics), to move in lockstep. So, when a change is made in one area, it does not have to be redone and rechecked for accuracy in another. That makes it simple, fast, cost-effective and something your business people can do independently from expensive and scarce IT experts.

"If this story was told to a company that was indeed driving or undergoing constant business change, we became almost unbeatable. It was articulating the strength of the DNA of the solution, its founding principles. If any of our competitors wanted to beat us on this, they would have had to start all over again; from the first line of code. It was impossible to copy.

"Two levers, however, can provide very strong differentiation, as well as defensibility. Network economies and counter-positioning. Network economies simply because of its exponential value component – the more people use your solution, the more valuable it gets. It's sticky. The concept has been around for a while, with Facebook possibly being the most well-known example, but today you still see new flavors of the concept showing their value.

"It reminds me of the big idea behind Snaphunt – a specialist recruitment agency, with no human recruiter. When I interviewed CEO Tulika Tripathi[7] and asked her about how she created defensible differentiation, she told me this:

> I realized that recruitment hadn't changed much over the course of my twenty-year career. Very senior, very talented individuals in search of their next dream job can find it extremely frustrating today. Besides that, employers don't know what talent is out there, and talents don't know what jobs are out there. So you have specialist firms that charge a lot of money to create a match.
>
> It taught me that there was an opportunity to leverage today's technology to do the same thing in a much more effective and scalable way. So, I saw this trend, and I felt rather than just putting lipstick on a pig by trying to reshape a traditional business, there was a phenomenal opportunity to create a new category. I could create what it should be, and could be, from scratch.
>
> That's the foundation of Snaphunt: a specialist recruiting platform sources and screens talent to provide employers with targeted shortlists for their open roles. It is a new category designed it to be massively disruptive: It brings down hiring costs by around 99% when you compare it to a specialist recruitment firm while also reducing time to hire by at least 30% and hiring effort by more than 50%.
>
> Where the defensible differentiation comes in is this: Instead of offering this as a next-generation recruitment suite to individual companies, we've created a platform. It's like a marketplace with multiple organizations on it. I believe that by having multiple players on it, we are able to spot market trends more effectively, we're able to see different companies competing for the same talent and start providing predictive analytics and predictive insights.
>
> Besides that, roles are changing very, very quickly. For example, we are starting to see a greater demand for marketing talent with a data analytics background as marketing is evolving to a much more

---

[7.] https://www.valueinspiration.com/product-innovation-recruiting-quickly-conveniently-and-cost-effectively-by-disintermediating-the-middle-man/

data-driven function. This is something we can start advising
employers on. As a result, the more organizations and talent joining the
platform, the more data we have, and hence the more value we provide.

There are more examples that follow this concept; for example, Collective[i]. The company has created what has been described as the 'Waze for sales.' Their application derives its value from the collective insights and data gleaned from its network of sales professionals and data that unearths B2B buying and purchasing patterns.

Or Xeneta, who have created a platform where buyers of ocean- and air-freight services make the pricing 100% transparent, enabling them to shorten negotiation cycles and focus on the strategic aspects, rather the price.

"But besides creating a network-effect, I also mentioned another concept: 'counter-positioning'. It's the art of finding a solution to an existing problem that you can offer in such a way that the incumbent simply can't follow because it would (for example) cannibalize their business or because this would simply drain their profits as their cost-structure doesn't support it.

"Let me give you two examples: inPowered and Fracta. Both of these companies have created a technological advantage that disrupts the status quo:

- inPowered[8] has transformed the way marketers go about digital advertising by eliminating the need to pay for (interruptive) ads (output), and switching the model to pay for engagement (outcome).
- Fracta[9] has transformed the utility industry by turning the traditional approach of modernizing pipe-infrastructures from simply replacing all pipes systematically based on age and break history, to one that's predictive; replacing only the pipes with the highest probability and risk of failure: far more targeted, manageable and cost-effective – and, most of all, scalable.

"Another example that struck me is at the level of business model. Matt Ward,[10] an angel investor, start-up advisor and entrepreneur, struck a fascinating topic in one of his blogs, namely 'defensible differentiation'. He compared

---

8. https://www.valueinspiration.com/product-innovation-how-ai-transforms-highly-ineffective-advertising-into-highly-relevant-engagement/

9. https://www.valueinspiration.com/product-innovation-how-ai-can-be-used-to-augment-engineers-to-solve-a-1-trillion-infrastructure-problem/

10. https://thinkgrowth.org/uber-is-going-to-0-and-benchmark-knows-it-1566fb51b308

Uber with Airbnb to point out that Uber's differentiation is not defensible, simply because the market for ride-sharing is local, and both drivers and riders have no loyalty.

"So no matter how compelling Uber's growth is now, the moment a better offer comes around in a city, everyone moves. They will always be on the defense, and have to spend tons of money to 'buy' their market – city by city.

"I am not sure how the situation is with you in Portugal, Rob, but what you see here in Spain with Uber is exactly pointing out the challenge they have. The constant fight with the government and the traditional taxi business has provided them with enormous challenges, where other, rather similar but local initiatives have taken off successfully.

"What Matt further pointed out is that the opposite applies to Airbnb, simply because of the network effect. Airbnb's market is about exploring – it's not just about the city you live in, it's about everything outside of it. That difference gives Airbnb massive differentiation, untouchable, no matter how many local competitors will stand up.

"The bottom line: solving a problem is not enough. In order to become remarkable, you need to solve a problem in such a way that it creates a shift in value perception, that's ideally delivered following a different, non-conventional path, and that can't be easily replicated by competitors."

Differentiation is subject to the moment in time

"Fascinating," Rob responded. "I already have some ideas on how to address the way we communicate our solution in the market. But if I understand you correctly, this is not just about marketing. Correct?"

"You're 100% right on that. With marketing you can do a lot; however, the moment you align everything in your business around your story and differentiation, you get leverage.

"This is as much a segmentation and positioning challenge as it is a development challenge," I continued. "You always need to keep reflecting. If the big idea behind your company is solid, it's a stretched goal, something that will be a continuous source of inspiration to keep evolving your value. Differentiation, however, is something that is always a moment in time. It could very well be that last year your differentiation was totally obvious, whereas this year, with the evolution of technology, or business models, its unique value evaporates like ice-cream in the sun.

"This is why many software vendors struggle. The digital banking platform you are offering today, Rob, is an excellent example of this. For decades the market of business solutions for banks was the automation of their core systems – their back office. Correct? That was 'the market' – that's what many vendors invested in, and it created a wealth of options for banks to choose from. Business was good for many software vendors.

"It was a stable market, no one was really looking for anything else, until Steve Jobs introduced the iPhone. That changed the norms about consumer convenience forever. It was now a matter of 'when' not 'if' new vendors would stand up to give these consumers a level of convenience to communicate with their bank that had never been deemed possible.

"Fast-forward to today and the power is fully in the hands of the consumer. The banks are not making the rules anymore, the customers are. If the convenience to transact, communicate, or keep abreast of our financial situation is not as simple as 'posting a status update on Facebook', we'll happily switch banks. Loyalty is gone. It's all about experience. At least that's the way I see it with the banks I am working with.

"So what has happened? The investment priorities of virtually every bank have shifted. Where they used to spend the bulk of their investment on their back office for efficiency, cost reduction and compliancy, they have now shifted their priorities to solutions that allow them to create the best possible experience across every possible channel. They actually use these solutions to attract new tech-savvy consumers and to grow their top-line by offering more services than they could ever do via their physical offices. Am I correct in my assumptions, Rob?"

Rob nodded. "Spot on," he said. "Most traditional core-banking vendors are indeed scrambling to stay in business. They have missed the next wave because they weren't paying attention. The ones I know which enjoyed double digit growth rates up to a few years ago, are now experiencing growth that has evaporated to single digit, flat or even declining rates."

"Correct," I replied. "It simply requires a different mindset. The problem starts again with the way you think about yourself. Many vendors in the banking sector that are now in trouble have always told themselves they were in the business of 'developing back-office systems for banks'. If they'd articulated this slightly differently, not about 'what' they are, but 'why they are in business', i.e. 'We're enabling banks to ensure their customers are always one step ahead in life and business' they'd had the freedom to evolve. That way the 'back-office' category would not have restricted them the way it has in the meantime.

"This is universal. I see it in the ERP space, the CRM space, procurement, HR – you name it. Many vendors that started in the era where their solutions were installed on-premise have lost their edge when the Cloud arrived. Due to the 'restricted way of thinking in boxes' the apparent belief for many vendors was that the transition from on-premise to the Cloud is merely a re-deployment challenge, i.e. their duty was to the same software available in the Cloud. At a 30,000ft level it might appear correct, but you and I know that there's much more at stake to drive success.

"When Cloud computing became popular in early 2000, it shifted the industry. However, as with all new things, it didn't happen overnight. Maybe at first the 'deployment in the Cloud' was *the* innovation. I totally get that. For the early adopters the core benefit at that point in time was to shift from CAPEX to OPEX, to do away with the upgrade nightmares, and benefit from enjoying the latest release.

"However, we all know that moving to the Cloud for the sake of 'just the deployment convenience' is something that's only scratching the surface when it comes to the value you can enjoy.

"Fact is, there are vendors that still think deploying their traditional solution in the Cloud is what the market is after. This might be the case today for the Late Majority, but not for Innovators and Early Adopters. They have come to the realization that deployment in the Cloud is 'table stakes' and that there's far more to gain.

"As such, what was once possibly a differentiator for the pioneers that moved the traditional back-office systems to the Cloud, it's not anymore. It has become a mainstream commodity, and something that only sells to the Majority who have plenty of options, therefore own the sales agenda, and only jump if the price is low enough. With that, no one wins.

"Just think about how you invest yourself, Rob. As they say: if it ain't broken, don't fix it. It's a mantra many businesses have. If everything is working fine today, no one will jump for just an incremental gain. It's just not worth the effort and risk. The only way to break this is to have convincing evidence that the gain is significant, i.e. it will double the performance, halve the cost, or, for example, create the ability the break with the barriers of linear growth in your business.

"This requires a different mindset. It requires vendors to constantly challenge their approach and choices. And many are challenged. It's another example of the issue that 'boxed thinking' brings, and in relation to that, the herding mentality within a sector I talked about earlier. With that you get complacency, all the vendors are simply copying their 'known' peers, and innovation comes to a standstill.

"This exactly the reason why becoming remarkable as a software business is not just about having a big idea, strategic segmentation, smart positioning and clear differentiation. These only define the first three traits of remarkable software companies.

"Remarkable software companies use that as their value foundation – the foundation the drives everything – from their product strategy all the way to their go-to-market.

"Remarkable software companies realize the enormous opportunities that are revealed when they pay attention to what's really going on. They make an orchestrated effort to look at the shifts from the customer's perspective. They pay close attention to why innovators 'jump' and take that risk of being first. These organizations go first because they are constantly on the lookout to receive and create significant leaps in value with their business, i.e. make the value bridge between 'what is' and 'what will be'.

"This value can be monetary, such as the opportunity to release substantial cost savings for themselves of for their customers. It can be growth related, such as an opportunity to introduce new business models or create new market categories. It can be brand related, such as the opportunity to take their perceived 'excellence' in their category to the next level.

"Remarkable software companies realize that the shifts in value they offer their ideal customers and the differentiation by which they deliver this will diminish over time. It's not a question of 'if', but 'when'. They ensure that they're always ahead of that moment and they do that by creating end-to-end alignment across their entire organization. It's not a differentiation point in itself, but one that ensures they'll protect their differentiation like the Crown Jewels – and that helps them to not only be, but also stay, remarkable.

"Patrick Collison,[11] CEO of Stripe, shared the power of this end-to-end alignment in an interview with Tim Ferris:

> If you have to compete on the merits of the product and just rely on people being honest about how well it works or doesn't, that kind of forces you to just build a product development organization that can

---

[11.] https://tim.blog/2018/12/20/patrick-collison/

compete. Maybe it's harder to get that initial traction, but if you can get there, you actually really have kind of an upper hand to the more traditionally incentivized companies, because they probably have gotten a bit lazy, a bit ossified, and it's just a bit less competitive on this axis.

Once you can make the battle about the quality of your product [i.e. the way it uniquely solves a big problem] you really have a huge advantage, and our experience was the incumbents just couldn't react. [...] It's such a deep cultural and organizational thing that it's very difficult for competitors to shift, whereas if you just have a better marketing campaign, that's super easy to copy. Anyone else can buy a competing billboard or pay more for the Google ads or whatever. We didn't kind of realize all this in advance. But I think that ended up really helping us.

Building the bridge between your value foundation and your product strategy

Rob reacted directly: "That's a valuable insight. I realize now this issue of losing your edge can happen to the best. The fact we were amongst the pioneers to create a new category in the market doesn't mean we'll remain the pioneer. Over time we'll risk becoming the legacy of a bank as well – just like the core back-office systems have become over the last decade. Food for thought, and ammunition to take into my board meeting next week.

"So this makes me curious," he continued. "What do you see as a proven tactic to start aligning everyone in our business? Is there 'this one thing'?"

"Good question," I responded, "and yes, there is. A common problem I see with many business software companies today is that brand experience and product experience do not align. And this is true for both start-ups and established software companies. All too often marketers try to position a product as something it is not, resulting in the brand promise being compromized, hence the potential of the company is impacted.

"As we have discussed, crafting a clear, simple and compelling brand/value promise is essential because it influences the way your customers see your brand, which informs their buying choices in the slipstream. Remarkable software companies understand that, they tune their brand experience into every aspect of their business – and they start with their product.

"Obviously the first thing every business needs to do is to create a product that's achieving product-market fit. If your product does not meet the basic requirements of your ideal customer then they'll be unwilling to put down money for it, hence you lose out.

"Now here's the key: A product can have an excellent product market fit, but the moment you bring brand fit and product market fit together you get leverage, i.e. that's where the magic happens. The question is: 'How and where do I start to bring brand-fit and product market fit together?'

"And the answer is simple: build the narrative before the product. Scott Belsky,[12] Chief Product Officer of Adobe, shared this in an interview with Tim Ferris:

> Sometimes, it actually helps to say, 'Hey, what should the brand be?' before we even get the team together, get a loan, or code something. We talk about the notion of product-market fit. We talk about product-founder fit. But what about product-brand fit?
>
> I think the greatest founders out there recognize that while the science of business is scaling everything that you can via automating and whatever, the art of business is the things that don't scale.
>
> Sometimes it helps to get 100% clear what the value proposition should be. It is okay to jump a few pages ahead and actually plan what your landing page should communicate, and how a product will strengthen your brand. You can do this before you even get the team together to start building the product.

"I totally buy into this. Far too many software vendors focus on branding, marketing and deployment in the final stages of software development. So, building a narrative before building the product provides everyone, including developers, with clarity about what the value proposition should be. It will steer your product in the right direction long before testing or implementation or verification. As a matter of fact, if you don't have the luxury of doing this, because your product is already in the market, it could help to course correct and tune your roadmap by stripping out all the 'stuff' that doesn't add value in

---

12. http://tim.blog/2018/09/13/scott-belsky/

order to stay remarkable in the eyes of your ideal prospects and customers.

"This is what I see happen in my workshops. Once the clarity around your big idea, your ideal customer, the shifts in value you offer them, and how you differentiate yourself become clear, the alignment follows by itself. It clarifies the reason for your business' or product existence. It clarifies where you are going, and why. This inspires, and as such others will want to come along on your journey. It's just that simple.

"Recently, during one of my workshops, a product owner acknowledged in the evaluation that he'd never realized with so much clarity what the company was all about. He had never taken the time to define this very essential foundation.

"With this knowledge came more insight. He realized that a large portion of his product backlog should be skipped as a consequence, providing him with new ways and resources to make the product market and brand fit even better, and with that, create happier customers and a more profitable business.

"It becomes your compass. If something is not working, you go back to brand promise and brand fit. If the product is not selling, you go back to that foundation. It all starts with the product."

At that moment we entered a tunnel. "Barcelona," Rob stated. "Gosh, that went fast. Three hours flew by. But I am not done with this, Ton," he said. "Let me buy you dinner before we hop on our plane to Porto."

"I am all into that," I replied.

Ask yourself

STEP 1: Reflect critically how you score your own ability around this particular trait by rating your organization on a scale of 1 (poor) to 10 (remarkable).

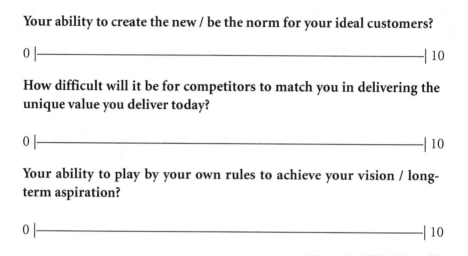

Your ability to create the new / be the norm for your ideal customers?

0 |—————————————————————————————| 10

How difficult will it be for competitors to match you in delivering the unique value you deliver today?

0 |—————————————————————————————| 10

Your ability to play by your own rules to achieve your vision / long-term aspiration?

0 |—————————————————————————————| 10

STEP 2: Take ten minutes to reflect on the next actions you could initiate to improve your score.

STEP 3: What's the single action from this list that would give you the biggest impact?

Take it to the next level

- Not only become remarkable, but ensure you'll stay remarkable as well by introducing the 'Remarkable Monday' habit within your organization. Download the three simple steps that will help you create and keep momentum: https://valueinspiration.com/RemarkableMonday
- Join the Remarkable Tribe Program to create accountability with other tech-entrepreneurs like you. Not only will you build traction to shape the business you aspire to be, but you will also obtain new ideas, create new contacts and will be part of a movement that defines what it means to be remarkable as a business software vendor:
  https://movement.valueinspiration.com

Hi, it's Ton, the author of this book

I hope you are enjoying my book so far and have obtained many ideas already to take the impact of your software business to the next level.

I'd like to ask you a favor: I'd love to get your point of view and as such, would you be so kind as to leave a review and rating on Amazon?

I believe that if more software companies would be remarkable in what they do, the world would be a better place. It's therefore my mission to help as many people like you, tech-entrepreneurs-on-a-mission, do exactly that. Your review on Amazon would help build that momentum.

Thanks for your review in advance!

Ton

Part 2

The Viability Lever – increase customer life-time value

Trait 4
Master the art of curiosity

The ingredients of a remarkable product strategy

The train slowed down, and we entered Barcelona Sants.

The hectic rush of packing and moving had already started and as soon as the train came to a standstill, the train seemed to burst open. "They are eager to go home, apparently," I mentioned as we left the carriage.

We walked to the exit, as I tried to book an Uber for the ride to the airport. 'Unfortunately, Uber is currently not available in your area' my app said. "This is what I meant, Rob," and I showed him the message. "This is what I meant when I talked about Uber and the need to have defensible differentiation. It's unbelievable how real progress can be stopped by the incumbent. It's a clear example of a business model that has got stuck – and the typical reaction is to fight change, rather than embrace it. They'll do everything to fight progress – asking for new regulations, striking, you name it.

"It reminds me of the shift in the 1990s when the transition started from on-premise to Cloud. How many vendors have fought the battle that this couldn't be real, that this would never sustain, that it was unreliable, not fast enough, not secure enough."

We walked out of the station at the north side. When we arrived at the taxi stand there was a long waiting line. It was cold, and a shower of rain came across Barcelona. "Just see how 'beautifully' this system works," I joked. "Everyone has to follow the process, there are not enough taxi's around because they have 'gambled' to be somewhere else in the city waiting for their new ride. And guess what, by the time we have our taxi, it's not exactly clean, the driver is frustrated, and it doesn't take credit cards. Long live progress!

"But where was I? Ah, yes, I remember; embracing new waves of technology.

"It all boils down to doing a couple of things right. The vendors that fought the Cloud as a new platform, are very like the taxi's we see today. They didn't pay attention, or maybe they did, but they waived it away as unimportant. It's complacency at its best."

"Agreed," Rob replied. "I see that in my industry as well. Most vendors of the core-banking systems are in that category. They didn't pay enough attention, and are now in catch-up mode, fighting to reclaim some of their position back."

"That doesn't surprise me," I replied. "It will be true for any platform change we'll see in the future. If your company was the go-to-brand yesterday, it doesn't mean it will be tomorrow for one simple reason: with every significant platform change, the norms change, and with that a reshuffling of the positions of power."

"Guess you are right," said Rob. "You mentioned that there are a couple of things you need to do right. What are those things?"

"Glad you asked," I said. "If I look at the ten traits of a remarkable software business, there are four traits that I'd assign to the Viability lever:

1. They master the art of curiosity
2. They create new possibilities, rather than evolving current ones
3. They create fans, not just customers
4. They focus on the essentials

"These four traits define the success of both start-ups and established software businesses. So it doesn't matter if you've just started, or if you have been around for decades, these four traits enable you, with the insights, the mindset and the drive, to

- create products that your ideal customers will love from the start;
- deliver a shift in value, not incremental;
- and to stay relevant in the volatile market we're in today.

At that point our taxi stopped in front of us, we got in, and I ordered the driver to go to Terminal 2 at El Prat, Barcelona's airport.

As soon as we drove off, I continued: "These four traits are about an entreperineurial mindset that enables these companies to regularly take a step back from their day-to-day reality and critically challenge their products and business models in order to validate if their ability to differentiate, and consequently their ability to deliver shifts in value, continues to sustain.

"Let's look at the meaning of 'differentiation' for a moment: *'It's the result of efforts to make a product or brand stand out as a provider of unique value to customers in comparison with its competitors.'* So, the answer is not entirely up to you – it is driven by the level of entrepreneurship around you in your category. That's what it will require from you as well: entrepreneurial thinking.

"It's about always being on the lookout for the next big thing. Because that next big thing could be your (next) tipping point. It's the same in big wave surfing. The next big wave could be at Mavericks in California, Puerto Escondido in Mexico or, like tomorrow, the biggest wave of all at Nazare in Portugal. It's not easy to predict where and when your next big wave will come, but if you have the right mindset and pay attention to the right things then you'll find it, and you'll be able to ride it.

"Let me plot the principles of these four traits on the big wave surfers that will be out tomorrow as the first heat kicks off at Praia do Norte. The ones that will write history tomorrow will be the ones that apply these traits in the best possible manner:

1. They master curiosity: And as such they are optimally prepared, have done their 'homework', asked all the critical questions, explored new techniques and the best board shapes, and know what it takes to disrupt themselves.
2. They create new possibilities: They will showcase perfect timing, know when to step in, even when it's not 100% perfect, and have the courage to make the moves no one has done before.
3. They create fans: Their preparation, combined with timing and courage to do new things, helps them to move the needle and exceed expectations of everyone out there. That's what they live for.
4. They focus on the essentials: They are resourceful and critically assess which wave to go for, and which one to leave.

"Here's why:

- No one will remember them if they just ride the small 'average' waves – everybody does that.
- No one will remember them if they are constantly too late for the optimal take-off point.

- No one will remember them if they 'play it safe'.
- No one will remember them if they don't go beyond what everybody else is doing.

"Let me bring this back to the business software space, because there's valuable lessons to learn from this. The four traits give you the framework to do the right things when it matters.

It's about daring to disrupt yourself

"Josh Linkner,[1] five-time tech entrepreneur and hyper-growth CEO, recently explained this in a thought-provoking interview with Tiffani Bova:

> *There's an old saying if you keep doing the same thing you keep getting the same results. That's actually worse because if you keep doing the same thing and everyone else is changing and evolving and innovating, you will not enjoy the same results. At some point you know that's going to crash. So, I think it's incumbent on all of us all to make sure that we are the source of disruption.*

> *There's an old saying in business, which I have always hated, which is: 'We can't cannibalize our business'. To me, that's such a foolish thing to say because it implies that you can prevent cannibalization. You've got to flip it upside down. It's our responsibility to be the cannibal, to make sure that we are the ones putting ourselves out of business, rather than waiting around for a competitor to do so.*

It's about timing

"Opportunities come and go – that's true for every company, but especially in the business software industry. Every five to ten years new waves of opportunity are building up that have the potential to change the world as we knew it before. And as with real waves, waves come in sets. One wave growing bigger than the other. Whoever reads the waves best has the opportunity to become the new champion. The opportunity with that is two-fold – the timing of your

---

1. http://whatsnextpodcast.libsyn.com/the-jazz-ensemble-of-innovation-and-reinvention-with-josh-linkner

product strategy, i.e. optimally preparing for the new opportunities that arise with the new technology wave building up, but also with positioning and repositioning your solution – since your customers' needs are changing all the time as well. They are in a fight as well to stay relevant in their industry as new waves of change are rolling into their industry.

It's about stepping in when it's not perfect

"Professor Erik M. Vermeulen gave some valuable advice in one of his blogs:[2] 'Waiting for perfection means missed opportunities or worse':

> *Just like the cloud in the late 90s, many recent technological developments in AI, blockchain and robotics are downplayed or dismissed based on the fact that the current version of such technologies is 'not yet' perfect. However, waiting for perfection isn't the smartest thing to do. You may miss the boat when (currently imperfect) technologies are deployed more broadly. History is littered with examples of companies that failed to act quickly enough when new imperfect technologies arrived and found themselves left behind by more adventurous rivals. Even if the technologies aren't flawless, they could very well offer significant improvements compared with our current experiences and ways of working.*

It's about courage

"I'd like to cite a quote from Xtian Miller, from his blog 'Take Risks. Break the Rules':

> *When a direction feels risky, it's probably worth it. It's a sign of the unconventional – the path that most would avoid. It might seem audacious or adventurous. You're creating something that most would hesitate to do. Perhaps it's a little outside of your comfort zone, but if you stick to your guns and take the leap, you'll gain knowledge at the very least. You'll learn more from a risk than playing it safe.*

"To me it's the essence of finding new unexplored market space and delivering remarkable impact.

---

2. https://hackernoon.com/are-you-ready-for-an-artificially-intelligent-future-b9df618d53b4

It's about moving the needle

"Here's a big one. We too often make it too easy for ourselves. It's almost like we like to be in a competition where we are OK when we're 'just ahead' of the competition because we have more features. CEO of Basecamp Jason Fried[3] has the following to say about that:

> Comparison is the death of Joy. The joy for business software vendors that move the needle is when they can focus all their energy on building the new, rather than fighting the old.

"Customers only move when they are convinced they will get a shift in value. It needs to move the needle, and therefore you should move the needle. This is all about mindset – it's the clear choice you and only you can make. And that leads me to the last critical element.

It's about exceeding expectation

"As I discussed when we started our journey, remarkable companies stay relevant in their category because they constantly evolve. A big recommendation here is not to do so by responding to 'the market'. Instead, respond to the evolving needs of your ideal customer segment. No one can ever find the resources or budget to respond to 'the market' effectively. It's too broad, to diverse. However, by being very articulate about what defines and drives your ideal customers puts all the change into context. It enables you to spot the signals early on by understanding shifts in their mindset, perception of value, urgency, and expectation. It allows you to optimally leverage your impact by aligning the trinity of product strategy, marketing, and sales. It will make decision-making easier, will make you resourceful so you can assign enough resources behind the things that create the biggest shift in value for your ideal customers (and give you an edge at the same time), so that you are always one step ahead. That will be noticed and rewarded."

"This is going to be an interesting evening if I continue to hear the passion in your voice," said Rob. "I can see some strong connection points, and agree with you on the traits you've just outlined. A good exercise to challenge my

---

[3.] https://tim.blog/2018/07/23/jason-fried/

team on again, because it's so easy to get bogged down in 'stuff', even if you are in a domain that's at the top of the hype-curve."

He continued: "From my background in the business software industry I have seen many examples of companies that had these traits when they started, but lost them over time. I assume you've seen this as well?"

"Absolutely," I replied. "Too often! The thing is, when you are a start-up you are building the future. This is the drive. This provides the energy, and this virtually all starts from the fact you see a big problem in the market that needs to be fixed. The problem, however, is that as we grow, we just enjoy the ride – we somehow believe this will last forever. And it doesn't, as you and I both know.

"Let me share an anecdote from Tiffani Bova,[4] author of the book *Growth IQ.*

We're growing! Let's change something!

"In one of her interviews this quote triggered me:

'We're growing! Let's change something!'

"I think this perfectly illustrates the mindset of companies that have the power to become – and stay – remarkable. It's illustrates the fact that remarkable companies anticipate their next big thing when they are still at the top of their game. They approach the category from an offensive, not defensive, position. If you start to think about your next big thing when you're in a full-blown stall of growth then the only way to finance it is with cost-cutting, layoffs, etc. Not fun, and not sustainable.

"Tiffani highlighted four categories of companies:

1. Rapid growth (Offense mode)
2. Seeing softness in growth (10% > 6%)
3. Flat – no growth but enough income to keep the lights on
4. Full-blown stall (Defense mode)

---

4. https://podcasts.apple.com/es/podcast/take-the-lead/id1229733551?i=1000429930348&l=en&mt=2

"The point she makes is this:

> *The best moment to make investments for growth are when you are growing fast. That's where you are acting from a place of strength. Your strong income can be used to invest in your next wave. So, don't just say 'we're growing, why change anything?' It's like 'We're growing, let's change something!', because you'll always want to anticipate that you may stop growing in whatever it is you're selling today, one, two, three years from now. If you start developing something new, when that one starts to decline, the other one, hopefully, is taking off. That's the ideal situation.*

"I fully concur with her advice. As I said, it takes courage, it's about timing, it's about stepping in when it's not perfect, it's about daring to disrupt yourself, it's about moving the needle, and most of all, it's about exceeding expectations. Nothing remains the same, it didn't in the 1980s, not in the 1990s, and for sure not today.

"Change happens from two angles, and it keeps accelerating in pace. It's happening in our own industry: technology shifts result in new ways to approach common and new problems. But it's happening at the same speed inside the business of your ideal customers as well.

"So we have to be very aware of not being 'run over' by a new competitor, and at the same time we have to assure ourselves at any point in time that our ideal customers would still place their bets on us, if they'd have to buy a new solution today.

"Tiffani shares a couple of tips to signal potential changes in growth. That it's all about keeping an eye on the data: customer sentiment, Net Promoter scores, term rates, growth rates, product adoption usage – etc.

"Her advice:

> *When you start to see them change don't just blow it off as 'oh it's because the economy is soft', or 'something's happening' or 'it's one or two specific things'. Take it seriously, because it's usually not that. It's a combination of a lot of things, things that are happening internally as well as things that are happening externally.*

"That's why the three questions I raised a number of times already are so important. There's a constant friction between value, urgency and expectation. How customers react to this, or what they expect, is dependent on a moment in time, the pressures they face, and the ambitions they have. To master this dynamic you need to master the art of curiosity."

Curiosity drives relevance

"I believe curiosity is critical in every aspect of a business software company. It's critical at the start when you develop the big idea and make it a reality, but it's possibly even more important as you grow and evolve. It's about staying at the top of your game, ensuring your customers will continue to see you as the 'go-to-source' that makes them successful. To achieve that you constantly need to stretch yourself. Chris Dayley,[5] founder of Dayley Conversion, once said:

> *To reach a goal you've never before attained, you must do things you've never before done.*

"Curiosity has always helped me both business-wise and personally. I recall back in the 1990s, very early into my career, and back then responsible for product management and marketing of an SME ERP product in the Netherlands. I always looked for inspiration on 'what's next', in what made other products remarkable. Back then I was fascinated with Microsoft's auto complete function in Office. My immediate reaction was, 'What if you apply this concept to book keeping?' How many errors could be avoided by non-expert users? How many hours of correction could be avoided by professional accountants? And how many hours could be regained by simply avoiding the time/effort to look up the correct double entry?

"So we built it, and it was that very feature that granted us lots of eyeballs at the annual Efficiency Beurs event at Amsterdam Rai – at the expense of the market leaders. Small effort, big impact. That what makes it so much fun!

"On the private side, curiosity is the very reason I live in Spain. It was Easter 2008 and I was driving with the family from the west to the east in the Netherlands to visit an entertainment park. The journey was one typical for the Netherlands – all four seasons in one hour. Rain, hail, snow, wind, clouds, sun – repeat. That triggered a conversation about 'the weather' – the never-ending complaint stream about the weather. Since for both my wife and I the glass is always half full, we turned the conversation into an opportunity: 'Why don't we just decide to live in a country where the sun is out 300 days a year?' And

---

5. https://www.eofire.com/podcast/chrisdayley/

that one question triggered a flow of answers – reviewing all the pros and cons. Once we arrived in Slagharen we had made our decision – let's do it.

"Did we know all the answers? No. Did we have worries and concerns? Yes, sure. But it's about progress. It's about exploring new paths to something better. Let's be honest – there's never a good time. There's always a 'but'. However, we wanted to avoid ever having to say 'we wished we'd had the guts to do it, but now it's too late'. You'll only know what you could've missed if you explore the opportunity. Just do it.

"That's what makes curiosity so powerful – growing that trait opens your horizons. It allows you to raise critical questions, to challenge the status quo, to explore. As Dr. Diane Hamilton shares in her book, *Cracking the Curiosity Code*:[6]

> *Curiosity is essential in all aspects of our lives because it ignites our desire for new experiences. As we develop our curiosity, we discover the things that make us happy, energize us, and create new opportunities. It's the spark that leads to motivation and to drive and for you to get anywhere with communication, critical thinking, leadership, creativity, teamwork, engagement. You name it, all the top issues that leadership struggles with.*

Rob nodded. "So true," he said. "That makes it so much fun, and talking about it now makes you realize we just don't do enough of it. It's so easy to get trapped in the treadmill."

"And that's not only an opportunity missed to make the most of our lives, and our business; it's also dangerous," I continued. "As technology and business advances, so do the expectations of our prospects and customers. It's that moment where curiosity plays a fundamental role to stay relevant and continue to stand out in our category. That's why its key to keep asking critical questions like 'Why is everyone doing it that way?' 'Why can't it be done differently?' 'What are the conventional beliefs that stop us from progressing?' 'What if we break with those beliefs and make it better?'

"Everyone believes it's impossible, but if it were possible, how could we do it? Asking those types of question could help reveal opportunities bigger than yourself.

"There's a story I must share with you with regards to that. It's the story

---

6. https://drdianehamilton.com/curiosity-code-system/

behind Susanne Baars,[7] founder of the Global Human Genome Foundation and CEO of Social Genomics. Susanne is known as the Dutch DNA Queen. She's a woman on a mission, which is *To create universal access to genomic knowledge for every human on our planet in order to prevent millions of people from dying every single year.* When I spoke with her this simple quote struck me:

'*If only we'd have known, we could have prevented this.*'

"I think this quote sounds familiar to all of us – for so many occasions that we've been involved in. But for Susanne this relates to memories about her childhood, where her dad, a doctor, who often came home after a day's work expressing these same words after someone had suddenly died. Fact is, every year millions of people are dying because of a lack of access to available data. Well, the data is available, it's just scattered all over the world, and impossible to get access to. It's like looking for a needle in a haystack. It could literally be that the answer to your disease is available in the hospital in a neighboring city, with a patient in a neighboring country, or a specialist that's an acquaintance of someone in your own network.

"So Susanne reasoned wisely:

> *I think that's just not right, and we should do something with this. Instead of focusing on problems and solving them, look around you and see the abundance, and really think about how you can use this to build the future. Dare to think big. It's knowing what you know, the unique knowledge that can make a change in the world, and to be able to think differently. Not linear or locally, but try to think, 'How would I like to see the future?'*

"Fact is, the essence of her quote impacts us on a day-to-day basis in our business live more often than we realize. How often do we see situations where we wonder out loud, 'If only we'd have known, we could have prevented this'. And to put that in perspective, how much opportunity is wasted as we keep wondering, without acting?

"Imagine we all took the mantra from Susanne: 'I think that's just not right, and we should do something with this'. If we decided to be curious, raise the right question and take action on it. What if every time we wonder about this

---

7. https://www.valueinspiration.com/saving-millions-of-lives-by-sharing-genomes-on-a-global-scale/

we stop and reflect on the bigger question: 'What would be required to prevent this from happening ever again?' What information would we need? Where's the source of this information? And how can we bring it together to make it really work for us?

"Everyone can do this. We don't have to wait for someone else to pick up the responsibility. And the solution is often right in front of us – we often just fail to see it. It just requires us to be curious."

Reading the signs on the wall

Rob responded with amazement. "Fascinating story; we should have more people like Susanne in our world. It makes you think why that's not the case. I agree with you, it starts with that very simple question of curiosity, 'Why?' What makes me wonder – also in relation to the success of my own company – is why, once businesses develop, they lose their capacity to be curious?"

"I am not an expert," I replied. "However, from what I learned when interviewing Dr. Diane Hamilton,[8] there are four factors that play a big role: fear, assumptions, technology and environment. She described the factors as follows:

1. *Fear: As far as fear goes, no one wants to look stupid, right? Nobody wants to ask that question that makes them look unprepared, or they don't want to be rejected.*

2. *Assumptions: That's the little voice in your head; you know, the one that says, 'Oh, I'm not interested. It sounds boring. Why is this even necessary? Why bother? It's too much work.'*

3. *Technology can be something that holds people back because either it does it for you, or it seems too overwhelming and you don't know where to start or how to learn it, especially if it's something you didn't grow up with. It can be overwhelming and sometimes it takes a lot of critical thinking skills. It's a problem for a lot of companies because people get behind or they aren't aware of the potential of what they can do with it. And that can be problematic for them.*

---

8. https://www.valueinspiration.com/cracking-the-curiosity-code-the-key-to-unlocking-human-potential/

> **4. Environment** is everything, from your family, to your teachers, to your work, relationships to your peers, and anything that you can think of growing up or in your current life. Just consider the fact if they cloned you right now and raised you again, even with the same parents, you wouldn't be the same person because your experiences would be different and your environment really can impact.

"Each of these factors impact our level of curiosity, and it appears that they are pretty evenly distributed. So as a business you want to influence those factors, to help curiosity to flourish in your organization. That starts by asking the simple question: 'What is holding you back from asking questions?'

"I share the same belief as Dr. Hamilton – that culture has to start at the top. If leaders think their people feel comfortable asking questions, but people really don't feel comfortable asking questions, that has to be uncovered. If leaders show really honest desire to improve curiosity, then they prove it by doing it themselves. You have to really mean it. If people still feel like they're being criticized, or don't feel the weight behind what they're saying, then it won't get anywhere.

"So, curiosity is something organizations should prioritize making part of their culture. It could be the start of something big and remarkable, but it's a critical ingredient in staying remarkable in the long run. The fact many business software companies lose their edge over time is often due to the fact they've lost their curiosity, not because they didn't have it. They've lost track of what's going on, and have become stale because of their own success.

"It's very often not one thing; it's a string of things. It's not about 'we're not creative' or 'we simply haven't got the ideas.' It's not about creating this one campaign to turn the ship – it's often much more fundamental. To turn the challenge into an advantage, the first thing to do is to recognize the symptoms, i.e. the underlying shifts that are happening.

"You should be looking at customer sentiment, Net Promoter scores, growth rates or product adoption rates, as already listed by Tiffani Bova. But let's add some more to that with other signals that should ring alarm bells for you because it often starts way earlier:

1) You're challenged to build engagement with prospects
2) You're less likely to be invited to the longlist – let alone the shortlist
3) When you are invited, you're not winning enough

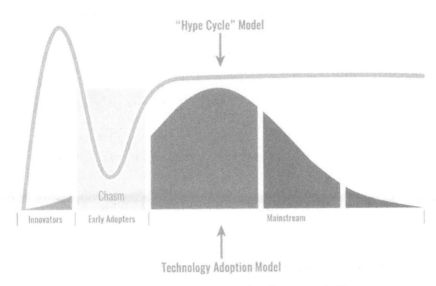

4) You're fighting a race to the bottom – the discount challenge
5) The balance of new business / existing business is shifting to the latter

"However, the problem is bigger than following these indicators though. There are companies that do, but still fall behind. We all know the Gartner Hype Cycle where they position the path of new technologies all the way from introduction to mainstream adoption.

"The same curve can be applied to companies. Virtually every software business starts on a 'high' – bring new innovation to market, growth is happening, the customer base is rapidly building up. However, at some point along the way the momentum shifts. We often believe our solution has what it takes to continue to be appealing to innovators, but the opposite is true. The market often shifts in front of your eyes, and we realize too late we have not moved with it.

"It strikes me every week when I publish a new edition of my podcast just how much contrast there is between the vibe in the new generation software companies and the established ones. You can feel it in everything – the big idea they are after, the focus they have, the determination to make a transformative impact, etc.

"Why? What is it that makes this difference so obvious? When I am working with established companies curiosity is often replaced by 'complacency', i.e. an uncritical satisfaction with oneself or one's achievements. That's dangerous. It's opening the door for the new generation to gain ground and take over. So, the question is: how can you avoid it? It all starts by sensing it. But sensing complacency seems hard, it's born out of self-talk, and often that takes over reality.

"Dr. Diane Hamilton had this explanation for it:

> *There's trait and state curiosity. Under trade curiosity, there's something called diversity which is motivated by boredom, like you're just aimless and you're not productive. Some jobs are just done mindlessly. Because it's always been done that way, when it doesn't have to be that way.*

"I have found other signals throughout my career that should raise alarm bells to fight complacency:

1) 'Our customers are not ready for this yet'

"Having an extensive network in the Enterprise Resource Planning space, I have heard this a lot. The problem, however, is not that their customers are not ready – it's because the PMs are not curious enough to challenge the status quo, step up and make things better. Sure, there's always enough to be busy with. But just because your customers are not 'asking' for it, doesn't mean they won't need it the moment it arrives! Consequently, too many traditional players end up in a vicious circle that seems impossible to break, opening the doors for a new generation of competitors to walk in and take advantage.

2) 'We always have to discount heavily in this sector to win new business'

"This is a typical source of evidence that should ring alarm bells. However, when complacency kicks in, this one is easily passed off as 'this is normal', putting all discussion to rest. What should be the case, of course, is to say: 'If we need to do more discounting to win a deal, this is a very strong sign something is wrong with the product. Discounting is never done out of luxury. It's done to buy the customer simply because the value is not clear enough (anymore). It's therefore not the sector; it's you where the problem resides. If the value were crystal clear, prospects would line up and be prepared to pay a premium over competitive offerings.

3) 'We're in a commodity market – it's hard to differentiate'

"The third sign of complacency is from the marketing side. It's the belief that because all solutions appear to do the same, one has to communicate them similarly as well. I have done dozens of messaging heat-maps across various industries – ERP, blockchain, digital banking, financial management, field service planning, not for profit, etc. – and the same pattern appears time after time: most vendors aim to lure prospects along the same lines: better, cheaper, faster, features. Guess what happens? The vendor with the largest budget wins. So, for the rest, they can merely hope they are invited to the longlist for comparison and be allowed to give a significant discount to win the deal.

4) 'We need this too'

"The fourth sign is internal complacency, a typical example of competing against the others, instead of for your ideal customer. One of the largest challenges business software companies face is the race to beat their biggest competitors. This leads to the deep struggle to keep up with both large companies and agile start-ups. This goes back to playing it by your own rules. The thing to do is to focus your curiosity on solving the biggest problems for your ideal customer, instead of doing the same as everyone else.

"Another variation of this is the shiny object syndrome. A common issue with many ISVs is to start their solution approach from the point of using specific cool technology. The current hype around Artificial Intelligence is a perfect example of this. The thinking is 'Because the technology is cool, the solution will be cool'. This results in the famous 'solutions looking for a problem.'

"The approach should be to focus your curiosity in your aim to make a dent in the market by redefining and solving an existing industry problem, identifying and solving a brand-new problem, or seizing a brand-new opportunity. Everything else is doomed to fail.

5) You're responding to specs, not to requirements

"Many ISV's follow the good principle of being customer-led. The problem starts, however, with the way you listen to your customers. Often, rather than listening and challenging them to uncover hidden needs, you're responding to the specifications they give you. Remember, your customers are not paid to create solutions, that's your responsibility. It's your job to find the needle in the haystack that could shift the value and impact they can make. This requires a different mindset – and starts with sincere curiosity.

6) You believe you're stuck in a trajectory of historic decisions

"I have seen many software businesses that follow a trajectory of investments that they know is a 'dead end'. Starting over seems too overwhelming, but continuing isn't the answer either. They're stuck in historic decisions. A big dilemma. As Nick Thompson,[9] Editor-in-Chief of *Wired* magazine, wisely said in an interview with Tim Ferris:

> *When you look at everything that goes wrong historically, you can see a deep chain of continuous mistakes that lead up to it. In a way, this is very discouraging. However, if you turn it around and think 'what if I did something right, right now', you are starting a whole new chain of actions that could lead to a fundamentally positive outcome. So even if you are going in the 'wrong' direction, everyone can stop, be curious, challenge the status quo, do something small, and turn the trajectory.*

7) You're not prioritizing with impact in mind

"Do you recognize this one? Your backlog looks intimidating, and, since you've always done it like this, you prioritize bottom up, rather than top down. As you evolve and grow your customer base, many ISVs fall into the trap of crushing their roadmaps with small features, maintenance, contractual obligations, etc. The result: this approach leaves no time, no budget, nor energy for the ingredients that will define your future, and not only yours, but also the future of your customers as well! It's the short-term that prevails. I have heard it many times: 'The long-term is about a lot of short-terms'. Correct, but that doesn't mean you should stop thinking strategically. To achieve your big ambition is a matter of many small, but rightly focused steps that bring you closer to realizing the vision. That starts with being curious and challenging whether your backlog is representative of that. Often it's not.

---

9. https://tim.blog/2018/06/26/the-tim-ferriss-show-podcasts-nick-thompson/

8) You've lost your Founder's Mentality

"Last but not least – the growth paradox has kicked in. Growth creates complexity and complexity kills growth. In the book *The Founder's Mentality*[10] by Chris Zook and James Allen, they state that 90% of issues with growth are internal due to loss of focus with the frontline, lack of accountability, and rigid processes:

> *Most large, successful companies began as insurgents – fast, agile and adaptable. They focused on customers. They hated complexity. But too many companies accept a troubling trade-off. They achieve scale, but lose their Founder's Mentality – the very core strengths and values that helped them succeed and grow.*

"Here again is where curiosity can be your way out. Staying curious around what you can do internally will help ensure you stay lean, fight complexity, and avoid complex decision making.

"Obviously there are more signals, but if you catch these then you're well on your way to changing course with success. It starts with people though. As a leader, you can't do it all by yourself. You need to create a culture where curiosity is something obvious. It's something that motivates people because they realize they can make an impact and help the company get closer to realizing its vision.

"Dr. Diane Hamilton's view on this is straightforward:

> *You should work on having people avoid being aimless by giving them goal-oriented problem-solving ideas. We want people to start thinking way ahead – asking the 'why' questions.*
>
> *You want them to be considerate of the moment they see something happening, and think, 'Oh, that's interesting, why is it doing that?' or 'Why doesn't it do that?'*
>
> *You want them to think 'What could happen? Where are we going?'*
>
> *You want them to reflect. Just think of things that you take for granted. Think of why something happens or something works a certain way. How could that mechanism of action be used for something else?*

---

10. https://www.bain.com/founders-mentality/

"All these little signs are signals that come from one or more substantial shifts. Sometimes they are blurred, almost hidden or even contradicting. Remarkable companies anticipate those shifts and act on them, because they are masters at staying curious.

"Or like Marshal Goldsmith once said: 'They realize that *What got them here, won't get them there.*'

Plan from your vision, not from your present

Rob responded: "It is so easy to forget that the problem is not necessarily what's happening outside, but what's going on inside. It's very much a culture and leadership issue. It's so easy to become arrogant when everything seems to fall into place, but that's exactly the moment when you need to be sharp and think ahead. So I recognize a lot in what you say.

"So what can I do in my company to stay sharp and inspire my staff to think different and ahead? Is there a framework you'd suggest?"

"Absolutely," I responded. "There are various aspects that will give you a framework to target curiosity at. Remember what I told you when we started our journey in Valencia this afternoon? It all starts with your big idea that consists of answering three basic questions:

1) What do you believe is broken in the world of your ideal customer that needs solving urgently?
2) Why would solving this provide a major shift in value for them, i.e. what's the opportunity?
3) How do you believe you can exceed expectations, i.e. differentiate?

"This is the foundation for crafting your vision. Framing that the right way gives you a stretched goal. It's the friction between 'what is today' and 'what can be tomorrow' that provides you the space to keep shifting value.

"So my first advice is to target your curiosity at 'what can be tomorrow', i.e. plan from your vision, instead of from your present. It's fun to dive into envisioning what tomorrow should look like for your ideal customers' point of view. Simple questions like 'What are the outcomes (not the outputs) our customers are dreaming to achieve?' will help you to disconnect from the status quo.

"Let me give you an anecdote from Doug Hatler,[11] Chief Revenue Officer at

---

[11.] https://www.valueinspiration.com/product-innovation-how-ai-can-be-used-to-augment-engineers-to-solve-a-1-trillion-infrastructure-problem/

Fracta. The company he represents started off with a clear vision to solve a potentially $1 trillion infrastructure problem arising from of an ageing water infrastructure.

"The problem is literally hidden, but eventually would impact all of us – in the end someone will need to pay for the damage, waste and disruption caused by failing infrastructure. I'm not sure how things are in Portugal, but where I live in Spain, issues with the water infrastructure is a regular source of frustration. It simply is not coping."

Rob smiled. "Same where I live. Regular cuts for hours due to broken pipes, faulty repairs and what have you."

"Exactly," I copied. "And this is what became the underlying driver for Fracta's vision. They realized the conventional approach to keep the water infrastructure functioning is not going work. Doug shared with me:

> By 2050, in the United States alone, we're going to need to spend close to one trillion dollars just to keep up with a one percent pipe replacement rate and projected community growth. Which means, if I have 1,000 miles of water main, I should be replacing 10 miles per year of pipe. However, 30 to 70 percent of the pipe that is taken out still has 'useful life'. If we just look at the low end (30 percent), you could be spending three million dollars a year replacing pipe that doesn't need to be replaced.

"On the question 'why?' the answer is simple: 'we have always done it this way'.

"So creating their vision around a large scale, global problem enabled them to step back, assess the issue with fresh eyes, and come up with an approach that's the exact opposite from what's currently happening: instead of finding a way to replace pipes faster, and cheaper – the conventional approach – they use technology such as AI to predict with extreme high accuracy which pipes need replacing and why in terms of risk. And this is revolutionizing the water industry as we speak.

"Fracta initially started their approach with a pipe-crawling robot, but quickly realized this wasn't scalable. That's when they decided to shift their approach towards Machine Learning. On that subject Doug offered a wise piece of advice:

> You should always keep challenging your approach – your initial idea might be the most obvious, but looking at the desired outcome in different ways might give you better routes to success – if so, be ready to pivot.

Manage for disruption, not for stability

"Greg Satell, author of *Mapping Innovation*, offered the following insight in one of his blogs:[12]

> *Today we need to manage not for stability, but for disruption. All great innovators actively seek out new problems to solve. In other words, they don't continue to hone in on their existing processes and practices, they actively look for areas where they can make an impact. These are, by definition, highly speculative and hard to predict, with lots of blind alleys and wrong turns, but they pay off in the end.*

Leverage the power of the crowd

"That brings me to another piece of advice that helps to make progress: leverage the power of the crowd rather than rely on your own experts only, i.e. use experts surrounding you in your network to solve complex problems. Thinking you have what it takes in-house is like entering all of your people in a smartness contest with everyone else in the world. And I can tell you one thing – they are not going to win, no matter how much money you give them.

"Too often we limit ourselves by controlling things too much. But we only know what we know. The good thing is, technology such as AI gives us the opportunity to explore millions of combinations, revealing new patterns, insights and, therefore, opportunities. This requires us to think bigger than the problem at hand and to open up to 'the unknown'.

"Anastasia Georgievskaya,[13] General Manager at Youth Laboratories, summarized this elegantly:

> *The future is in the collaboration. You need to be flexible and find a way how you can integrate and collaborate with everyone – customers – fans and skeptics, partners, platform players, etc. Every person can't be a specialist in everything. We consult a lot. I just want to stress that there is so much undiscovered right now and we just can't think of it because we don't have an idea about that.*

---

12. https://www.inc.com/greg-satell/ive-studied-hundreds-of-organizations-heres-why-most-cant-innovate.html
13. https://www.valueinspiration.com/how-ai-is-helping-to-increase-confidence-and-life-quality-for-all-of-us/

"So instead, find smart ways to utilize the combined brainpower and diversity of people outside your organization. You could, for example, start a contest around a specific challenge. You'll be amazed by the perspective shifts you'll see. And that's what it is all about."

At that point the taxi stopped. We were there already – El Prat Airport, Terminal 2.

I paid the taxi driver, then Rob and I collected our luggage from the trunk of the car and walked into the terminal.

"Let's go through customs first, and then find a place to get some tapas," Rob suggested.

Luckily, the queue at security was short. As frequent travelers, we unpacked the liquids, laptops and other electronics rapidly, put everything on the conveyor, and moved through the scanner without any interruption. Three minutes later we were on the 'other side'. I rapidly checked Foursquare for some recommendations and we were off to Enrique Tomas to get some authentic Iberico dishes.

On arrival at the restaurant we selected a table and sat down. We ordered some Jamon de Bellota, some chorizo and Salihichón, and each a nice glass of Verdejo wine, and continued our conversation.

"Where were we?" I asked out loud.

"The framework you use to focus curiosity in our organization," Rob replied.

"You're right, so let me continue with the second angle to explore: major shifts – and in particular the macro-shifts your ideal customers have to deal with. What are the trends and external pressures they have to deal with today or in the near future that can or will impact the course of their business.

"This is an excellent technique to stay ahead of the curve. And it keeps you focused on the price, i.e. the most pressing problems your customers are or will have to start dealing with. It's these challenges that should be the inspiration to your solutions of the future. As motivational guru Tony Robbins always says: 'Losers react, winners anticipate'.

"If you pay attention, the opportunities are plenty. The very concept of work is being redefined as different generations enter and exit the workforce amidst a rapidly changing technological landscape. Borders are disappearing, and ecosystems will do away with the traditional industry borders. This has an impact in three big ways. Let me give you some examples:

'Organizational impact'

"Many people think the hierarchical system that we know today is going to disappear because organizations have to become nimbler to remain competitive/relevant.

"Accenture's research about the organization of the future showed that 67% of executives agreed that the future workforce would be structured more by projects, i.e. work focused on joint goals completed in collaborative teams, rather than by job function.

"The growing mix of contingent workers, as well as freelance employees, provides employers with the opportunity to pull from a global talent pool to source the skills and expertise when and where they are needed, resulting in more flexibility and less risk.

"And last but not least, Harvard believes that by 2020 the manager will no longer be the manager and that organizations will shift into spiderwebs of interconnected employees, coaches, leaders, and mentors.

"This could mean that the organization of the future will be one that's more self-guided, quickly configured (around projects), fluid, location independent (virtual), has distributed teams, and is composed of a mix of fixed contract and freelancers.

"The Institute for the Future[14] gave this a name by coining the label 'superstructed organizations'. To 'superstruct' means to create structures that go beyond the primary forms and processes with which we are familiar. It means to collaborate and play at extreme scales.

'Technological impact'

"Without any doubt, technology will be a crucial component in the process to reimagine how work is done. McKinsey & Company revealed that organizations that showcased above average growth had two capabilities that stood out: First, they used data and analytics to squeeze out incremental growth on the margin, and second, they leveraged their ability to collaborate cross-functionally to work in an agile method.

"Data will continue to exponentially grow, and therefore by utilizing this data, we'll have a wealth of new options to identify opportunities and risks faster, and with more precision. This fuels an organizations' ability to drive not only higher

---

14. http://www.iftf.org/uploads/media/overview_READER.pdf

organic growth (top and bottom line), but also to create more timely, relevant and personalized experiences for both employees and customers.

"This collective intelligence and access to virtually unlimited resources through technology enables us to achieve the kind of scale and reach previously attainable only by very large organizations. In other words, where ideas used to take years to introduce to the market, today this can be done in a fraction of that (days).

'Eco-system impact'

"As sector borders dissolve, new business ecosystems emerge. This means no company can be an island, and success in any market requires that organizations learn to co-create value with other firms. Companies that leverage this in the best way – the so-called orchestrators who own the data – will have disproportionate power over the whole value chain. So we are not just seeing value chains merging faster than ever before, but also the shift of value across these value chains is much faster than we have seen. And this creates a huge challenge for any company or organization who is involved in serving clients or distribution, because it requires them to reinvent their strategy at a much faster speed, looking at a much broader horizon than ever before.

"As a result of these three shifts, not only we, but also our ideal customers will have to rethink what it means to be competitive, how partnerships will play a role, and how we'll have to innovate the value chains in which we operate. The 2020 workplace will be one that's networked, flexible, integrated, open, and innovative."

At that point our dinner was served. Two plates of Spanish delicacy. Mouthwatering.

Rob and I toasted on the fact we'd met on our journey before he said: "I agree with these shifts you see, but what's puzzling me is what we should do to keep abreast of it? I mean, you can spend time researching this full time, but we have a business to run as well."

"I am with you," I continued. "And the good news is, there's plenty of research and guidance on these topics. But there's one book that provides a useful framework to guide and inspire your actions. It's called *Understanding How the Future Unfolds*.[15] In this book the authors Mark Esposito PhD and

---

[15]   https://www.amazon.com/Understanding-How-Future-Unfolds-Megatrends-ebook/dp/B01N4OZQ8C

Terence Tse PhD reveal a framework called DRIVE, introducing five different lenses through which to view the next mega trends for any organization:

1. Demographic and social changes
2. Resource scarcity
3. Inequalities
4. Volatility, complexity, and scale
5. Enterprising dynamics

"When I interviewed Mark,[16] his conclusion was straightforward:

> *Utilizing the five different lenses enables organizations to understand how to position themselves in the next few years.*

> *For me, more than a competitive advantage, is a position in advantage. We've been doing a lot of work in how organizations position themselves in the market, and that market is changing. The DRIVE framework enables leaders to feel empowered in that they understand. They don't feel they have to sit and wait for what happens because that, of course, is a vendor's game to play. They can proactively create the future they want to have. For me it's more about their competitive positioning that is different in comparison to before. Previously, positioning was happening primarily through either trends that tend to be a replication of the past with some marginal optimization to the future.*

"Taking one of their lenses: resource scarcity was the underlying story on how Caitlin MacGregor[17] created her company Plum. This is what she said:

> *In the second business I helped build from scratch, I was tasked with making our first hire. My executive coach warned me that a failed hire at this stage of our company could cost our business $300,000. I decided to use psychometric testing and I was blown away by how*

[16.] https://www.valueinspiration.com/the-secret-to-creating-a-position-of-business-advantage/

[17.] https://www.valueinspiration.com/product-innovation-how-ai-can-help-any-organization-hire-top-rather-than-mediocre-performers/

accurate it was at predicting how somebody was going to behave on the job. I learned that a lot of the data that we use right now to evaluate talent, like where they went to school and previously worked, hardly predicts whether someone will be a top performer in the role. This skills and knowledge data can determine eligibility for a job, but cannot predict if they'll excel.

I started relying on this data to be educated in the field of industrial organizational psychology. What struck me was that there's 10,000 industrial organizational psychologists in the world, and the only way a company really gets access to them is through consultants, or really expensive, custom, one-off types of software. That's where the idea came to democratize access to this highly accurate data by turning it into software as a service. That's how Plum was born.

"This aligns nicely with the conclusion from Mark Esposito:

As much as you benchmark, most disruption doesn't happen from your own industry. It happens from outside of your own field of vision.

"This is what triggers new companies to arise, and what gets so many companies into trouble; because they're so focused on what's happening in their own market/industry, they simply don't see the threats or opportunities coming timely enough. As they say, innovation is in most cases not introducing something we've never seen before. Far more often it's about combining elements that we all know very well, that, when blended into one solution, delivers remarkable value and has the power to create completely new categories."

"I cannot agree more with that," Rob replied immediately. "It's that very point that has created the market I am in with my company. It's about helping banks to tune in to the channels their customers use day to day – virtually all those channels already existed. It's now about blending the experience."

"Yes, isn't that fascinating?" I replied. "And see what value is being created as a consequence of that. And this is just the tip of the iceberg, because once you have picked up the macro-shifts, then you can start to challenge the status quo again by looking at the micro-shifts."

Identify the micro-shifts

"Where the macro-shifts are all about picking up on the big trends ahead of us, another aspect to focus your curiosity on is the micro-shifts. If you've carved out your big idea in the correct way and if you have segmented your ideal customers correctly, this should come naturally, simply because you are so close to what's going on."

Shifts in business priorities

"One thing I always look for is the visions of your customers. Where are they today, and where do they aim to be in one, three, five years. Often this is related to the macro-shifts happening in their market, but what it results in is micro-shifts that are going to be crucial to their success.

"Paying attention to this is a very good start to pick up on two important things: first, the shifts in priorities, i.e. how their business goals are evolving. It could very well be that one moment your ideal customers were hyper-focused on cost management to be ultra-lean. You see that in markets where margin is very thin. However, due to shifts in the market, their priorities shift 180 degrees towards top-line focus – or, for example, customer experience."

"That's exactly what happened in the market I focus on with my business – banking," Rob replied. "They were always in a position where they were in charge, customers were loyal, and the focus was on margin optimization, not at all on customer experience. Today that's exactly the opposite. Loyalty is gone, customers are in charge, and banks are battling for a position of relevance with their customers."

"Agreed," I replied. "And, consequently, you've likely seen that their shift in business priorities has also led to a shift in their challenges to achieve those priorities, correct?"

"Absolutely." Rob replied. "Many new challenges! Just think about the changes they are dealing with operationally in meeting new customer experience expectations in terms of speed and quality: the shift from single channel, their physical office, to omni-channel; their ability to attract new customers, and maybe even a bigger challenge, retaining existing customers; the new skills they need to build; finding ways to invest a higher percentage of their revenue to innovation to compete with FinTechs, and so on."

"Exactly," I replied, "all of these challenges are the reality of today. They are the internal roadblocks they have to overcome, one way or another. And that's where the opportunity will be for the time to come – and this makes it so important to anticipate this. Because if you can offer a solution that exceeds their expectations based on this new reality, then you become the go-to-source for them. That Is what defines remarkable business software companies from the rest."

"I get your point," Rob replied. "So my question is, what are the tricks to being ahead of the curve? What should everyone in my company be sensitive for?"

I sipped my wine and responded. "Excellent question, Rob! And the simplest way is just to ask. What drives them? How are their ambitions changing? What are the new expectations they have to live up to from their customers, their partners, or their shareholders? What problems hold them back from delivering upon those expectations? In other words, what do they need to do to stay relevant in their industry? This tells you everything about the shifts they are undergoing, and as such, how the problems you solve today are evolving."

Where is value being destroyed/created?

"Another very strong approach to look for micro shifts is to ask the question: 'Where is value being created' or 'Where is value being destroyed?' These questions force you to look critically at what's going on. What's the status quo? And is this resulting in loss of resource, speed or quality which is perceived as 'normal', or is it undermining potential, i.e. nothing is really going wrong, but with today's technology advances, it could be so much better. Making a list of this would be a strong starting point to finding your next big thing.

"Let me give you an example of a company that was founded on this principle: SalesChoice Inc., a Canadian SaaS and predictive AI analytics company. When I interviewed Dr. Cindy Gordon,[18] CEO of SalesChoice Inc., she said:

The problem we are solving is that 30 to 60% of sales professionals don't make their sales plan targets or quotas in the B2B market segment. This high cost of performance yield, if focused on the best sales opportunities with strong propensity to purchase insights, can unleash trillions of new value into our global economy.

---

[18] https://www.valueinspiration.com/product-innovation-how-ai-can-help-sales-teams-beat-their-numbers-every-month-quarter-year/

A clear example of an area where value creation is being undermined is by avoiding to challenge the status quo. The process is broken and no one is really challenging this. It has always been like this. We have done all we could to automate by implementing CRM suites, etc. We've become complacent to it. Edwards Deming famously phrased: 'When you see something broken, don't assume that it's the people; there's something in the process or something you can't see that might be hurting your discovery.'

"And that's exactly the point Dr. Gordon challenged. She found that:

It's not only information overload at the customer/consumer side – the same is true on the sales side. 30% of sales professionals suffer from attention deficit disorder. And if that's not enough, in the past 10 years, the human attention span has dropped by 50% since the advent of mobile technology. So, what's happening is that the speed of acceleration in our world dynamics is becoming 'the age of distraction' where sales professionals have one of the hardest jobs in the world because of the increasing 'noise interruption' factor. As a matter of fact, our attention span is less than ten seconds, less than a goldfish, which is eight seconds.

This is why the sales process is ripe for transformation. Not by removing people from the process, but by improving our human/machine interfaces that combine the best of people with the best of technology. It's about guiding sales in real-time by removing the noise interruptions, and replacing them with richer insights and next step best actions, fueled by AI. With our AI approaches, we have been able to achieve over 95% predictive accuracy on sales forecasting, and also in predicting our client's wins and losses before they happen. With this type of foresight, there is no question that companies applying AI in successful ROI outcomes, will outperform those who don't use AI.

"Dr. Gordon finished with wise advice:

Everyone knows that to succeed you have to stay focused. Possibly more important is to stay curious. One needs to be constantly looking around the next corner for new market dynamics and unique edge plays. Ensure that you and your people find time to pause, reflect and have quality time to think. This form of reflective intelligence will

*separate the winners from the losers as our world increasingly becomes
smarter, it is what most don't see that allows you to see more clearly.*

"Another way to look at the question is to take it from the value destruction
side. Just challenge every relevant process at your ideal customer and ask the
question 'Where in the process is value being destroyed?' Look at it from the
perspective of 'What's the problem it's trying to solve, and how has this
approach to the problem really evolved for the past decade(s)?

"Very often you'll find spots where nothing has changed. It means we've
become complacent with the approach. We just take it for granted. It's been
resolved once based on the state of the technology available at that time – or
because it seemed the most obvious then. But times have changed. And
consequently, following the old approach results in waste – waste in time,
speed, and quality – at a massive scale.

"So challenge it by asking 'What would you do if you had a clean sheet of
paper?' What's stopping us from taking this fresh approach? To create differentiation, you have to break with traditions.

"Let me give you an example from my time at Unit4. We were heavily
focused on people-/service-centric industries. I have had many discussions
with my product management team where we asked 'Why does a billable
consultant need to put in their timesheets manually? Why do we have to spend
the precious private time we have to submit our business expenses every
month? Why do managers have to surrender their Friday afternoon to deal
with piles of approvals? Isn't there a better way?'

"We leave so many trails on a day-to-day basis, and so much of what's
required to deal with this smartly is already available inside enterprise systems.
Isn't there a way to make this all go away? The answer to this is yes, it can, and
yes, it should. The target is not: 'let's build the most user-friendly and sexy
[name your task] app,' the target is: 'let's use technology smartly so that's we
never have to enter [name your task] at all.'

"In my interview with Ivo Totev,[19] President Line of Business (LOB)
Marketing at SAP, he made a strong point regarding this:

*With the rise of Artificial Intelligence, Machine Learning, Deep
Machine Learning, now we're getting into a phase where business
software actually understands what I am up to, and can*

---

[19]. https://www.valueinspiration.com/how-to-change-the-nature-of-the-backbone-that-drives-the-global-economy/

pro-actively help me. Conversation is not bound to me just being able to say very particular words and sentences. No, I can stop talking out of context, or in context, and the system would be able to make sense with that.

This is so revolutionary. This changes so much that, I'm sure in ten years, we'll be looking back and saying: 'The Internet was a great foundation and Cloud was also a great foundational element in their first generations, but none of those technologies or movements really changed the way we see business software as much as this latest revolution.'

Our vision [at SAP] is to be the first ones to provide a hands-free ERP. Our vision for the next three years is to reduce the interaction between people and the business systems by 50 percent.

"This is a very good step in the right direction. It's about challenging the status quo of how we are doing things today as to where value is being destroyed or not optimally created. I strongly believe we can deliver big impact if we design business software that's totally 'silent'/'invisible'. Too many software companies continue to stick to the mantra of delivering yet another 'better' user interface. That's old thinking, we've been doing that for multiple decades now – and what did we really gain?"

Where are people under-utilized?

"A slightly different approach from the value creating/destruction angle is to ask the question 'where are people under-utilized?' rather than just looking at the process itself. Sometimes the process is running fine, and totally optimized, but there's an opportunity to drive more value by focusing on making the strengths of people even stronger.

"It's my strong belief that too much focus is being spent on automation. It can be because it's the closest to what we've always been doing, it's evolutionary, but that doesn't mean it's the most valuable. Besides that, it creates a negative hype in the market. Just Google the phrase 'AI and Robots are going to take our jobs' and you get an idea of the incredible amount of focus and negative buzz surrounding this topic. Folks are worried that in a world of fast-moving technology, all the smart bots are about to put us out of work."

"You have a point there, Ton," said Rob. "I think we're guilty on that as well in the focus we have with our Digital Banking Platform. We already get questions from operational staff at banks who realize 'this is a task I used to do in the past'. And that's sometimes quite a difficult discussion."

"Spot on," I commented. "This is exactly where the problem lies, and it doesn't have to be this way. We have, at our fingertips, a huge volume of human resources, and they are not living up to their full potential simply because they've been cornered into doing work they were not supposed to do in the first place, i.e. doing many non-value-adding repetitive tasks, day in, day out.

"Remember when I talked about Ryan Falkenberg, CEO of CLEVVA? He phrased it perfectly:

> *Currently, human beings are not differentiators. They're a scale problem. Human beings are currently trapped in the role of robots. In most companies, we give them fleshy interfaces, but we ask them to be robots. Based on our company 'formula' we ask them to ask certain questions, based on certain answers. They need to do certain outcomes, based on compliance, based on rules.*

> *The problem is, my company 'formula' is non-differentiating because, as soon as a competitor captures a similar formula, it can scale as quickly as I can.*

> *Human beings should become the way I differentiate. That's going to be an interesting change for organizations. Many have tried to mitigate human involvement because it adds risk to their formula. I see a future where human beings are becoming an opportunity to fundamentally differentiate.*

> *Until we can augment the brain with digital intelligence that relieves them from worrying about replication, people are caught between having to learn it so they don't make an of error, yet knowing that by learning it they become more redundant, or more problematic. This is really the opportunity.*

"Do you see where I am going with this?" I asked Rob. "We are often creating the problem ourselves. The way we've approached automation has always been about making the process smoother, not the people better. Artificial Intelligence has, to a great degree, been about that same thing: Further automating the process, to the extent that people are not required anymore. And to an extent that's good, as this will free people from the mundane tasks. But it's not where the big shifts in value are created. That's happening when we apply Intelligence Augmentation to people in order to make them better, i.e. enable them to deliver value perceived impossible before."

"So, if I understand you correctly, I should start focusing my R&D efforts towards intelligently augmenting operational staff at banks to go above and beyond?" Rob said.

"Yes, that's a good example," I replied. "And you'll see that's also just the tip of the iceberg. You could equally provide that power of intelligence augmentation to the banks' customers. Guess what that will do with their ability to exceed expectations? And in a way that's much more scalable as well.

"That brings me to another angle to focus your sensors as you look for opportunities to create shifts in value: changing working relationships.

Changing working relationships

"One of the major shifts in the market is the fact that organizations will get flatter and flatter. Hierarchies are disappearing, work becomes more project-oriented, and opportunities are created by orchestrating work in such a way that it's creating the optimal blend of cross-departmental employees and external contract workers. Organizations will start to blend in a higher percentage of freelance workers for scale and flexibility. And at the same time something else is happening: millennials tend to change employers faster to pursue their career aspirations.

"All these changes result in new challenges your ideal customers have never had to deal with before. For example, how are they going to capture and protect corporate knowledge? How do we bring that knowledge back into the organization to increase competitive edge? How do you control quality on work that's done by mixed teams of internal/external workers? How do you optimize communication? How do you mitigate risks around meeting the outcomes your customers expect? The list goes on and on. All opportunities for innovation.

"And that triggers yet another angle to look for innovation opportunity: Sources of Uncertainty. Efrem Hoffman,[20] CEO of Running Alpha,

---

20. https://www.valueinspiration.com/how-human-machine-combos-can-be-used-to-avert-financial-tornodos/

founded his software business on the principle of uncertainty. He said this:

> *How could you actually use uncertainty in the markets not as a bad thing, but as a competitive advantage? I keep on hearing people on the TV saying: 'There's so much uncertainty, we're not going to make any decisions. We're just going to wait until all the uncertainty goes away.'*
>
> *We all know that it never all goes away. We're living in a time where it's definitely heightened. So maybe what people really mean is, let's just wait until it goes back to somewhat normal levels.*
>
> *But the problem is, by the time you wait for it to actually have a mean reversion to the normal, which is always a dynamic thing anyway, that involves another prediction that you can actually get right, you end up losing out on opportunities. That's a big issue, because managers and fund managers and investors get paid for making decisions. If you're not making decisions, you don't get money in exchange.*
>
> *So the opportunity lies in finding an answer to turn something that's really negative to the marketplace as uncertainty into clear competitive advantage.*

"If you pay attention to sources of uncertainty amongst your ideal customer base you can uncover new innovation potential that will give both you and your customer significant competitive advantage. So it's worth paying attention to."

Then Rob interrupted me. "Now I see what you mean with the point we spoke about earlier, 'the risk of defining your company too narrow.' If I'd define it as 'we're in the business of delivering omni-channel platforms to banks' versus 'we're in the business of enabling banks to ensure their customers are always one step ahead in live and business' then the latter option would give us the focus to constantly hone in on what drives most value to our customers' customers. In the financial services world this indeed is a lot about dealing with 'uncertainty.'"

"Exactly," I replied with a smile. "An interesting twist on the topic, but that's exactly what I meant. Which reminds me of yet another angle to spot innovation opportunity: moments of truth."

Moments of truth

"You're point about the banks' customers is all about that. It's an under-explored terrain full of innovation opportunity. Let me explain. Just picture how we think as consumers of services or products. We have a certain expectation that things work, that they won't break, and that they will deliver us a certain value as we consume them. That's what I'd call 'table stakes'. That's the norm. Every respectable vendor will deliver a product that meets those simple needs. So you can put all your efforts and investments on making incremental improvements around your 'table stakes', but the fact is – it will go unnoticed. So, after you've reached a certain point, every additional effort is a waste in the eyes of your customer, no matter how proud you could be yourself in delivering it.

"Where the real impact is made is when you focus on becoming the best in so-called 'moments of truth'. The defining moments in a process that are the most risky or costly in terms of failure. The moments where you have to deal with exceptions. The moments where you have to deal with peaks of volume. Name it. We can all think of many examples ourselves.

"Those moments of truth can become the differentiators for your customers. Just think of your bank's customers. What are the moments of truth when they need their bank most?"

Rob was clearly thinking. And then he replied: "If their bank card gets stolen. Or if they are in urgent need of credit."

"Exactly," I responded. "Two examples I have in fact experienced myself. Well, these are moments you can make a difference as a solution provider. You can make it super simple for the customer to fix the issue of a stolen card themselves digitally, and automate all the underlying actions of ordering a new card, etc. Just make it super convenient and ensure the problem is fixed in a day, rather than the typical two weeks. You can be pro-active to customers in avoiding the need for credit by giving active guidance throughout the month around spend/save behavior. You can provide intelligent guidance, i.e. coach bank employees as they are on the call, so that they can focus fully on the experience and empathy they provide, rather than the typical rules and regulations that go with this (which should be hidden from the customer). The point is that you are 'there' at the moment of truth, and exceed expectations in that very moment. That's the opportunity.

"A company founded on exactly that principle is Cogito. They built a platform that can listen to conversations and help individuals understand how they can speak differently in order to have better conversations. Skyler Place,[21] their Chief Behavioral Science Officer, gave some valuable insights on this when I interviewed him:

> *One of the hard choices that we made is, we decided that the real value of this approach was in the real time feedback. From a technical perspective, it is easier to provide coaching after the call, or to create the reports and hear all of the things that you could have done in the call that would have led to a better outcome [but] psychology literature and the behavioral science really supported the idea that to drive the right behaviors in call, we had to give feedback in the moment as it was happening.*

"The point is that we all get away with a 6 or 7 rating if you'd have to score the user experience. But what's the value of a 6 or 7? People would only recommend something when it's a clear 8, 9 or 10.

"Why? Because then it exceeds their expectations. They experience remarkable value. This is why Cogito's choice was easy: to deliver remarkable value we have to deliver 'in the moment' guidance, not after the fact. Much harder, but exceptionally better.

Shifts in job profiles

"Last but not least I want to hone in on the evolution of jobs. Micro-shifts can be found by exploring how the job profiles that your ideal customers put out are changing. Olaf Growth,[22] author of *The Solomon's Code*,[23] made some clear points on this when I interviewed him:

> *There are various different statistics out there, with astounding numbers on how many people are actually unhappy in their jobs. We have an opportunity to shape jobs such that they are not just more productive, but also much more enjoyable.*

---

21. https://www.valueinspiration.com/how-ai-helps-call-center-agents-be-their-best-selves-and-create-customers-for-life/

22. https://www.valueinspiration.com/product-strategy-solomons-code-humanity-in-a-world-of-thinking-machines/

23. http://pegasusbooks.com/books/solomons-code-9781681778709-hardcover

So to create the solutions of the future you should anticipate the job profiles of the future. [...] Symbiotic intelligence could be the right cure to fix as it brings together the best of machines and the best of people – and as such allows for more human inspiration, more visioning, more ideation, more theory development, more empathy, more creativity, and overall, to have just a lot more purpose on the job.

The time to act is now to be thoughtful about this. I hope that people are going to say: What's my role in all of this? What does this emergence mean to me in my everyday life and how I run my day? How is my day going to change? Which decisions am I willing to delegate, and which do I want to make myself? This is of critical importance.

The challenge is not to get it right, and nail it down to the T, but rather to have the dialogue. Once you have the dialogue, you create relation-ships, concept and trust. That is really what we need to do in this new world of thinking machines: recover and strengthen trust as the most important currency in society. Trust is so much more valuable, easy to lose, and hard to regain than clicks, likes, eyeballs or cash.

"Olaf's advice is straightforward, but he admits it will take much effort and collaboration among many stakeholders to get there:

1. *Develop a landscape map of the organization in terms of what the work is that is being done, where the value is being added, along multiple activity axis: routine and non-routine, expressed in digital and non-digital data, productivity enhancing and purpose enhancing.*

2. *Then try to understand where humans and machines could collaborate much more elegantly, based on their strengths, in a much more integrated, complementary fashion.*

3. *Then ask yourself, what does each job look like in five, seven years out, and describe the symbiotic enhancements, including where the symbio-pairs of humans and machines could reach higher levels of joint performance.*

4. *Then try to design a development program for the people in those jobs, for migrating people between jobs, or for people who might be*

better suited to take symbio-jobs. Importantly, this has to be done with employee representatives, not hush-hush behind closed doors, which would be the most effective way to destroy trust and create paranoia.

It's an evolving process. You want to be prepared from a defensive perspective and from an offensive perspective.

"Wow," Rob said as he finished the last of his chorizo. "I have something to work on with my product management and R&D team. It's so easy to just follow the day-to-day 'busyness' and become blind to all these opportunities."

"I agree with you," I responded. "But finding new sources of innovation is where it all starts. That's where you'll continue to find inspiration to keep evolving and stay relevant to both new as well as existing customers. That balance is critical. It's not only good that your existing customers keep coming back, you have to stay so relevant that they'd buy *again* if they had to make the choice today. That's hard work – but rewarding work."

"So true," Rob replied. "And let me take the bill for this, Ton. It's on me."

We paid for dinner and then walked towards gate 32.

Ask yourself

STEP 1: Reflect critically how you score your own ability around this particular trait by rating your organization on a scale of 1 (poor) to 10 (remarkable).

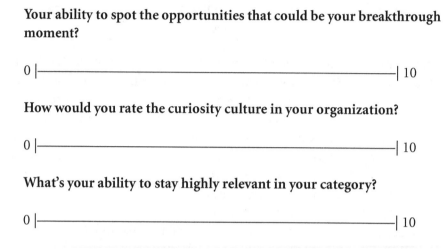

Your ability to spot the opportunities that could be your breakthrough moment?

0 |———————————————————————————| 10

How would you rate the curiosity culture in your organization?

0 |———————————————————————————| 10

What's your ability to stay highly relevant in your category?

0 |———————————————————————————| 10

STEP 2: Take ten minutes to reflect on the next actions you could initiate to improve your score.

STEP 3: What's the single action from this list that would give you the biggest impact?

Take it to the next level

- Not only become remarkable, but ensure you'll stay remarkable as well by introducing the 'Remarkable Monday' habit within your organization. Download the three simple steps that will help you create and keep momentum: https://valueinspiration.com/RemarkableMonday
- Join the Remarkable Tribe Program to create accountability with other tech-entrepreneurs like you. Not only will you build traction to shape the business you aspire to be, but you will also obtain new ideas, create new contacts, and will be part of a movement that defines what it means to be remarkable as a business software vendor: https://movement. valueinspiration.com

Trait 5
Create new value possibilities

Creating value perception shifts by changing our mindset

As we walked to the gate, Rob stopped me and asked: "If you had a company like mine, forty-five people in size today, growing rapidly – once we have done our homework on what should be next, what should we do differently development wise?"

I thought about it for a couple of seconds before I replied. "There's no straight answer to that. There is no silver bullet, but I can give you a framework to guide your decisions. Here's the thing: the world is changing extremely rapidly. You can see that in your world, I mean, digital banking platforms didn't exist three or four years ago, and now it's the single biggest priority on the agenda of many banks around the world. It's because their world is shifting in front of their eyes, and keeping up will mean they'll become irrelevant.

"It's that level of pressure that sets the bar for you, and your competitors. That's what you should have front and center in every decision you make: how can you plan your product investments so that you can drive shifts in value towards their biggest priorities, and how can you exceed expectations in doing so? And this requires a different mindset.

"Let me give you an example of Nadine Hachach-Haram,[1] plastic surgeon

---

[1.] https://www.valueinspiration.com/how-augmented-reality-helps-surgeons-add-value-from-anywhere-in-the-world/

and founder of Proximie, a UK start-up specializing in augmented reality technology empowering clinicians. She said this:

> I work in the National Health Service in England and we have
> growing pain points around supply and demand of surgical expertise.
> It's no different in the US. It's no different in parts of India. We are all
> challenged with it. The question is: 'How can we deliver care to the
> most people with the resources that we have?'
>
> To solve this we have to get smart. We have to think about new
> disruptive ways to do that because our historical traditional ways of
> doing that are no longer working. We're at crossroads now, where
> technology can really, really transform health care.

"I believe this summary applies as much to banking, education, and not-for-profit professional services just as much as it applies to healthcare. We have to start thinking differently. Once you can step away from the specs and requirements, you can start to see things clearly. You can start to see why things that we have become accustomed to don't work anymore, if you honestly assess them. We're often trapped by our own beliefs. And that's limiting what we can accomplish.

"Why do we keep improving processes incrementally, instead of aiming for a 10x impact?

"Why do we keep inventing new User Interfaces, instead of aiming for making technology invisible, i.e. why not challenge why we need the UI in the first place?

"Why do we keep focusing on output, when we could unlock superior value by focusing on the outcome?

"Why do we keep focusing on automation, when creating human-machine scenarios would develop superhuman powers where people could accomplish things unimaginable before?

"Why do we only focus on just our customer, when focusing on our customers' customer would help remove the real roadblocks?

"Why don't we allow ourselves to do the things that would potentially disrupt our own business, and instead leave that 'honor' to our competitors?

"Too often we approach the problems in the market too linear. That is stopping us from breaking away. I know customers and prospects always have a lot of resistance when it comes to dealing with change. But isn't that something we create ourselves? If they only experience marginal increases, they'll fall back on the typical mantra 'If it ain't broke, don't fix it.' A significant difference is necessary to convince them that it's worth the resources and risk to shift. And to deliver that, you need to think differently from the start.

"Therefore, trait number five of a remarkable software business to me is: they create new value possibilities. They think exponential – a 10x impact, not just 10%. They think in win-win-win situations: their customer, the customer of their customer, and themselves. They support moments of truth. They make technology invisible. They focus on solving the hard things first, and so forth. The technology is there, it just needs our creativity to leverage it.

"As Jon Shalowitz,[2] CEO of LiftIgniter, stated perfectly in my interview with him:

> A company like LiftIgniter would not have been possible six years ago. Without the advancement in cloud infrastructure, such as provided by Google, by Amazon, by Microsoft, by Oracle, you know, this type of product would have been impossible. The thing that cracked the code that made this possible was the amount of raw horsepower and the amount of computational work that has to get done. It is immense, it is massive.

"Michelangelo Buonarroti once said: 'The greatest danger for most of us is not that our aim is too high, and we miss it, but that it is too low and we reach it.' There's a lot of truth in this (ancient) quote. How often do great ideas pop up and then what happens is we tone them down until they become mediocre. So with that in mind, the challenge all business software companies have is: Are we doing enough to exploit the advantage we have at our disposal?

"I believe the answer lies in the under-utilized concept of exponential thinking."

In the meantime, we had arrived at the gate. The boarding process had already started. There was a massive queue; it was going to be a full flight.

"What seat do you have, Rob?" I asked.

"16C," he answered. "Exit row, next to the aisle. That's where you can always find me," he smiled.

---

2. https://www.valueinspiration.com/product-innovation-how-ai-solves-both-data-privacy-and-customer-experience-challenges-in-real-time/

I laughed. "Ha, ha, another globe-trotter! Funny we've never met before – it's the same place you could have found me over the last eighteen years. I actually thought 'who stole my seat?' last night when I checked in. So guess what? I got 16D, other side of the aisle. Isn't that a coincidence!"

We boarded, moved to the middle of the plane, parked our hand luggage, and sat down left and right of the aisle. From there the conversation continued.

Incremental versus Exponential mindset

"Where was I?" I wondered out loud.

"The under-utilized concept of exponential thinking," Rob answered.

"You're right," I continued. "And let me explain why this is important. It's often overhyped, and dropped into the conversation too easily. As I said, the difference between a remarkable business software company and 'the rest' starts with having a different mindset. I like the definition *Harvard Business Review*[3] gives this:

> *The incremental mindset focuses on making something better, while the exponential mindset is about making something different. Incremental is satisfied with 10 percent. Exponential is out for 10X.*

"Now, exponential thinking for your business could involve focusing on improving a current product to deliver exactly what your customer base wants and needs, and then do one or two specific things that exceed expectations in a way no one else in your industry is doing or has done. If that delivers a shift in value for your customer, you're on the right track.

"Most business owners, as well as individuals, have an incremental mindset – meaning that they see a very clear linear path of steps they have to take to get from point A to point B. Each step builds upon the one before it. Progress is made by marginally improving different elements on that path.

"There isn't anything wrong with this way of thinking. Chances are high that it has helped you get where you are today. However, real success is going to come from making the shift and starting to think more exponentially, i.e. getting the same or better result, but doing things differently.

[3.] https://hbr.org/2016/07/how-to-create-an-exponential-mindset

"Exponential decisions have a different effect on your business. They provide you greater long-term success. It isn't about having a hundred new users tomorrow; it is about having a million users in the next two years. As you can imagine, what you need to do to accomplish each is totally different.

"But it's not necessarily something that's more difficult, or requires more investment. Here's what Astro Teller, CEO of X,[4] mentioned in an interview with Tim Ferris:

> *When you shoot for 10% better, you are putting all of your people in a smartness contest with everyone else in the world. They are not going to win! It doesn't matter how much money you give them.*
>
> *But if you push them, if you give them the expectation and the freedom to be 'weird' – that's moonshot thinking. Then they can do the perspective shifts. And not only that, if you shoot for 10X bigger instead of 10% bigger, it's almost never going to be 100x harder, and the payoff is 100 times. So, you already know that you've got a better return on your investment. But sometimes it's literally easier – because that perspective shift is actually cheap, relative to being smarter than everyone around you.*

At that moment the security announcements kicked in. We both waited for the moment the flight attendant had finished his pitch, and the stewards had passed to check if we'd fastened our seatbelts, and satisfied themselves we didn't have any additional baggage stowed that could block the exit. We were ready to go. The plane started moving backwards from the gate in order to start its journey towards Porto.

"You've made me think, Ton," Rob said. "I've never really considered that creating a 10x impact could actually be easier than creating a 10% impact. It's indeed all about mindset."

"Yes," I continued, "it's about that, and it's also about combining with four other ingredients:

---

4. https://tim.blog/2018/04/18/how-to-think-10x-bigger/

1) Disrupting your mind

"Remember when I talked about, Timothy Willis,[5] COO of Aerobotics? He told me that when he sat down to brainstorm some ideas, he realized that starting with 'why' leads to better results. Idea generation should be focused on creating a positive outcome, not a positive output. Solve the 'why' and solve the outcome; don't leap straight to the product.

2) Make theoretical practical

"Big changes happen when innovative thinkers transform simple concepts into honest practicals. Every problem has a theoretical and practical approach – use them. Think about Susanne Baars again, the founder of Social Genomics. When she came up with the idea to make "genomic knowledge available for every person on Earth,' her theoretical idea was to save lives. Her practical idea? To make genomic information widely available.

3) Ensure scale

"Exponential thinkers are able to understand scale. Big things have small beginnings, and in business software that is no different. Airbnb[6] began as a few cots on a floor in San Francisco. Now, Airbnb has operations in nearly two hundred countries. Understanding the scale of an idea is critical for exponential thinkers. Airbnb identified a problem in the industry – the lack of a marketplace for private lodging – and scaled up.

4) Narrow it down

"The best ideas are the ones that can be targeted to a very real problem. Airbnb tries to solve the lack of a marketplace for privately owned rentals. Susanne Baars tries to solve the lack of access to genomic information. Spot-specific targeting means finding a slice of an industry that needs help and crafting a specialized tool to exploit it.

---

5. https://www.valueinspiration.com/how-ai-is-intelligently-augmenting-farmers-to-exponentially-grow-yields-and-efficiency/
6. https://www.cnbc.com/2018/01/02/airbnb-from-1400-guests-on-new-years-eve-2009-to-over-3-million.html?

"With this in mind, just challenge your laundry list of 100 to 200 things you think you need to deliver with your solution to please your customers. You'll see you'll be able to identify the ten that will indeed move the needle. That's the simple, yet critical, thing to do to outlast your competition. By narrowing down your focus, you'll be able to deliver remarkable quality and impact that people will remember. And that's what it is all about, right?"

Rob smiled. "Yes, so true! I have a question though. Given your experience of working with the many pioneers in the industry, can you give some examples that inspired you?"

"No problem," I replied.

At that moment the plane started its acceleration and we were heading down the runway in order to take off for Porto.

Exponential impact by taking a one-to-masses approach

The plane shot up into the air and within seconds quickly started to curve to the left.

"If I look at the various examples of exponential thinking, I actually see two major streams. One is about transforming technology in such a way that can be made available to an exponentially larger audience than ever before. I had an inspiring conversation with Maurizio Vecchione,[7] Executive Vice President at Global Good and Research. He shared his vision of removing the traditional barriers to solve global problems across three angles: making solutions more affordable, applicable and accessible. He said:

We are using the words catalytic invention to indicate disruptive new technologies that are more than just a new technology; They truly have the ability to catalyze a sea-change in a problem, i.e. catalyzing a change in disruptive behavior that allows an improvement, not just for the developing world but across the board.

If you solve the issues that those people [the bottom 5 billion people of the world] have, what you typically see is that, if you can do it for them, you can do it for everybody. Therefore, it will drive incredible innova- tion and prosperity for the rest of the world as well.

---

7. https://www.valueinspiration.com/a-different-approach-to-innovation-to-accelerate- change-action-and-impact/

"I concur with his ideas. From the people I have worked with throughout my professional career I can clearly see that this concept applies to virtually every industry and challenge we face. Too often we focus our efforts on just one aspect of the three. However, if we challenge our solutions around all three angles this would drive a lot more innovation, and more importantly, more value. But let me illustrated that with a couple of examples.

"I talked about 'scarcity' already when I addressed the various sources at which to direct your curiosity. And the story I am about to share with you is a good example of a solution that was born out of that very topic. Many things are scarce, and sometimes this could lead to life-threatening situations. In the Ted Talk[8] Dr. Nadine Hachach-Haram gave in December 2017, she highlighted an example of how countries like Sierra Leone suffer from an unbelievable shortage of qualified surgeons: one surgeon for every 600,000 people – can you imagine that?

"So in my interview with her we zoomed in on how the technology created by her company Proximie augments medical expertise to truly scale across the world. The big idea behind Proximie is to enable surgeons to virtually transport themselves into an operating room anywhere in the world so they can share expertise and maximize patient benefit – just by using the technology we all have at hand: a computer, tablet or mobile phone.

"Her solution is ticking all three A's:

1. Accessible: She's democratizing access to healthcare, solving some real scarcity problems in many countries around the world, including the UK and US.
2. Affordable: She's making it extremely cost-effective since no one has to physically move or travel.
3. Applicable: She using technology we all have at hand, i.e. mobile phones, tablets or PCs, to enable specialists to perform their work with the right level of quality.

"For me this is a clear example of a solution that creates an exponential impact and has the potential to reach effect masses of people. It brings us closer to solving the problem of the scarcity of medical experts in a completely new way."

---

8. https://www.ted.com/talks/nadine_hachach_haram_how_augmented_reality_could_change_the_future_of_surgery?language=en

"Fascinating," Rob replied. "I am already thinking how I can apply these three simple concepts to deliver catalytic impact to the banking world and their customers."

I smiled. "Let me give you another example – one from an interview I conducted with Peyman Nilforoush,[9] co-founder and CEO of inPowered. inPowered is transforming the digital advertising industry by taking a catalytic invention approach. This is what Peyman told me:

> *The journey leading up to inPowered was essentially inspired by advertising not working. In '99 the number of people clicking on a banner ad was still 10%. Today you're looking at an average of 0.05%. Not 0.5%, not 5%, but 0.05% click-through rate on any banner ad. And that's after using tons of technology and targeting and everything that you can imagine.*

> *If we can't make advertising work online [then] digital publishers are going to die. Facebook is going to die, Google is going to die and nobody's gonna be able to pay their bills. So we thought: There's gotta be a better way to do this to actually add value to the consumer. And our idea of that was: We all love reading – so what if instead of putting up banners that interrupt our experience we actually turned articles, reviews, or blog posts, i.e. content, into an ad?*

"Challenging the status quo allowed inPowered to find solution to a 'hidden' problem and turn the model upside down by triggering consumers with material they already love: relevant content. This shifted the model from low clicks to high engagement and allowed even underdogs to increase consideration by 65%, thereby outperforming any form of advertising ever done.

"inPowered saw that and was actually brave enough to create a true outcome-based monetization model around this: pay for engagement, not for impressions. It's a win-win for everybody – for the consumer (better content), for the supplier (very efficient use of your marketing budget and the right triggers to create meaningful content), and for inPowered (differentiation power). All the pointers are targeted at doing the right thing right. Be honest –

---

9.   https://www.valueinspiration.com/product-innovation-how-ai-transforms-highly-ineffective-advertising-into-highly-relevant-engagement/

until now the only ones that really wins with online advertising today are Facebook and Google. Advertising has turned into 'who shouts the loudest', and 'who bids the most to get top-ranking' – irrespective of the results a customer actually gets.

"So, can you see the three A's again?"

"Yes," Rob replied. "It's indeed fascinating what we can achieve when we start thinking exponentially and use technology to accomplish things we've never been able to before."

"There's one more example that I have to share with you," I continued, "and that's the story of AJ Abdallat,[10] founder and CEO of the artificial intelligence company Beyond Limits. Beyond Limits is on a mission to use science and technology developed for space missions to make life better for all of us on earth. He told me:

> When you are trying to send a robotic mission to space, for example Mars, you're really dealing with a very complex, dynamic, and unknown environment where you have situations you're not familiar with and data sometimes does not exist, or it is missing, or corrupted.

> With conventional AI, like machine-learning, if you have a missing rule, or the data is misleading, that's where it stops. You cannot do that in space. In space, you have to continue the objective of the mission. At Beyond Limits, we believe that those same conditions and problems that exist in space can be applied to complex problems here on earth.

> The problem we identified is that many organizations have experts that developed expertise over decades. They are receiving many requests from different parts of the organization; and as you can imagine, are very hard to scale. The only way to cope is to prioritize.

> In the space business, you really have very experienced and seasoned scientists. However, quite a few of them are close to retirement, so you really want to capture their knowledge and experience, and transfer that to the younger generation. The same is true in many large-scale industries.

---

10. https://www.valueinspiration.com/new-ways-ai-helps-scale-human-talent-to-solve-global-problems/

For example, energy, specifically upstream in oil and gas. They are operating in very harsh environments with zero tolerance for failure. Safety is therefore extremely important.

This is where we believe the collaboration between man and machine comes in. We are taking the knowledge of a highly skilled individual and scaling that across the organization where we're allowing less skilled individuals to utilize it and take their value to the next level.

"What AJ's company is doing is another example of solving scarcity, by making unique knowledge and experience accessible (forever), applicable (very special, highly valuable use cases), and affordable. It's a very interesting aspect of Intelligent Augmentation as it is actually capable of filling in the blanks in situations where not all data is available – extremely important in zero-tolerance environments."

Rob nodded. "Fascinating. I've never thought about it this way. Food for thought!"

"Talking about food," I responded, "do you fancy something? The service crew is approaching us in the aisle."

"Good idea. Coffee for me," Rob answered. "I still have to drive home when we arrive in Porto."

Exponential impact by taking a masses-to-one approach

As the service crew stopped at our seats, I ordered two 'freshly brewed' cafés.

Then Rob said, "Earlier, you were talking about two major streams of exponential thinking. So what's the other one?"

"Yes, lets continue with the opposite angle," I responded. "I refer to the other category as 'masses-to-one'. Here's why: From all the podcast interviews I've done with tech pioneers, I found a lot of examples on how technology helps to augment individual people with insights we never had.

"With technology, individuals can now benefit from the knowledge of thousands or even millions of sources – interviews, tests, events, experiences, behaviors, you name it. Make that knowledge available to a single person and you have the recipe to deliver remarkable value.

"The authors of the book *Machine, Platform, Crowd*[11] perfectly quoted the opportunity we have:

> *The success of a venture almost never turns on how much technology it can access, but how its people use that technology, and on what values they imbue in the organization. Today, we have more freedom to do things that simply could not have been done in earlier generations. Rather than being locked into any one future, we have greater ability to shape the future.*

"As you can imagine, this is what inspires me. To me AI is a fantastic invention. However, I get particularly excited about the AI scenarios that are about intelligence augmentation, rather than automation. The automation scenarios are good, but they typically only address the aspect of efficiency and cost. Automation scenarios are often (rightly or wrongly) connected to the negative hype that AI is going to take our jobs. People get very defensive if they talk about the automation side. There's certainly reality in that, but I believe that in the majority of automation scenarios, AI will do what Vinnie Mirchandani phrased as 'The three 'D's – the Dull, Dangerous and Dirty', i.e. tasks we don't like to do anyway.

"But enough on automation. Intelligence Augmentation to me is about opportunity – it's about unlocking value we've never held possible before. Here's where we can raise the bar on all levels. It's about creating human/machine scenarios that are all about 1+1=3 (or more). That's positive news. And it's these examples that I put front and center in my weekly podcast.

"So, let's dive into the details and share some examples.

1) An exponential increase in speed

"This is the first angle I'd like to share. We all know the good old Microsoft slogan 'Information at your fingertips' – a vision they laid out in 1995. And even today this is still an area of innovation. In more and more cases these days, having the right information available in a split second is what's required – it can actually be life-saving.

[11.] https://www.amazon.com/Machine-Platform-Crowd-Harnessing-Digital/dp/1543615791

"Andreas Cleve,[12] CEO of Corti, shared an excellent example with me on how AI is augmenting medical experts with split-second advice and insights from thousands of other situations. This allows medical experts to spot the real issue while on a 112/911 call, in order to save that live, at that exact moment. As Andreas said:

We found that in the pre-hospital setting there were some quite good use cases of scenarios where time was critical. One of them was detecting cardiac arrests on live emergency calls.

When a sudden cardiac arrest happens outside of a hospital, you have only about 10 minutes to make sure to get the right treatment, which would be proper CPR or a defibrillator that actually helps them read- just the heart rhythm. That can only happen if they end up detecting it.

The best 911/112 agents in the world will be able to hit detection rates around 73 percent. That's actually quite high since we as bystanders, the people who experience somebody else having a cardiac arrest, might be quite biased and give wrongful information since it's, of course, happening in a rush.

So, we challenged ourselves to see if we could decrease the amount of cases where it wasn't detected where it actually should've been. That's the foundation of Corti. What Corti is trying to do is to build a symbiosis between the medical professional and technology. Corti isn't built to replace anybody, it's built to amplify somebody.

What we do is this: we listen in on patient/doctor conversations, or conversations between medical professionals and patients. We try to help them pick up the different signals and alerts that's hidden in the conversation that might not be apparent to a human, to help the medical professional come to the right conclusion, preferably faster, and preferably with a higher precision.

We'll do what computers do best: computing large sets of data and try to look for angles that might seem obscure to the single human being that might only have heard or seen or participated in a finite amount of conversations.

---

12. https://www.valueinspiration.com/how-to-save-more-lives-by-augmenting-911-112-agents-with-ai/

We will never be better than the dispatchers. That is not the point. But together with the dispatchers we can be quite powerful.

"Fascinating story," Rob interrupted. "Really a case that we could not imagine possible five or six years ago, and today these cases are all at our disposal to transform the way we do work and deliver value."

2) An exponential increase in accuracy

"The second example I'd like to share about how technology can create shifts in value by intelligently augmenting people is this one from Unanimous AI, who are taking accuracy in decision making to the next level. Louis Rosenberg,[13] their CEO, said this:

There's a scientific name for what we do: Swarm Intelligence. In nature, Swarm Intelligence is the reason why birds flock, fish school, and bees swarm. They're smarter together. The inspiration for me was to say, "Well, if birds, and bees, and fish can get smarter together, why can't people do it?

The opportunity this raises is beyond imagination – mainly because we can apply this to so many things in our day-to-day professional life. Just think about forecasting (sales, financial, projects), making assessments or judgments, and overall decision-making in general.

For a long time we worked on how technology can improve or enhance the ability of individuals. It becomes far more interesting if we look at how technology can enhance the ability of groups. That's how we founded our company.

We use AI to connect people together and enable similar amplification of intelligence. We use AI to turn network groups of people into artificial experts that can act as a superintelligence. We connect people in real time, and then use AI algorithms to enable them to make more accurate forecasts, more precise predictions, better assessments, judgments and decisions. So instead of trying to take people out of the

---

[13.] https://www.valueinspiration.com/product-innovation-how-amplifying-the-intelligence-of-groups-with-ai-is-the-formula-to-create-breakthrough-improvements/

system, and just replace them by crunching big data, we're coming from the perspective that the most important data out there is the data that exists inside people's heads.

The results we achieved even early on were remarkable. We could take a group of people and make them so much more accurate by connecting them together. For example, with Stanford University Medical School we connected a group of seven doctors and radiologists to diagnose chest X-rays together, all located at different universities. We reduced the errors in diagnosis by 36 percent.

We took a group of financial analysts who are looking at markets and made 26% more accurate predictions about market trends. Why? We underestimate it, but in our minds we're keeping information up to date, every second. If you're a financial analyst, you're up to date. You have a sense of the context and the mood [of the market] and we just need to value that. When we combine the patterns and facts AI can give us, with the context and market sensitivity that humans can bring to the table, that's where we start to unlock remarkable value.

We believe we're just scratching the surface of how smart these systems can be when we connect people together.

"Another fascinating story indeed," Rob replied. "I agree with the reasoning that AI performs at its best when it has access to many, large datasets. The bigger the better. However, it will never be able to do something with the data we have in our heads – so here's an enormous untapped opportunity waiting to be unlocked. I wonder what we can do with that thought in our market?"

"Absolutely!" I replied. "And if you liked the big idea behind Unanimous, you'll like this one as well. I talked about augmenting individuals through speed and accuracy, here's an example of creating leaps in value by increasing the scale we can operate in as an individual."

3) An exponential increase in scale

"A third story comes from my interview with Ilan Kasan,[14] CEO of Exceed, an AI-led company that's delivering a solution that has the power to increase sales productivity, and thus scale, by over 80%.

> *In my time at CISCO, as a Senior Director, Product Management, I was exposed to what I would say was the middle of the funnel, and realized how difficult it was to manage a huge stream of leads. I saw how much time reps were spending in qualifying, getting back, trying to set appointments, and talking to the wrong people. How many leads marketing created where nobody would do anything with them, or even follow up one.*
>
> *I understood there was a real problem here that was not necessarily related to the size of the company, but rather the nature of the business. The problem is that when you get all those leads at the top of the funnel, you get a lot of noise.*
>
> *An expensive rep will actually go and talk to a lead, qualify them, and understand what they're looking for. That takes a lot of time because it's a very manual process. That's where my partner and I said: There's real money involved, it's repetitive and nobody likes doing it. So let's see if we can solve it.*
>
> *So we're now using a combo of AI, natural language understanding, and natural language generation technology, and we're able to increase the number of qualified meetings for each rep by 81%. So instead of 36 meetings per month, we're able to give a sales rep around 60 highly qualified meetings per month. Now, you can say 'Okay, how come the reps now suddenly have the time to meet with 60 qualified leads?' That's because we are able to free up their time wasted on all those communications, viewing and sending emails. So in return, they were able to spend that time meeting with prospects. It's a double win.*

"Do you see how we can now use technology to scale individuals? Another story around the same topic of creating exponential increase in scale is Collec-

---

14. https://www.valueinspiration.com/product-innovation-how-the-combo-of-ai-and-a-sales-rep-can-increase-sales-productivity-by-80/

tive[I], a company that uses Robotic Process Automation (RPA) and other forms of artificial intelligence like machine learning to optimize outcomes in sales by aligning the sales and buying process. Their technology has been referred to as 'The Waze for Sales.' Here's the story that Collective[i] co-Founder and Chairperson, Heidi Messer[15], told me:"

> *The entire enterprise will be transformed using a combination of data networks and artificial intelligence. And when I say transformation, I don't mean automation. That's a common misconception. Those of us on the cutting edge of this massive change are driven to identify all of the areas where humans are underutilized – areas where their jobs have become something other than what they were originally intended to be.*

> *We looked at the revenue management side, and in particular sales organizations as a ripe place for technology to completely reorganize and allow human beings to shine and show their true talents.*

> *Just to give you a sense of the scope of the opportunity, here in the United States, it is estimated that one in eight people are in the field of sales. Sales professionals spend roughly 70% of their time on non-revenue producing activities. That is astonishing, especially when 100% of how they are compensated is related to revenue and outcome.*

> *And so that dichotomy – they are hired and paid for their ability to understand and persuade buyers but instead spend more than two-thirds of their time on tasks and meetings, each having to create a map of a buyer that has been sold to before – that was something that we wanted to eliminate and allow for not only those individuals to apply their talents, but to do so in a way that fueled their success, their company's success, and their buyer's experience. Here's how we do that: First we free people from mundane non-value adding tasks. We automatically log activities into systems like CRM (so-called "rigor") to free time and improve data quality. We also provide managers with transparency and teams with collaboration tools aimed at minimizing the need for internal meetings.*

---

15. https://www.valueinspiration.com/product-innovation-how-ai-is-positively-influencing-the-science-of-buying-and-the-art-of-selling/

The second thing we do is we surface insights around how buyers are buying. That's really our secret sauce. We operate as a global network, analyzing massive amounts of dynamic data about what's happening in the market at large. We can use machine learning to spot patterns and identify important connections. As such, we're able to surface insights around the buying process that help sales leadership, operations, and professionals align their process and be responsive to what buyers are thinking and doing at any given moment. It's counter-intuitive, but when you use science (data and artificial), it turns out that companies operate a lot like people. Each person, function, and department exhibits different patterns around how they manage and make purchases. A procurement department tends to take a similar amount of time to negotiate contracts, certain buying clusters operating in certain ways. And so when the machine spots those buying clusters, it's trying to classify them based on what type of buyer they are. It's literally looking at the pure data and saying: 'here's what's likely to happen with this buyer cluster.' That's a much more effective way to help guide a seller. Another example would be bias known as 'loss aversion'. It takes a sales professional three times as long to lose a deal as it does to win a new one. And so one of the things our system is able to tell those sales professionals is when the odds have dropped below an acceptable level that it's worth spending their time.

The third thing we do is provide technology that enables a much more efficient and modern way of working. Today it is essential for companies to be more agile and connected to their customers. That requires transparency and collaboration (often between people in different time zones, countries and/or offices), and that also leverages human connections, intelligence, and relationships. Sales is an inherently social profession – personal networks directly correlate to accelerating sales cycles and improved odds of winning. Our application, and the graph we've spent years building, connects people who might not realize they can help each other.

All of the above is a good example of the beauty of machine learning – you can 'reimagine what can be' rather than iterate on what was. Combining automation, augmentation, collaboration, and social networking can be incredibly powerful, impact the lives of one in eight people, change the way companies do business, make revenue much more predictable, and therefore avoid some of the cyclical economic swings that inflict tremendous costs on job creation, corporate competitiveness and social stability.

"Fascinating, right?" I said. "The technology forces we have at our disposal to augment individuals are beyond imagination and by applying them together, the powers multiply."

At that moment an announcement was made to fasten our seatbelts. We were entering a low-pressure area which was going to cause turbulence.

4) The power that unlocks when multiple forces join

"As I said, another example of forces building up," I commented to Rob with a smile. "Very likely one of the reasons why Nazare will have these huge waves tomorrow. The reason why Nazare gets so big – the record surfed has been a massive 80 foot, or 25-metre wave – is because multiple forces join at that specific location, creating incredible energy.

"First there is the Nazaré Canyon, which comes closer than one mile to the shore and reaches a depth of around 16,400 feet at its lowest point – 10,000 feet deeper than the Grand Canyon. When the sea floor falls like that, waves gather more energy as the water rushes to fill the space. But when the biggest waves form at Nazaré, it's a product of two swells – one coming from the canyon and one from the shallower continental shelf. At Nazare they converge, so essentially, the waves are getting so big because they are two waves stacked on top of each other.

"In addition to the canyon, a small channel pushing water outward from the shore augments the already impressive wave height. Add in the Atlantic storm that's been growing over the last week from Greenland and you get the perfect cocktail for big wave surfing.

"This is exactly what happens with all the stories of innovation I have just told you about. These innovations optimally leverage several underlying forces to create the perfect 'wave', and with that, create leaps in value. Many of the examples are about use cases we have become used to for years, decades. Most use cases have benefited from several solutions that provided 'OK' value, nothing mind-blowing, and over time improved through small incremental gains. To connect that back to surfing – it's your average groundswell, that creates smooth, but small waves.

"It's those moments where multiple forces are bundled where the true 'big waves' are created, exposing forces we've never seen before. They change the norms. Companies that have the ability, i.e. the mindset and curiosity, to spot the opportunities of value creation, have the opportunity to create new possibilities. They become remarkable because they see the big problem amongst their ideal customers, connect the dots, reimagine what can be by blending technology and people in new ways, make the bet, align resources and execute.

"Those companies create the big waves their customers want to ride because of the push it will give them. Those companies have the ability to take a market by surprise.

"I believe every company can create such big waves of value. And the conditions, to connect it to another big wave surf aspect, have never been better with the rapid growth of data, computer power, infrastructure, and evolution of intelligent technology.

"Having said that, let me give you one more example; it's about a Norwegian company called Xeneta."

5) An exponential increase in scope

"When I interviewed Patrik Berglund,[16] co-founder and CEO of Xeneta, I was impressed by the approach he took to his company. In short, they are transforming how the logistic world – in particular the container trade – buys and sells. He told me this:

> To us there appear to be two problems. There's a lack of transparency in the market that's highly volatile. We found it very tricky, peculiar and inefficient that so many container boxes – 70 percent of global trade – were traded, bought, and sold with almost no visibility. Secondly, the way they're buying and selling is absolutely crazy inefficient. We realized that in order to solve anything about the second problem, we had to provide visibility and transparency.
>
> If you think about prices going up or down all the time, meaning it's a volatile market that is opaque, then you realize how difficult it is to be a buyer. I mean, one container is equal to the next when you simplify

---

16. https://www.valueinspiration.com/positively-impacting-the-global-economy-by-trans-
forming-buying-selling-dynamics-of-the-logistics-industry/

it. It felt very strange that it wasn't more transparent and we couldn't access market info more efficiently than by using emails and phone calls. The whole dynamic between the buyers and the sellers was awkward to us.

This is a very relationship-driven industry. And even while it was technologically possible to make it transparent, the incentives for doing so haven't been there. From the selling side, if you and I were the only one selling coffee beans and you didn't have any reference points to what it should cost, I would dictate the market. I will tell you what it costs. And that's exactly the problem going on in the container logistics market. The sellers dictate the price – route by route.

This is where I got together with my co-founder. We looked at the landscape from both the buying and selling side and concluded we had to go to the buying side in order to fix the transparency challenge. They want transparency. This is where we came up with the idea that we could get all this pricing data if we'd just crowd-source it from the buyers – companies, anything from Continental Tires, Electrolux, Nestle or Unilever.

After two-and-a-half years, we started to see critical mass and visibility in the main trade routes in the world. From thereon out, we actually productized our solution and started selling. The beautiful thing with our crowdsourcing structure, this network, is that it took us these two-and-a-half years to reach two million prices. The subsequent two-and-a-half years, however, that two million grew to fifty million. It was difficult to get to that basic level, but then it just started taking off, because we provided value.

Today, buyers and sellers are using our market data, acknowledging that this actually is the market. And when you have buyers and sellers doing that, then why on earth would you buy and sell in the same, similar, old-fashioned way you used to do? We wanted to create a proper dent in this industry and you don't do that by making it 'just' transparent: you do it by changing the fundamentals of how it works. That's what we're doing today: we are changing the way they buy and sell.

We take care of pricing for them, meaning securing that no one is ripping anyone else. This means that the buyers do not have the best price and the sellers do not scheme everything they can from the customer. Instead, they can focus on their five-year horizon, switching the discussion to long?term value, such as supply chain optimization, instead of handling back and forth on an additional discount of 50 or 100 US dollars per box. This is fundamentally changing how the game is played.

Connecting the dots

"Do you see what they did? They looked at the market with a curious mindset – asking simple questions like 'why is this market behaving like is?' On the outset it seems impossible to solve, but if you look at what both parties want – long-term value – then it's obvious you have to take the tactical noise out of the way. And this is what they did.

"As you have seen, creating exponential impact happens across specific angles, such as speed, scope, scale, accuracy towards individuals – the intelligence augmentation we just discussed. It also happens at the level of making solutions far more applicable, accessible, and affordable. Regardless the path you choose – or combinations of that – there are some underlying swells that are worth noticing. These underlying swells build the strong foundation that lead to the shift in value you created. Let's me share them with you.

1) Start with what's truly broken

"For all the cases we discussed the core ingredient that spurred the big idea was: there was something truly broken in the market they target. A growing scarcity of medical specialists (Proximie), a growing deficit of skills and experience (Beyond Limits), only 0.05% ad conversion (inPowered), Sales spending +70% of their time on non-revenue generating activities and massively missing targets (Collective[I]), etc.

"The bigger the problem, the bigger the opportunity to create a solution. Often, these problems are right in front of our eyes – we just don't see them. That's why the curiosity trait is so important. Because once we actually see the problem, only then can we create solutions that deliver exponential impact. That's the recipe for long-term success."

2) Leverage abundance

"As you have seen from the Xeneta story, the core value of their solution is the global transparency of data. The data was always available, just in silos – company by company. Xeneta decided to break that restriction and create a network to bring all the insights together in one single offering through crowd-sourcing – i.e. by getting buyer after buyer on board to anonymously share their data. Once they hit a certain level of data, suddenly there was a shift in value, and it took off. Buyers now have full scope of what the market looks like. It's trusted – fair. It shifts the focus from being process-centric to data-centric. And that changes the game from tactics to strategy.

"But I have shared more stories today that are based on this principle of focusing on abundance. Think about the story of Social Genomics, led by Susanne Baars. She said:

> Instead of focusing on problems and solving them, look around you
> and see the abundance, and really think about how you can use this to
> build the future with.

"That's exactly what she did. Her moonshot is all driven by the abundance of data – the genetic and medical data that every person on earth hold for themselves. Bringing that data together will 'empower every patient around the globe to find their cure faster, together.'

"The story of Collective[i] presents yet another similar case. Their network is their secret sauce. A shift in value is created by taking an 'outward' – and not just an 'inward' – focus. By pulling together aggregated and anonymized data from thousands of companies around the globe, and then using machine learning to spot patterns, Collective[i] is able to unearth insights previously unattainable to any individual or organization. Hence their name, short for Collective Intelligence – the sum of what is knowable translated into intelligence that exponentially augments what they know as individuals. Through this concept, they are able to understand the buying process scientifically and are able to help sellers align their process to what buyers are thinking and doing at any given moment to create a win-win-win. Companies, sales professionals and their buyers work in harmony. This is where sales performance goes up dramatically.

3) Deliver outcomes, instead of outputs

"Another underlying swell that helps to shift value creation is achieved by focusing your solution on delivering on impact, rather than just more output. If you look at companies like Corti, Unanimous AI, Collective[I], inPowered, and Xeneta, but also examples I talked about earlier on, like Aptage or CLEVVA, they are all setting new benchmarks by focusing on the outcome.

"They all realized that it's not about incrementally improving the process. It's not about making the work easier. It's not about delivering more of the same, just with less effort. They realized that value is created where we improve the outcome of our work.

- Delivering outcomes instead of outputs places a different focus on the challenge, and that is what helps to create new possibilities and break with the limitations of the past.
- Corti doesn't make the 112/911-agent make more calls, it helps them to save more lives by increasing the speed and accuracy of their judgment on each call.
- Xeneta doesn't enable buyers of container logistic services be more efficient in their purchase process, they help them to shift from tactics to strategy, and as such negotiate the best possible long-term contracts.
- Unanimous AI didn't focus on just another dashboard to empower individuals, they enable individuals to solve the largest business problems in the shortest possible time.
- Aptage doesn't enable project managers with just another KPI report, they target uncertainty in projects and guide them proactively with the single goal to raise project success rates across the board.
- Aerobotics doesn't give crop-tree farmers just pictures to make inspections of their farm more efficient, they give pro-active guidance with the single goal to increase crop yield.
- And Collective[I] doesn't just make managing and growing revenue easier by removing tasks They have crafted their solution to deliver the key ingredients to support improved outcomes for every part of their ecosystem: companies, their employees and buyers.

"Many business software products exist to help people do their jobs in an easier and more effective way. But creating a new product that allows them to do that job just a bit better, cheaper or faster won't cut it. Remember, people will only switch if the impact you create is exponentially better to what they have today. So keep the outcome in focus, not the output or process. People want to sell more, not just sell more efficiently. They want a competitive advantage, not just a job done.

4) Do the opposite of the norm

"A slightly different angle on the outcome principle, but no less important, is this one: doing the opposite of the norm. The ability to challenge the status quo, to see through the established rules and practices, and say 'enough is enough', takes courage, but is rewarding.

"I mentioned before that my background is in the ERP industry – Enterprise Resource Planning. The concept of ERP has been around for decades. It's ultimately about automating the back office of virtually every organization on the planet.

"Over the years I have been involved in the various technology shifts – and that always led to 'just another user interface' to automate a task we've been doing as long as we've been at work. Timesheets, expenses, billing, payroll, invoice reconciliation, you name it.

"Doing the opposite of the norm is the only way to disrupt this. It's asking the question: Why are we doing this process in the first place. At Unit4, the company I used to work for, we started to have this discussion many times around 2014. Very interesting debates that were not about 'yet another UI', but about 'the best UI is no UI'. This led to landing the term 'Self-Driving ERP', which resulted in solutions where, at the end of each day, your timesheet is actually proposed to you by a digital assistant – simply because we leave all the trails anyway. Employees shifted from 'load oriented' to 'exception based', and could actually be automatically paid salary at the end of the month without the intervention of a payroll clerk if everything was accurate and in line with rules and regulations. Expense claims would be proposed automatically, based on recognized patterns, email receipts, etc. That's about doing the opposite of the norm.

5) Make people better, not redundant

"This brings me to another underlying principle: Leveraging technology to make people deliver value never held possible before. Virtually all the stories I shared are founded on the principle that in Business to Business, impact is made by people, and hence the opportunity is to focus on making them shine.

"This reminds me of my conversation with Vinnie Mirchandani[17] about his book, *Silicon Collar*. He shared this insight:

> *When I interviewed all these executives, I didn't hear any one of them who said 'I'm doing this because I want to replace 1,000 employees.' They said they did it because, 'it'll make our workers more productive.' Most people start off the augmentation mentality, not a replacement mentality.*
>
> *Over time, they will be able to replace. Most companies have become realistic that automation doesn't automatically just deliver the labor savings that you may start off with. Some of them start off with that intention. For various reasons, automation does not majorly reduce in labor savings. It's much better to start off saying, 'How do I make my workers much more productive?' As I call it, how do I make them super workers?*

"This is exactly the underlying theme in the many stories I shared with you – and that separates them from the pack. They are using the available forces and combine manpower with machine power to take the outcome of a typical user's work to the next level. They're leveraging the opportunity to make 1+1=3.

6) Change the business model, not the business process

"The last underlying force worth mentioning: changing the business model, not (just) the business process.

"The story about inPowered is a perfect example of changing the business model, not just the process. As their website states: 'We deliver attention, not clicks'. This is the difference in thinking behind their solution, and with that they are transforming the digital ad world. The don't make digital advertising easier, instead they guarantee engagement. And that's what you pay for – the outcome.

[17.] https://www.valueinspiration.com/an-optimistic-perspective-on-humans-machines-and-jobs/

"Aerobotics is another one. The power behind their solution could affect how fertilizer companies go to market (pay for yield growth), how insurance companies go to market (pay for the level of risk you carry), and even how the upstream supply chain operates, because it allows retailers on the other end of the world to anticipate the tiniest shift in supply risk. That's valuable, and that drives adoption."

"Wow!" Rob responded. "Lots to digest, but revealing. It's very valuable to have these 'mirrors' when evolving our business. I think it really will help to dig deep and get to the core of what's really important. We're guilty of not doing enough of this."

"You're not alone, Rob," I responded. "For each of those cases it's not easy to do – if it was easy everyone would be doing it. But as such a clear case of building defensible differentiation. Just think about all these examples. Whether you are in sectors like the container-shipping industry, healthcare, agriculture, or in domains like sales, HR, accounting. The opportunities are up for grabs everywhere."

"Fully agree," said Rob. "We have to spend more time reflecting. Step away from the day-to-day rush and challenge the established unchallenged rules within the ideal customer segment we target. That's a big opportunity if you ask me."

"Spot on," I replied. "And that is how all the examples I have shared with you started. With a single spark of wisdom they gained from simply reflecting. In doing so, each of them is changing the norms by creating new value possibilities. They deliver a shift in value for their ideal customer compared to the established alternative. Their solution is about getting 10% better, but instead going for the 10x impact. This fascinates me and in particular the techniques behind it.

"These companies, each in their own category, create the big wave their customers can only but want to ride. Heidi Messer summed it up perfectly:

You realize you cannot sit on the sidelines. The idea of being a fast follower doesn't work in AI, because the advantages are so far superior.

Ask yourself

STEP 1: Reflect critically how you score your own ability around this particular trait by rating your organization on a scale of 1 (poor) to 10 (remarkable).

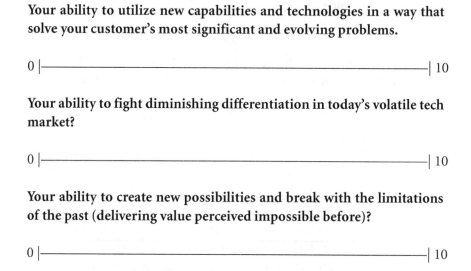

Your ability to utilize new capabilities and technologies in a way that solve your customer's most significant and evolving problems.

0 |————————————————————————————| 10

Your ability to fight diminishing differentiation in today's volatile tech market?

0 |————————————————————————————| 10

Your ability to create new possibilities and break with the limitations of the past (delivering value perceived impossible before)?

0 |————————————————————————————| 10

STEP 2: Take ten minutes to reflect on the next actions you could initiate to improve your score.

STEP 3: What's the single action from this list that would give you the biggest impact?

Take it to the next level

- Not only become remarkable, but ensure you'll stay remarkable as well by introducing the 'Remarkable Monday' habit within your organization. Download the three simple steps that will help you create and keep momentum: https://valueinspiration.com/RemarkableMonday
- Join the Remarkable Tribe Program to create accountability with other tech-entrepreneurs like you. Not only will you build traction to shape the business you aspire to be, but you will also obtain new ideas, create new contacts and will be part of a movement that defines what it means to be remarkable as a business software vendor: https://movement.valueinspiration.com

Trait 6
Create fans, not just customers

The power of fans

"As you can see, Rob, the traits to become a remarkable software business are all layered on top of each other. The more traits you can master, the bigger your impact will be. And based on what I just told you, if you create new value possibilities, you have the opportunity to get a lot of attention and attract an audience that's prepared to pay a premium."

"I totally agree," Rob replied. "And what I like about the examples is that it gives me a spectrum of angles to first of all explore and find those new value possibilities, and secondly to find different ways to execute them so as to create maximum impact. I love that!"

"There's one thing I need to add to this, however," I interrupted Rob. "There's a lot of value in curiosity, and there's a lot of value in exploring exponential thinking in executing on the opportunities you'll find. But the devil is in the detail. There's a fine line between creating customers, and creating fans. And it's the fans you want. That's why I have defined 'creating fans, not just customers' as the sixth trait of a remarkable software company."

At that moment the service crew came by for a last opportunity to get something to drink. We had already been in the air for over an hour. "Time flies, Rob," I commented. "Would you like another coffee?"

"OK, one more won't hurt," Rob replied.

I ordered two coffees, and then continued my point.

"From my experience in the business software space, and all the podcast interviews I have conducted with pioneering CEOs, I have gathered a range of compelling stories on the topic, and a lot of value comes from working very closely with your ideal customers to trigger that 'yes!' moment.

"A lot can be done by simply thinking logically and reflecting on which products you love yourself. For all those products simply reflect on exactly 'why' you love them. Why you recommend them to others – and why you don't do the same thing for other, quite similar, products in that category. You'll find it's often not about the facts, but about the feeling.

"Let's link this back to big wave surfing: What makes me, and so many others, such big fans of big wave surfing? It's not just one factor. With big wave surfing the moment fans are created is the moment the perfect cocktail is served. Multiple forces come together – the location, the tide, the massive groundswell, the passionate positioning of the surfers, the growing wedge, the moment it is about to break, and then . . . the commitment.

"The masters commit at points where others chicken out. Commitment to go 'all in' gets you points, credits. Taking off at the steepest point on the wall. Taking off straight and deep into a barrel. Knowing that if they wipe out there's a painful consequence, a combo of millions of liters of water crashing down upon you, and often a sharp ruthless reef only 60cm underneath you on the other end.

"It's that cocktail of elements that's memorable. That thrill you get from it. It's not the individual components. It's not the surfer. It's not the big wave by itself – it's the unique moment when they all come together. The moment when it's all or nothing. And that memorable, no – that remarkable moment is what everybody will always come back for, no matter how far they have to travel, no matter the price. That's when fans are created – fans for life.

"It's the same with business software – possibly the atmosphere and context are different."

"You bet!" Rob said with a smile. "But I get your analogy. It's indeed those magic moments that have the power to turn average customers into raving fans. That's what remarkable software companies – at least the ones I know – understand really well."

"It all comes back to the very simple unit of three: value – urgency – expectation, as I explained earlier," I continued. "It always fascinates me how much more value you get if a customer becomes an advocate of your business. When they start referring you to others without even asking them. Fans go the extra mile. They drop what they are doing just to be part of the momentum you create. They'll stand up to defend you to critics as if they were working for you. That's priceless.

"The magic sits within this triangle. If you strike the right balance with these three criteria, and continue to do so, you'll create fans. You'll create value worth making a remark about.

"But the big question is: what turns them into a fan in the first place? What I have come to realize over time is that the devil is in the detail. Having the big idea to fix something that's truly broken in your market is one thing. It puts you on the right track. But then comes the part around exceeding expectations. That's where something average can turn into something remarkable."

Rob nodded. "I thoroughly agree with that. Creating something average is the easy part. But that's often where we stop. The mantra 'it's good enough' plays a big role here. Often because we have to move on, there's a time or budget constraint, or simply because we actually believe 'it's good enough'."

"So true," I responded, "but creating something remarkable doesn't have to cost more, or take more time. You 'just' have to play it smart. You have to strategically choose your bets – and if you know what to look out for, that becomes a relatively easy thing.

"So let's pick it apart – what are the things to watch out for in creating that new product, that new module, or even that new feature? If I reflect on my previous work and all the hundreds of examples I've explored over time, I end up with seven examples that matter:

1. Be there when it matters most
2. Think in Win-Win-Win scenarios
3. Make it magically happen – i.e. make it all invisible
4. Focus on the result, not the process
5. Surprise
6. Change behavior
7. Make it sticky

1) Be there when it matters most

"The first category that comes to mind is 'Be there when it matters most'. It seems like an open door, but how often do we use a solution to realize that at the moment supreme, it's just not up to par with what we need, so when it gets difficult, you're on your own again.

"It's identifying those examples where you can create your biggest fans. Examples where the solution you use really helps you out of a challenging, time-pressured situation without dropping you.

"The story from Corti comes to mind again. Remember how they are using AI to help 911 call agents uncover the 'real' issue in a split second? The agent could perfectly handle the vast majority of the incoming calls, but it's that extra help in moments that matter where Corti makes the difference. And it's often those moments where the user can become the hero in the eyes of their 'customer'. In the case of Corti, that could literally mean a life-or-death difference. That's valuable. So, solve those moments, solve the hard parts first, that will give you credits.

"This reminds me of some advice Andreas gave during the conversation I had with him:

> *'If you really want to bring 10x value to a use case, I think you need to go quite deep and really understand it well. A lot of Machine Learning is getting a bit generic and is taking a more horizontal approach to creating value. Those who create the most value are quite good at going very deep.*

"The part around 'going deep' is all about exceeding expectations. It's not that you have to do that in all parts of your solution, but if you want to deliver something remarkable, do it when it matters most.

"The other example that immediately jumps to mind in this same category is one I told you about earlier on as well: Cogito. It's again a solution that has focused on 'being there when it matters most'. Their customers are providing customer support – which is full of opportunities (for them) to turn their customers into fans. What stuck with me from my interview with Skyler Place was this quote:

> *What we are most proud of is this: when we go on site and visit our customers, the agents who were making these calls all day talk about how Cogito is the favorite piece of software they have on their system. It's the only one that's there trying to improve both their experience, as well as the experience of their customers. It's wonderful to build software that not only can support an organization's goals, but can also support the well-being and work environments of their employees.*

"I believe that you have these moments with every solution. And sure, it's not always as potentially critical as with Corti, but those moments are plenty. Skyler stressed that this happens a lot in the insurance world:

What we're finding is that the most important conversations are the ones when your customer needs something from you; they have an unexpected medical bill, or they have been in a car accident and it's the first time they're making a claim.

Those are moments where the customer wants to talk to a person and the success of those interactions determines if that individual will stay with that company or if they will switch.

It's in those moments where having agents who are empowered with the best tools to have a strong empathic conversation with a customer, the organization is going to win, retain and grow their revenue and customer base.

"See how basic this can be? We often don't realize it, just because it is so basic. If you have insurance, you hope to never use it. But when you do, it's those moment that define everything.

"It's those moments where you hope to get a resolution quickly. Where you hope to get some empathy. What we expect is frustration though – and that's the opportunity. It can be as simple as taking a frustration away that occasionally happens, but one that defines the overall perception.

"It brings back memories of an example with my previous company, Unit4. It will resonate if you are familiar with financial solutions, and in particular with, for example, the 'reversal of an incorrect General Ledger transaction'. The focus typically is on making it simple to enter/create those transactions. However, what if you'd made a mistake? That typically was always was a nightmare to resolve. I think you'll understand what I mean and how this works counter to creating fans."

Rob nodded. "I can think of plenty of those situations," he smiled.

"So my recommendation is really to reflect on your current solution: What's the experience your customers face when the heat is really on? Does it stand the test? Always think about this from the perspective of the customer, or even the customers' customer, as with the example of Cogito. Have you ever received a 'big thank you' call or mail from your customer because your solution made the difference in such a situation? Those are the moments.

"Remarkable software businesses think differently. They don't see those moments as an exception but as the rule. They see these moments as opportunities for their product and brand to shine, and therefore as a way to differentiate and grow in new and unique ways.

"This reminds me of my interview with Toby Allen.[1] He's a specialist in virtual reality and augmented reality. He shared some inspiring examples of how business solutions could evolve beyond what we know today – and become truly effective 'at the moment when it matters most':

> *The ability to visualize your worlds in a hands-free capacity, augment it with holograms, and information, and viewing that information in a new way is absolutely incredible.*

> *There are a lot of people that don't like sitting in front of a computer and actually want to be outside doing things or being 'in the action', whether that's being on a set in a theater production, being in the wild saving rhinos, or studying marine life.*

> *Think about the amount of accidents or errors people make on the job. What if you could instruct or train people 'in the action' and avoid the problem. The compound effect of all this is that you start reducing those errors and start being more efficient. Companies would not only make/save more money, but would also start reducing things like insurance premiums.*

> *I think we're at the point where all these technologies can provide a better set of tools for these people to perform. This could lead to results that we've never seen before.*

"Fascinating, right? I mean, just think about your own business, if we take a different perspective on designing the business solutions we're using on a day-to-day basis. Why do we always have to be in front of a screen? Why can't we blend the essence of these solutions with the moment of action – when we're in the field, in meetings with our customers, on-site working on a project, running a workshop, etc.

"We're starting to see this happening now. In the business software space Microsoft Dynamics[2] 365 division has been the first to blend the transactional with the virtual experience. Instead of 'just' focusing on automation, they're

---

[1]   https://www.valueinspiration.com/product-strategy-the-value-we-can-unlock-when-we-combine-mixed-reality-ai-and-blockchain/

[2]   https://dynamics.microsoft.com/en-us/mixed-reality/overview/

actually guiding people on the job by bringing augmented and virtual reality into the moments where the work is happening – it's fascinating to see where this can take us. It gives a totally new dimension to making software 'hands-free'. And although that's just scratching the surface of what's possible, I can imagine this is going to create quite a number of fans."

2) Think in Win-Win-Win scenarios

"The second category I'd earmark as high potential to turn customers into fans are those scenarios where you can really take the benefits for your customers' customers to the next level. Remarkable software businesses often don't just think about what is good for them or for their customers; they think about what is good for everyone – including their customers' customers.

"How often do we stop too early and solve just the problems at hand for our customers. Although that's OK, and obviously what's expected, there's a missed opportunity here. Think about what makes your customers thrive: it's where they can make the difference for their customers. That's what I'd call Win-Win-Win.

"What you do is to translate the problem forward. You can solve the challenge your customer is facing in such a way that it will make them look like the hero with their customers. Abhay Gupta,[3] CEO of Bidgely, had a fascinating story about that. They are transforming the utility/energy industry, not only by focusing on streamlining the core business of their customers, but actually by enabling their customers to create shifts of value towards their customers. This creates a compelling competitive advantage. This is what he said:

> The primary business for most of the utilities in the world has been around how to keep the lights on, how to build power plants, how to keep the distribution and transmission of the energy correctly happening. That's where they shine. But in this changing world, where everything's about data, the majority of the industry does not specialize in extracting value of the data. They're all collecting the data but not utilizing it.

[3.] https://www.valueinspiration.com/product-innovation-how-ai-is-shaping-a-better-future-for-all-of-us-by-transforming-the-utility-industry/

With over one billion smart meters around the world today we have so much data coming out of every single home. This is the opportunity for the utility and energy industry to completely change and morph themselves into something, what I call, at par with the Googles and Amazons of the world.

So at Bidgely, we make this absolutely fabulous lens to empower both the consumer and utilities themselves with intellectual decision making. The opportunities go as broad as enhancing their shareholder value, by reducing the cost of operation, creating new revenue opportunities, and personalizing the customer experience. The latter makes their customers a lot more loyal.

With AI we are able to tell each consumer where they're spending energy, on what appliances, when. We effectively change how people consume energy by providing them timely insights and making them conscious via email, SMS, or voice via Alexa or their Google Home appliance. We make them aware on things like 'How much money did I spend on air conditioning the refrigerator, the hair dryer or the dish washer' – and more importantly – we give them recommendations on how they can improve or cut down this spend.

The goal here is to support the changing industry and create value for both the utility industry and their consumers by making things personalized.

"Fascinating indeed," Rob commented.

"Exactly. And think about it: the prime reason for existence of every organization is the unique value they deliver to their customers. Remarkable business software companies seem to understand this extremely well. They architect solutions by taking away the pains their customers face in delivering beyond the expected value to their customers.

"Think about customer experience in the context of a call-center again. It's about getting the right and relevant answers, empathy, and about on-the-spot creativity to solve their case. All too often organizations use technology to automate. But if your target is to increase customer experience, automation will only get you halfway. Ying Chen,[4] Chief Product and Marketing Officer at

---

4. https://www.valueinspiration.com/how-to-create-breakthrough-business-results-by-augmenting-people/

Luminoso Technologies, former Head of Platform Product Marketing at Pega-systems, summarized this really nicely when I interviewed her:

> *Organizations need to think from the place of 'What is the experience, the journey that you want to improve?'*
>
> *It's not about 'How can I reduce the number of agents?' – It's about 'How do I not make my customers wait?'*
>
> *It's not just about 'What are the things I can automate?' It's really about 'What are the things that are either intended or unintended that I'm doing to make my employees' jobs difficult that gets in the way of delivering great experience for my customer?'*
>
> *It's all about making sure that you have improved employee experience that will lead to greater customer satisfaction.*

"As you can see, Rob, it's a subtle difference, but an important one. I strongly believe we should ask the question 'How does this solution, module, or feature contribute to growing the differentiating value our customers deliver to their customers?'

And here's where today's technology really comes in handy, and particularly the scenarios where we can create the ideal human/machine combinations in order to deliver 1+1=3 outcomes. With that everybody wins."

"This is absolutely an area where my company has a huge opportunity," Rob said, smiling. "Virtually every bank in the world is in a fight for relevancy amongst their customers. And this is where we can help them make a very big difference. Thanks for reminding me about that!"

3) Make it magically happen – i.e. make your technology invisible

We could already feel we were approaching the airport of Porto. The pressure on our ears was building up and the flight attendants were walking through the aisle to collect the garbage.

"You know what?" I started. "You indeed have a very large opportunity to help your customers in banking win the war for relevancy amongst their customers. And another way to start looking at that opportunity is by thinking 'what you can make invisible?'.

"Often the way to get people to become your fans is not to create the next easier, better, slick UI, but to completely remove the UI altogether. Let me connect this back to the timesheet process again. Do you have a policy inside your company to register time?"

"Yes, we do," Rob replied. "All our consultants do, obviously, but so to do staff working on projects in order to track how we are doing compared to budget. Why?"

"And do your employees like it?" I asked Rob again.

"Well, what do you think? They despise it. But it's a necessary evil. Without that insight there would be no invoices, and without invoices there would be no income. It's that simple."

"Agreed, and this is how it has been for decades," I continued. "With every technology shift – from DOS to Windows, from Windows to Web, from Web to Mobile, or simply after every two years of 'evolution' we have 'invented' yet another, better, UI for this process that everybody would love to be released from in the first place. And the aim was always to make it 'less frustrating', or as my dear friend and colleague Thomas Staven at Unit4 used to say, 'They'll hate it less'.

"And that's exactly what we started to challenge early in 2014. Instead of coming up with yet another trick to the UI we asked out loud, 'What if we removed the need to enter a timesheet altogether?' That's how Wanda, Unit4s digital assistant, was born. Instead of making timesheets[55] easy to enter, she now simply 'proposes it' based on all the trails it can uncover; 90% of the time that's simply correct.

"And since it's self-learning, it will just get better and better, up to the point you don't have to bother about it at all anymore. It's simply done, or even better, gone. It magically happens, by making the technology invisible. End result: users happy, project manager happy, and customer happy, as there are virtually no disputes anymore about incorrectly entered time.

"Think about it – most customers don't want to deal with technology. They just want to make progress and be productive. Today's AI and Machine Learning technology is perfect for that. Looking at my own business, I am using around ten AI solutions myself, and I love it. Things just happen, and that not only gives me valuable time back, but in a range of cases it actually allows me to do things I could not have dreamt about before.

[5.]   https://vimeo.com/277648863

"So if you really look carefully at what we 'want' you'll see we want seamless tech that works so hard for us that we don't even notice its presence. Instead of downloading a handful of apps to get the job done, we want technology that's our peer, taking care of things and enabling us to always be one step ahead. Correct?"

"Spot on," Rob replied.

"Indeed, so the words for that are the best UI is NO UI. Period. Talking of this, Omar Tawakol,[6] CEO of Voicea, gave me an example of how his company 'magically makes things happen'. Voicea is an AI-powered platform that transforms your meetings into time well spent. When I asked about their approach to turn customers into fans, he said this:

> *Given how much time we spend in meetings, it's one of the largest time sinks of all knowledge workers. I saw there was an opportunity to help democratize the skills of great executives – helping people get the best skills from the best executives – that's how EVA (Enterprise Voice Assistant) was born.*
>
> *The core starting point is: 'EVA has our back'. You and I can have this conversation, I don't have to have my laptop open or take notes, it's going to record it, transcribe it and identify the implicit moments that look like the actions and decisions you made.*
>
> *There's a second area of value though which is super interesting: The change in people dynamics. A lot of people go to meetings because they have a fear of missing out. But they don't really intend on participating, they just kind of show up with their laptop open. What we tried to do is transform that from 'The fear of missing out' to 'The joy of missing out.' This means you don't have to go unless you are going to participate: EVA will go for you and you'll magically get the summary. This transforms those meetings to meetings that are focused and where people are fully engaged.*
>
> *The consequence of this is that our viral coefficient is quite large, it's getting close to one. Here's why: If you are able to invite EVA to a*

---

6. https://www.valueinspiration.com/product-innovation-the-difference-ai-can-add-in-making-our-meetings-worthwhile/

meeting, and you share notes with a couple of people, they get intrigued and as such want it as well. Seeing it in action is the core reason for our rapid growth.

"I want that! So simple, yet so powerful!" Rob interrupted.

"Agreed," I replied. "And the moment you think about it, there are so many use cases where we can 'make things happen' magically. Another example that springs to mind is one we all benefit from every day once its powers are applied at work. It's a solution from Opas AI. I spoke with their CEO, Mohit Gupta,[7] about their vision to create self-healing systems. The way it came about was the stress Mohit and his co-founder had in their previous IT operations jobs at Amazon and other large infrastructure players. This is what he said:

We can win customers. We can buy contracts. But winning credibility is a long-term process. You may be doing very well for the last five years; however, a two-hour outage will basically wipe that credibility away.

A few minutes outage on your site becomes a massive PR issue and the cost is not only the lost revenue. The bigger cost is negative PR and loyalty crisis that follows. And God save you if you are providing service to other SaaS providers. That's where it multiplies.

In the world of IT and SaaS, every major company has a huge operations team whose primary goal is just to make sure system services are never impacted, no matter what time of the day, no matter what kind of load you are running.

But is this something we can keep up with? Is adding people and monitoring systems the answer in the long term? Traffic volumes will just increase, complexity of services will just increase due to interlinked services, and norms of what good looks like will increase as well. So, with current approaches being all very reactive, in a world where repair time is limited to hours, or even minutes, that's not only costly, but more worrying, a very big risk.

And this is exactly the problem Opas AI set out to fix: solving the problem of 'reactivity' so IT operations can sleep peacefully. It uses AI and Machine Learning to detect the application performance issues,

---

[7.] https://www.valueinspiration.com/product-innovation-how-ai-delivers-the-dream-of-every-it-operation-self-healing-systems/

then employ past analysis and future projections to find, and then automatically fix even the toughest application problems. This is what we call 'self-healing systems'.

"As you can see – another example of taking a different approach to creating solutions. Not by creating more tools, more monitoring systems, more dashboards, but 'simply' a solution that solves the problem magically by making technology invisible.

"Have you ever read the book *Blue Ocean Strategy*?" I asked Rob.

"Yes, I have. Why?" he replied.

"Well," I continued, "if you can remember, the framework they use is to make distinct decisions about what you Create, Eliminate, Reduce, or Increase. I have used this technique plenty of times in positioning and market segmentation exercises, and even in pricing projects. But at the start it's a framework for product managers. And where we always think we should simply 'add more stuff', the power of many solutions is actually to reduce the stuff, or even eliminate it.

"That's what this category is all about. Carefully looking at the work we do. Challenging it by asking 'Why should we do this in the first place?' or 'What would this look like if we just made it magically happen?' In many cases you end up with the response 'Thank you, you've made my day' because people simply hated doing it in the first place. That's a good signal to turn customers into fans."

4) Focus on the result, not the process

We were approaching the landing strip of the Francisco Sá Carneiro Airport in Porto and within a couple of minutes we'd be touching down.

"Where's your hotel?" Rob asked me suddenly.

"Near Aveiro," I answered. "I wanted to make sure I'd be heading towards Nazare already tonight, so I can be there first thing in the morning when the first heat starts. I expect that will be around 8 a.m."

"I get that," Rob responded. "How will you get there?"

"I'll simply rent a car," I answered. "Seems like the most obvious thing to do, correct?"

"Well," Rob responded, "what if I take you to your hotel? I live in Olive-irinha, which is just 8km east of Aveiro. And another thing; if you like, I'll join you tomorrow. It's been a while since I've seen the monster waves of Nazare. I have an appointment in Lisbon at 11 a.m. with some friends of mine, so I can take you to the event as well and watch the first heats unfold prior to that."

"Wow," I responded. "That would be fantastic! I'd love that. Thanks!"

"Deal!" Rob said as he put up his hand for a high-five.

At that moment the plane shook. We'd landed.

The plane braked to cruising speed, and from there taxied to the gate.

After a minute of taxiing it stopped and parked. We could already see two busses approaching the plane to park on each side of the left wing. The 'seatbelt' light turned off, and everybody jumped up to pack their stuff.

"Now on to the last part of the trip," I said as I checked my WSL app. "Looks like the conditions are going to be perfect tomorrow. They expect waves of between 40 and 45 feet, so well over 10 meters. And they plan to start at 8 a.m. sharp, with heat 1 including some of my favorites, Kai Lenny, Billy Kemper and Grant Baker. With waves that big, the heat will be on since it's just a one-day event and as such you only have one shot to move to the next round. Fifty per cent get eliminated in round one – so it's all about results, and nothing but results."

The doors opened, and the plane started emptying from the front and the rear. Since we were seated at the 'Exit' row, we'd be the last to leave the plane.

"That, by the way, is one of the key differences I see between remarkable software companies and the 'rest'. They clearly focus on the result, not the process," I said as we slowly moved towards the front exit door.

"Remember the case about Onsophic – instead of building yet another Learning Management System that focuses on the output, they built a platform that guides each individual in a company to achieve better results fast. In other words, addressing the learning gaps that stand in the way for each individual to achieve this outcome in the shortest and most impactful way.

"And think about the story I told you about First.io. Instead of building yet another 'better CRM' they focused on the outcome – recommending people that are actually in the market to buy or sell their house. With that real estate agents can focus on closing, and do away with losing out on 60% of the opportunities that are actually closing without them knowing."

At that moment we reached the bottom of the stairs and walked towards the first bus. It was packed, but there was still some room at the back. We both got in and a seconds later the doors closed and the bus drove off.

"Another story that comes to mind is one from Politecnico di Milano," I said. "I spoke with Federico Frattini,[8] Professor of Strategic Management and

---

8. https://www.valueinspiration.com/product-innovation-how-ai-empowers-new-generations-of-business-minds-with-the-knowledge-and-skills-they-need-to-succeed/

Innovation. They were amongst the first, if not the first, universities in the world to launch an AI-powered, personalized, continuous learning platform called FLEXA. Here's what he told me:

The basic idea is to give our students exactly the knowledge they need to achieve their career goals faster and to make them more employable. It's something that represents a big change in the traditional business model of a business school or of a university.

We started to think how to make professors at our school able to amplify their knowledge by tapping into this distributed, mostly free knowledge landscape. This was one starting point. The other was linked to the fact that we have a growing number of students. We realized that each student is unique in terms of background, education, and aspiration for their career. However, we didn't know their skills. We didn't know their strengths and weaknesses. And as such, up to today we offer them more or less the same program.

So we raised the challenge: How can we amplify their knowledge experience in our school and after they graduate by using the knowledge available outside our boundaries? This is how FLEXA was born.

FLEXA doesn't only use our knowledge, our courses, and our programs, but on top of that we're integrating contents, expertise, events coming from any angle in the world. All the book platforms available on the web like Harvard Business School Publishing, MIT's Sloan Management Review, the Instituto de Empresa Learning Resources, Gartner, New York Times, Financial Times, etc.

We are aggregating all these high-quality, certified knowledge sources. Through FLEXA, we bring to our student exactly the piece of knowledge they need, when they need it. FLEXA amplifies the knowledge of our students by giving them personalized, tailored, digital and physical learning experiences. With that they'll be able to achieve their career goals fastest.

"See what I mean, Rob?" I asked. Once you start focusing on the result, the outcome, you can find new and fresh ways to break with processes that have been around for decades. And the funny thing is, it all seems so logical once you hear about these examples. But as you can imagine, for the education sector, FLEXA is introducing a 180-degree turn in how 'the business' of education works.

"By applying intelligent technologies to the learning process, any university can make the shift from delivering graduated students to employable students that can directly start to make an impact and be self-sustainable in society. That's a true shift in value. And beyond that, linking effort to tangible results (i.e. employability) will, from my perspective, add more meaning, and as such lower the number of drop outs, and help students to accelerate their education process, which is a win-win for everybody.

"To me this is just the first step in accelerating a large-scale transformation in education. Matching curriculum and content with student aspirations is one side of the coin. Imagine what happens when employers start to engage in the process? That way you have the perfect platform to match demand and supply – and, as such, critical information to perfectly tune curriculum development. It's turning the curriculum process from top-down (education system led) to bottom-up (market led).

"If you know what employers really search for, and what this actually means to the expected knowledge and skills students need to be of the best value, it means that for the first time the education system can start to anticipate and follow the shifting demands in the real business world, resulting in new ways to close the rapidly growing skills gap as well as the gap between students and placement.

"That's what makes focusing on results so powerful, Rob," I concluded. "It's incredibly powerful in turning customers into fans. And as a by-product of this process you'll see that this impacts the monetization side as well. Be honest, what option would you choose?

- Pay for financial software to manage your transactions, or pay for the actual change in annual profit?
- Pay for managing the enrolment process of students or pay for every new student you win as a consequence of better enrolment experience?
- Pay for managing the project delivery process, or pay for the physical impact it has made on reduction of project leakage or increase in utilization?
- Pay for managing the fundraising process, or pay for the actual growth of the average gift per donor?

At that moment the bus stopped. We'd arrived at airport arrivals. The door opened and together we headed for the exit.

"Strong point," Rob said. "I've been in the business software space for a long time, and up to now I've virtually only seen the traditional thinking around process automation and managing transactions. This is all changing now at a rapid pace, simply because the expectations are different from what they've always been."

"Correct," I replied. "And technology is playing a big part in it, accelerating it even more."

5) Surprise

As we walked through the baggage area, Rob suddenly said, "Gosh, the suitcases are already coming in. That was fast! And wait, there's mine already."

He walked towards the conveyor belt, picked up his suitcase, and we walked on.

"Not a single second's delay," he said.

"The fact you are surprised says a lot," I replied. "Surprise always helps to create fans. And now you see why. It's actually a component of all the situations I mentioned before, but I believe it should stand by itself as a key component to focus on.

"Surprise comes in many flavors – and its power is that it goes beyond the 'average'. It can be as simple as a nudge for a valuable insight – remember when I told you about Nudge? It can be an alert that helps you prevent or actually accelerate something – remember the story I told you about Aptage? The right technology can sometime surprise us, because the answers are counterintuitive. Our 'fast' thinking processes are sometime wrong and our gut feelings can steer us off course. It can be many things. But the fact it 'surprises' you in a positive way is where the power lies.

"I'm actually using a solution myself that fits into this category – it's from an AI start-up called CliClap, they use Machine Learning to predict and apply the next best action for each of your website visitors. What's unique about it is that the platform builds journeys for each visitor which are optimized for engagement and conversions, thus producing more leads in higher quality, hands-free. First of all, for me it does magic since I no longer have to worry about what content to put where on my website. But more importantly, visitors to my website get highly personalized recommendations that are surprisingly relevant for them for the point where they are on their journey. So every time I see it in action it brings a smile on my face. And that's what you want as a business software vendor, correct?"

"Absolutely," Rob replied. "That's exactly where my company has a fantastic opportunity. So it's good you 'label' it. It's so easy to approach certain features as 'cool', but at the end it's not the feature, but the experience they give we need to put the focus on."

"Correct," I continued. "This reminds me of a company that's revolutionising the recruitment space: Eightfold.ai. Ashutosh Garg,[9] their CEO, shared with me the big idea behind his company:

> *While I was at Google, I saw how important people are to the organization. The success and failure of any company depends on the kind of people they hire. The other thing was, as a candidate, I also realized how hard it is for one to find the right job. And once you find the right job, it can completely transform your life.*
>
> *The problem is, 80% of the people today end up applying to the wrong job.*
>
> *And since employment is the backbone of our society, everything depends on that. That tells us how big a problem it is, how widespread the problem is. That led me to found Eightfold.*
>
> *Instead of people applying for a job, we recommend them. When people are looking for a job, they are not switching the job to do the same thing they have been doing. But they want to do something more, something different, they want to grow in their career.*
>
> *And through AI, what we can do is predict what someone is likely to do next in their career. For example, the system can highlight and present that based on what you have done, it looks like you can be a great product manager tomorrow. The system can predict that people who did information theory in the earlier years actually have all the training required to be Machine Learning scientists today.*

---

9. https://www.valueinspiration.com/product-innovation-how-ai-transforms-the-recruitment-process-in-a-win-win-for-everybody/

This helps us understand who will be a good fit for this role in which organization. That enabled us to connect people to those opportunities. So, we've changed the paradigm: Instead of people applying for a job, we go and recommend them: John and Lisa, these are the three jobs in our company that our most relevant to you. If you're only looking to hire people based on what they have done, not what they are capable of doing, then you're losing value proposition. Everyone deserves the opportunity and we want to enable that in people.

"Fascinating, right?" I asked Rob.

"Definitely! Surprisingly fascinating! It's turning the entire process on its head. Something I should look into myself, ha ha."

"Indeed, systems like this keep surprising you in a positive way. And the good thing is, they just get better and better because they keep learning."

In the meantime, we walked out of the airport, crossed the street and walked into the car park.

As Rob searched for his ticket, we headed for the ticket machines to pay the car park fee.

"All set," he said. "Let's walk to the left towards the end. My car is in the third bay."

6) Change behavior

A minute later we arrived at Rob's car, stalled our luggage in the trunk and drove off.

"That story around Eightfold inspired me," said Rob. "It's a tangible example of how we can create more value by challenging the status quo and the established so-called 'unspoken rules.'"

"I copy you on that, Rob," I replied. "It's what you get when curiosity is at the right level and when you start asking the right questions. We're all so engrained in our day-to-day busy life that we simply don't see the wood for the trees anymore. Ashutosh raised the simple question 'Why do 80% of the people today end up in the wrong job?', and then started backwards engineering the process. The rest is history. They created a solution that's changing the status quo for the better for both employees and employers.

"That brings me to another key element that helps in the process of turning customers into fans: changing behavior. Remember the story I told you earlier on about First.io, the company that's using AI to ensure real estate agents never lose another customer?"

"Sure," Rob replied.

"Well, Mike Schneider,[10] their CEO, gave me this anecdote on the need to change behavior – and the potential that has to turn customers into fans:

> *The big takeaway is that though some of the tech today didn't exist ten years ago, the same problem still exists in terms of how to change behavior.*
>
> *When I sit down with our users after they've been on the platform for seven months and ask 'How is it going?' 30-40% of them will reply 'Well, I haven't really gotten around to it.' Then we pull up their app and reveal that from the 150 people that have been recommended, 42 have already sold. Well over 25% ... and they missed all that value by not taking action.*
>
> *The key take away: With any of these platforms, behavior change is hard.*
>
> *That's why all of our product focus today is not on improving the power of the analytics, but instead on how to create a delightful experience for the parts that people use on a day-to-day basis. What parts can we take off their plate, or gamify to help them build routines of doing actions we know are important to drive outcomes. When we pair the negative of loss aversion with positive gamification, that's where we're see adoption shift dramatically.*

"A similar story arose during my conversation with Adam Martel,[11] CEO of Gravyty. He said:

> *When I started selling our solution, and it was selling well, but what we found was that it drove the frontline fundraisers back into their old 'system'. Our platform was perfect in predicting which donors were*

---

10. https://www.valueinspiration.com/product-innovation-how-human-ai-combos-creates-disruptive-competitive-advantage-in-real-estate-sales/

11. https://www.valueinspiration.com/how-ai-redefines-the-impact-of-fundraising-in-not-for-profit/

going to make the next biggest gift. From there the frontline fundraisers should take over and approach these donors. But they didn't. They weren't sending the emails out and trying to communicate with the donors. What we learned was that we had to use artificial intelligence to change behavior. It wasn't good enough just to provide insight.

What that really meant was that we had to deliver an 'AI first' experience. It had to be where the frontline fundraiser was working. We found we could actually write the email on behalf of frontline fundraisers. We branded it 'First Draft' because fundraisers weren't comfortable with essentially having a self-driving car. They wanted to be able to change the emails. They wanted to be able to edit them and personalize them.

Being able to write the first draft of the emails, we found we could change the behaviors of the frontline fundraisers. That changed the course of our company.

"Do you see what I mean? Your solution can do its job perfectly, better than anyone else, but if the users of your system don't change behavior, the impact is undermined, sometimes even totally wasted. That's why making the extra effort to change behavior can make such a difference. Taking out the friction that stops people from achieving the full value. That can be something very simple. For Gravyty it was as 'basic' as writing the draft email. That kept the ball rolling. That's where their users started to fully appreciate the true value.

"But changing behavior could go far beyond business value alone," I continued. "Danny Saksenberg,[12] CEO of Emerge, shared this with me:

We've been building solutions for some of the big insurers. Tools that allow them to provide green lights to a certain proportion of their claim applicants, just based on their questionnaire data. Making that process simple makes a big difference to the insurer, as well as to the client, because you do not have to go through an endless process if everything is 'OK'.

---

12. https://www.valueinspiration.com/product-strategy-whats-required-to-solve-the-worlds-biggest-problems-through-technology/

Lemonade made a big splash in setting a world record of paying a claim within three seconds of being submitted. This really changed the experience. It's an example of where AI is changing the way we do stuff. Sometimes stuff we've done for hundreds of years because, fundamentally, banking and insurance haven't changed at all.

However, now that you can have claims done in no time, the last major area of application that we have really boils down to behavior modification. What I mean by that is this: At a more fundamental level in insurance, if I'm ensuring your life, I would like you to eat healthy food and exercise regularly. What can I do to get you to become 'a better risk'? If I ensure your car, I'd like you to drive more safely and less recklessly. How can I incentivize you to behave in a way which is actually better for both insurer and the policyholder?

Developing customized, individualized interventions that will get every individual policyholder to behave in a way that is actually better for everyone. Neither the insurer nor the policyholder wants a claim to happen. It's in everyone's interest to improve the quality of the risk. That's where there's a big opportunity for technology to help change behavior.

"As you can see from these examples, Rob, we can create solutions that basically address a problem or challenge. But the biggest impact comes when at the same time it helps change the behavior of its users. That's were magic happens and where customers turn into fans. It creates an effect that's larger than the sum of its components."

"I never thought about it in this way," Rob replied as he nicely merged onto highway A4 towards Aveiro. "I see another clear case for us to explore with our solutions for the banking world. There must be a sea of potential in using our technology to change the behavior of the customers of a bank – and if we help do that, we create value for both bank customers, as well as the bank itself. The value will translate onto them. That's competitive advantage."

7) Make it sticky

"Talking about competitive advantages," I said, "there's one more aspect on my list of ingredients that has the power to turn customers into fans, and that's making your application sticky. Just see what apps like Facebook, Twitter and Instagram have done in the consumer world – people are constantly checking in so they don't miss out. And because they always find something new and interesting, it becomes their favorite application.

"That's what you want to achieve in B2B environments as well. You want to incorporate something in your applications that users keep coming back for."

"Agreed," Rob replied. "If an application is used often it helps to grow brand experience. That's key to the banks we serve – especially the traditional ones. For them it's key to win the war for relevance with their customers. If they fail, then they run the risk their customers will switch to other banks that provide the experience they're looking for. I indeed think 'stickiness' is a core element to strive for in our designs."

"Yes, and it's not only the applications that are addressing the frontline, like you are doing, Rob," I replied. "I have an example from the HR space, so pure back-office, i.e. not the most exciting type of B2B solutions. When I spoke to Robert Bromage,[13] CEO of IntelliHR from Brisbane, Australia, he told me this:

From a mission perspective, we actually want to not only be the most valuable, but also the most addictive, especially in the business. We believe if we can increase adoption and usage of our platform, then we're increasing value for our customers and the very users that are actually using it.

We see a lot of businesses that don't provide people with the tools to be able to communicate and connect effectively. Just realize that the pace of change is speeding up. It's no longer about setting a 5- or 10-year plan and head in that direction. It's constant iterations of business models. There it all comes down to how people work together.

A lot of leaders think that the way to get performance is from the top down, but it's really about empowering people bottom up. So our development focus is on connecting staff with their leaders to enable

---

13. https://www.valueinspiration.com/product-innovation-how-to-create-the-most-valuable-addictive-technology-for-every-person/

really meaningful conversations and supporting them to be aligned around expectations. What you'll then naturally create is a circle of understanding. One way to achieve that is by increasing the level of transparency for both the staff member and the leader.

To give you an example: We've built a pretty good sentiment analysis tool where in real time we're predicting sentiment on qualitative statements on a minus one to a positive one writing where we can then identify highly negative things and highly positive things. We're able to see something as simple as someone feeling bullied or being very aggressive around performance.

It really puts a business in the driver's seat to be able to react to things. Equally, some of the data on highly positive things gives them a really good understanding to see where those high performing outliers are, and where that actually sits.

As a result, we've seen customers increase marketed levels of engagement across the business – over 20%. Completion rates of one-on-one catch-ups and goal setting with managers hit record highs – all in the 97, 98, 99 percentile range. Completion of important tasks has gone up, and more importantly, results in financial performance.

It's all in how they're using the product. They're constantly tweaking processes in response to how the staff are actually interacting with them. Due to the results it's become addictive.

"So what the IntelliHR team achieved is a solution that, unlike other traditional HR solutions, is not about the transaction and the administrative process. Instead it's about enabling the business to become a high-performing organization. Where it's about alignment and full and continuous transparency on what's going well and not so well in. It's a system where constant feedback is the backbone to make things better and help everyone grow in their job. The result is that people start to see it as their source of the truth – therefore it's experiencing extreme high adoption amongst its customers. It's sticky.

"Another example of stickiness that comes to mind is iThrive. The company name already reveals where this is going: helping people thrive in their job and in life. This example nicely aligns with the 'change behavior' topic, but at the end it's the stickiness of their application that's core to creating the shift in value. When I interviewed CEO Nadja Muller[14] on the big idea behind iThrive, she told me this:

People that are thriving are strong, they're successful, they're healthy, they're balanced.

However, when you look at longitudinal studies that have been studying people for a long time seeing how they're changing their behavior, you realize that actually only 10 percent of the time we succeed on our own.

Whenever you start something new and big, you always need a lot of help. People that were able to succeed either had a coach, a supportive partner, a mentor or something else that was a really strong supporting figure in their life.

That's basically what we are aiming to do with our virtual assistant 'Jean' – at scale, low entry barrier way, everywhere available, 24/7, at a very low cost.

There are a couple of things we learned. When we started talking to hospitals and looked into the research of many of the lifestyle diseases we see nowadays like obesity and diabetes, the need for an effective behavioral change solution is huge. This is like an avalanche that's coming towards us. It's really important that we have something available that people can use on a daily basis, wherever they are. It has to be something that's always with us – such as our phone.

That's how we started – but we realized quickly that building an app wasn't good enough. Feedback from the users was clear: The app is nice, but what we really want is 'someone' to talk to. So we pivoted. In terms of software development this meant we had to start from scratch again. But it paid off. Every week we get feedback and we're perfecting the conversations. Most of the time it's all about rapport, deepening the relationship, the empathetic relationship, between our chatbot and the user.

---

14. https://www.valueinspiration.com/product-strategy-how-ai-can-help-our-productivity-quadruple-by-transforming-counterproductive-habits/

Today we're getting regular feedback from individuals on how Jean has turned into an amazing companion. We see how amazing change happens when a whole group starts using it, including their team leader. That they're having much more honest conversations, much more transparency, and a clear positive effect on the entire team. When people are thriving, you're preventing stress, you're preventing burnout, you get 37% less safety incidents and productivity can go up by +400% percent.

"This kind of returns happen when there's an optimal blend of user and application. Once an application is sticky, users want to come back all the time, simply because it brings them value. In the case of iThrive it helps them to become their best selves."

How do you know you are on the right track?

As we merged onto the A1 heading for Aveiro/Lisboa, Rob raised a question: "This has been thought-provoking, Ton. We too often get too obsessed with the solution, its features and what our competition is doing, where the only thing that really matters is if what we do turns our customers in to fans. I've made a mental note to throw this into my management meeting on Tuesday next week.

"What makes me curious though is this: how do you know you're on the right track? I mean, if I look at our business, I believe our customers are pretty happy. But the real question is: are they really? What's your take on this?"

"Good question," I replied. "And one that more business software companies should ask themselves. To me the best question you should ask is this one: would your customers care if you ceased to exist today?

"Just think about it. It's an incredibly sincere question. One you might not like at all. However, it's not about whether you like the question or not. It's about whether you dare to ask the question, and what you are going to do with the truth, once you know the truth."

"Wow," Rob responded, "that's indeed a pretty direct question. But I agree, if you want to be among the best in your category, it's a critical one to ask."

"Exactly," I replied. "Obviously we all want our customers to care. We go the extra mile to make that a reality – every single day. We want to be perceived as remarkable in what we do, and we want customers to be a testimony of that. That way everybody wins!

"I've realized, however, that sometimes we have a very different internal perception on this topic than our customers. All the signs might tell us we're doing fantastically well, while our customers feel they are being kept 'hostage' and are simply waiting for the right moment to jump ship. I mean, let's face it, your software business might be very lucrative to you. You might make tons of money, you're highly profitable and on a steady growth trajectory every single year – all signals that should indicate you're on the right track, correct?"

"Correct," Rob replied.

"Well, you'd be surprised how often customers would answer the question 'Would you care if we ceased to exist today?' with a short and firm 'No.'

"I believe there are a number of things why this difference in perspective creeps in. Sometimes things grow in directions that shift the pendulum from one side to the other side. The focus shifts to 'we', rather the customer. The focus becomes short-term (i.e. profit), not long-term (i.e. value). Throughout my career I've seen plenty of examples where this has happened.

"I've seen it happen when companies change ownership structure – for example if a company switches from private to being publicly traded. Suddenly the whole dynamic changes, and the focus becomes short-term profit and keeping shareholders happy.

"I've seen it happen when companies change leadership – when they grow from one stage to another. With new leadership come new rules, new strategies, and often a lot of change that doesn't always end up with just good things for the customers.

"I've also seen it happen when companies change business model – the shift from license to subscription is a clear example of that. As you and I know, in the 'old days' when we implemented on-premise systems and sold a license, the risk was 100% at the customer side. Today, in a world where everything becomes a service, that risk is 100% on the supplier side – and that does things to the way the business thinks and acts. And I can assure you, that's not always in favor of customers.

"There are many more scenarios to think of. There are many more reasons where the love and care for the customer gets traded for a model that keeps them 'hostage'. In the long run, this is not sustainable."

"I concur with your observations, Ton," said Rob as we crossed the Puente de Arrabida bridge. "I've worked for companies earlier in my career where these shifts indeed happened. It's funny how these shifts always seem to creep in without management even noticing. Do you have any tips on what to do to keep sensitive to this? What could I do tomorrow, for example, that would be a reality check for my business?"

"Sure, I have plenty of ideas," I replied. "Do you conduct customer satisfaction surveys?"

"Yes, we do," Rob replied. "We aim to do one per year."

"That's what I would imagine," I returned. "Here's my first tip: Ask 'the' question. Most businesses conduct their annual, bi-annual or even quarterly 'Customer Satisfaction Survey.' The mistake they make is the following – they ask dozens of carefully crafted questions. The problem is, however, that most of these questions hide the truth. In reality, there are only two questions that matter:

1) Would you recommend the solution you use to your best friend?
2) Would you repurchase it if you were in the same situation again?

"Nothing more, nothing less. There's possibly one more question you could ask and that is: 'If you we're the CEO of my company, what would you change/do differently?' But that's it.

"Also, don't get hung up on NPS index rates where people score you a 7 or something in that range. A 7 is a polite answer for 'you're OK, but if I find something else, I'll move.'

"Here's another one: What percentage of your customers reference you … unasked? This is related to the topic above, but it is even more powerful because even if you don't do your annual survey, these customers spread the word for you. So, do you know who they are? Do you know why they reference you unasked? And most importantly: Are you happy with the percentage you uncover? If not, this is an excellent starting point to change course. Customers that reference you unasked can help you find your spark. Make that your focus for specific initiatives to turn more customers into fans. Every fan counts, right?"

"Right," Rob replied with a smile.

"Another tip to consider: what percentage of your case studies … samples a shift in value? This is one that tells a lot about the quality of your relationship with your customer. I don't want to open a can of worms about all the case studies that were done out of compliance because 'it's a clause in your contract.' No, let's take the general message from case studies with customers that participated out of free will.

"What I often see is that the bulk of these case studies are about the name recognition this customer brings, and hardly ever about communicating how this customer received shifts in value from your solution. Quotes like 'We're now very efficient', 'We can make more informed decisions', 'It's very user-friendly', or 'We're pleased with the people that implemented the solution' should ring some alarm bells. Your customer is just polite, not a raving fan. If this is what you see, use it as a trigger to challenge the status quo and start working with your customers to get them from 'efficient' to 'excellent'. I mean, if they really believe they get a shift in value from your solution, they will proudly tell you so. It makes them the hero. Who doesn't want that?

"Another angle, but one that matters: what percentage of your customers embraced your latest new module? How eager are your customers to add the new capabilities to their contract ... if they have to pay for it? They all happily use the new features that came freely with the summer release of your SaaS solution. However, when it's chargeable, how many will then call you and say, 'What we are experiencing on a day-to-day basis continues to positively surprised us, so we expect this next thing to do the same – bring it on!

"If you are not happy with the numbers, use the signal to challenge your product strategy, and course correct it to ensure your next release surprises even your worst competitors.

"Here's a question to ask that should speak for itself but is often forgotten: Are the online reviews about your solution worth a press release?

"In other words, are you getting enough reviews on software review platforms like G2Crowd[15] and TrustRadius[16] – and what's the sentiment? Let's put it this way – are you proud enough with the results you'd be willing to send out a press release to shout the results from the roof?

"Alternatively, would you dare to publish the latest stream of reviews live on your website? If you are, excellent, you're on the right track! If not, it's a sign you have work to do. We're living in an experience economy, and these platforms are used more and more to drive the initial long- and short-list. So, I'd use this as an opportunity to get input from both your fans and your critics. Their insights are gold dust to have as ammunition to tune your strategy and turn every customer into a fan.

"Last question to raise – again, one that requires guts: are you confident enough to let your customers ... control their contract? This might be a strange question to ask, but it tells you everything about your own belief in

---

[15] http://www.g2crowd.com
[16] http://www.trustradius.com

your strengths. Remarkable software companies use commercial models that enable the customer to be entirely in control. The mantra is: 'If they stop the contract, it's a sign we've failed.'

"However, on a day-to-day basis I see alternative models being used to prevent this artificially.

"Why do some vendors enforce minimum contract terms of 3+ years?

"Why is only annual billing available, instead of monthly billing?

"Why are there stringent contract clauses about what can or cannot be changed?

"So my take is this, if we are confident we have the best solution in the market, then why not let our customers be the judge of that? Instead of creating contracts that protect our weaknesses, ask the question: what do we need to do to be confident enough our customer will think twice before cancelling their contract?"

"So true," Rob replied. "I must say, I am going to put a number of these questions on the table with my management team. I am sure we'll be able to identify a number of things to change rapidly. Thanks for this."

"It's about being honest with yourself about what you aim to achieve. It keeps coming back to the three core ingredients:

1. Is what you offer valuable (not just interesting)?
2. Is it urgent (i.e. high on the priority list for your ideal customer)?
3. Are you exceeding expectations in delivering it?

"Remarkable software companies use these three criteria to create fans, not just customers.

"It's a mindset, it's a culture, and it defines everything they do.

"Remarkable software businesses have customers that do care when they cease to exist: not just one, but the majority.

"The don't aim to be best for everyone, but instead, focus on the special one.

"They tell a story that their customers are sharing because it resonates.

"They focus, to be the best at what they promise.

"They do that by carefully selecting moments that matter.

"They don't do half work; they do the hard work.

"The solve the valuable problem, not the interesting problem.

"They think in win-win-win scenarios.

"They create shifts in value."

Ask yourself

STEP 1: Reflect critically how you score your own ability around this particular trait by rating your organization on a scale of 1 (poor) to 10 (remarkable).

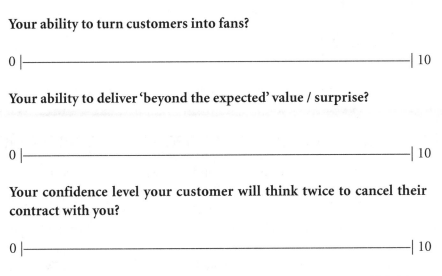

Your ability to turn customers into fans?

0 |——————————————————————————| 10

Your ability to deliver 'beyond the expected' value / surprise?

0 |——————————————————————————| 10

Your confidence level your customer will think twice to cancel their contract with you?

0 |——————————————————————————| 10

STEP 2: Take ten minutes to reflect on the next actions you could initiate to improve your score.

STEP 3: What's the single action from this list that would give you the biggest impact?

Take it to the next level

- Not only become remarkable, but ensure you'll stay remarkable as well by introducing the 'Remarkable Monday' habit within your organization. Download the three simple steps that will help you create and keep momentum: https://valueinspiration.com/RemarkableMonday
- Join the Remarkable Tribe Program to create accountability with other tech-entrepreneurs like you. Not only will you build traction to shape the business you aspire to be, but you will also obtain new ideas, create new contacts and will be part of a movement that defines what it means to be remarkable as a business software vendor: https://movement.valueinspiration.com

Trait 7
Focus on the essence

There will never be enough people to do the work

"A thing that's been going around my mind for a while, Ton, is this: I learned a lot today, and it has provided me with loads of inspiration to apply to my own business, but we're a relatively small company, so what's your take on execution? I mean, the first thing I always get thrown back from my team is 'we need more resources.'"

I laughed. "Yes, I have dealt with this question many times as well. I've literally sat in hundreds of product planning sessions throughout my career having a fight with R&D, product management team members and even board members on why certain features should be prioritized. It was always about 'more', never about 'less'. And although everyone has logical arguments on why to put something on the planning, it's often driven by their own (short-term) agenda, not the long-term vision to own a specific market.

"It requires a strong leader to keep the focus on the signal, i.e. the long-term vision. I am sure you've heard about the famous words Steve Jobs once used: 'I am more proud of the things we didn't do than the things we did'. Saying 'No' is the hardest part of creating meaningful impact. Saying 'No' frees capacity, and that capacity is critical to do the things that resonate in the market.

"At the end it all boils down to being resourceful, and that's a core trait again. Remarkable business software companies master this: they focus on the essence.

"Honestly, the cry for resources will never go away. It's driven by a universal problem: our never-ending urge to be 'innovative' which in reality often only means we're trying to catch up with the stuff our competition has already released. What we're actually delivering is just a bunch of new features that remove some friction, close some functional gaps and only incrementally grow the value of our solution.

"We're often overrating on the topic of 'innovation', and that's not giving the industry a good name. Why do we always aim to do more and more (breadth), instead of focusing on becoming the best in an area we can truly own (depth)? It's impossible to please everyone. If you try to please everyone, you please no one.

"Seth Godin[1] raised this dilemma in one of his short blogs:

How big is your unfillable hole? It doesn't really matter, does it?

All of your bad habits (and some of your good ones) exist to fill that hole, or to protect it from being seen. And as long as our mission is to fill the hole, and as long as the hole remains unfillable (and after all this time, if it's not filled yet, good luck with that) it doesn't really matter how small or trivial or unmentionable the hole is. It still drives us. The first step to living with it is to acknowledge it. You can't make it go away. But you can learn to dance with it.

"Spot on," Rob replied. "I recognize this so much. The easiest way is always to ask for more. And if you give into that request, you'll grow in size, but not necessarily in value."

"Exactly," I replied. "And it will only get worse. Chief Product Officer at Box, Jeetu Patel,[2] said something that's key in respect to this:

There's the half-life of business models and products and businesses in general, and at the velocity with which they move, the half-life is shrinking down quite dramatically: Your business model is changing every seven to eight years. You see that the business model completely resets within the company, and as a result, every seven to eight years you as a company have a choice of disrupting yourself and moving to the next wave, or being disrupted and not being in a relevant company. And by the way, the half-life of a product is actually going down even faster. Within 18 months the product gets dated.

---

1. https://seths.blog/2019/03/how-big-is-your-unfillable-hole/
2. https://podcasts.apple.com/es/podcast/ai-at-box-with-chief-product-officer-jeetupatel/id1399642701?i=1000430660835&l=en&mt=2

"See what I mean? The only way to stay ahead is to follow your own path. We've discussed many aspects to achieve that already – the importance of creating your big idea, starting from the point of solving a big problem in the market. Be rigorous on segmenting who you're for, and who you're not for. And then the three fundamental questions that keep coming back. Is what you offer valuable to your ideal customer? Is it urgent (i.e. is it a clear priority)? And lastly, can you exceed their expectations in the way you execute? If you get this right, you're well on your way to becoming very resourceful in your execution, and will be able to keep up with the shrinking half-life of business models and products.

"Elon Musk once famously said: 'Focus on signal over noise. Don't waste time on stuff that doesn't actually make things better.'

"Greg McKeown wrote a very relevant book about this titled *Essentialism: The Disciplined Pursuit of Less*.[3] This is how he defines it:

> *The way of the essentialist isn't about getting more done in less time. It's about getting only the right things done. It is not a time management strategy, or a productivity technique. It is a systematic discipline for discerning what is absolutely essential, then eliminating everything that is not, so we can make the highest possible contribution towards the things that really matter.*

"To me, the idea can and should be applied in much broader terms. I strongly believe, and I have learned this the hard way throughout my career, it's getting to the essence that creates the strongest value propositions, the strongest product strategies and the strongest sales pitches. It helps to stand out, to draw attention more effectively and to get action going.

"Focusing on the essence is important because you will always underestimate how much resources product development will need. I've never had a conversation with an R&D director that told me the release was done in half the time. You?"

"You have a point there, Ton," Rob answered.

"It's human. We see the solution in front of our eyes and then make an educated guess as to how long it will take to deliver the feature set. The agile

---

3. https://www.amazon.com/Essentialism-Disciplined-Pursuit-Greg-McKeown/dp/0804137382

movement has made this a lot better, but still we always have to compromize. With that comes the aspect of Product Market Fit. What you believe is Product Market Fit almost never is. So that pushes you back to putting in the extra effort. It's all worth it, but you better have the resources to execute on it.

"Over the years I've encountered three typical challenges within business software companies that struggle to deliver products that both their prospects and customers find worth making a remark about. Here's what I see:

1. The big idea is missing
2. Their inability to make bets
3. They waste precious developer time

"After doing ninety-plus podcast interviews with technology pioneers across the world, the word 'focus' was one that's a red line throughout all the interviews. Here's what I see in virtually all interviews:

- **They start out with a clear** vision about the change they want to make
  - ° The vision is not about them, it's about the ideal customer
  - ° They align everyone in their organization to focus on realizing that vision – from product development to marketing, to sales, to services and support
- **They follow clear, but simple criteria to make decisions**
  - ° It's about creating a shift in value (not something incremental)
  - ° It's about making a change that's critical, i.e. urgent to their ideal customer
  - ° It's about doing exactly those things that enable them to exceed expectations
- **They are resourceful**
  - ° They focus on doing those things that are hard but *only* they can do to make the difference in the moments of truth
  - ° They either buy or partner for the parts that are not core
  - ° They realize they don't have to deliver the vision in release one – but instead focus carefully on their plan so all their steps get them closer towards that vision

At that moment Rob slowed down and turned onto the upcoming exit. "Time to fill up the tank," he said with a smile. "Do you want anything?" he asked me.

"A bottle of water would be perfect, thanks. Other than that, I'm fine."

Rob parked the car next to a pump, jumped out and started filling up.

I too jumped out of the car and asked him, "How far are we from Aveiro?"

"About thirty minutes," Rob replied as he took out the nozzle.

He then walked into the store to get the drinks and pay.

Your vision clarifies your path

A couple of minutes later Rob returned and we drove off again.

"What you just told me about resourcefulness struck a chord," he started. "But what makes me curious is, are there any do's and don'ts here that would give me a framework to use on a day-to-day basis?"

"Sure thing," I replied. "As I mentioned, what I take away from my own career and my many podcast interviews is almost too simple to be true: you need to know where you are going. Remember when we started our journey in Valencia and I asked 'What's your big wave?' It all starts there.

"To focus on the essence, you need that North Star. That's not something like 'We want to be the leader in XYZ' or 'We will be a billion-dollar company by 20XX', or other examples I often see in that genre. Forget about that. It needs to be outside-in. And that's starts with defining what's broken in the world of your ideal customer that, if you could solve it, would introduce change they could not live without once they've experienced it.

"Let me illustrate this with a story. It's an example from a company that's disrupting the Financial Auditing space called MindBridge AI. I spoke with their CTO, Robin Grosset,[4] about the big idea behind their company and this is what he shared:

> *Our vision is to make a positive impact in the world by building solutions that revolutionize the way we analyze financial data. Here's why: Each year vast sums of money are lost to the economy world-wide due to unintentional errors and intentional misstatements in financial data.*

---

[4]. https://www.valueinspiration.com/product-innovation-how-human-centric-ai-can-help-cpas-find-15x-more-fraud-irregularities-and-misconduct/

The existing ways that we are analyzing or auditing financial transactions are inadequate because with the rules-based system, you're only going to find something that you anticipate.

The problem with that is this: The Association of Certified Fraud Examiner's estimate the amount of fraud, misconduct, irregularities that are caught each year to be about $200 billion a year. But they also estimate the amount we don't find, i.e. the issues which are not detected by any method we have today. That amount is somewhere north of $3 trillion per year. That means we only 'find' 7%. A massive 93% is not detected. If you put that number in perspective, that's about a little under $500 for every person on the planet – every single year.

So imagine if you could go under the surface, find things that aren't being found right now and return that value to the economy. That would make a huge difference. That's what we want to solve. We intend to restore confidence in financial data.

"As you can see, MindBridge defined a clear vision that was about solving a valuable problem, had and has a great sense of urgency, and they believed that with their team, with their skills and their devotion, they could exceed expectations for their ideal customers. And that's what is actually happening as we speak. Robin illustrated that this way:

When we started this process, there were a lot of people saying 'No, that's not necessary. That's not the standard. That's not how we work.' But today, and this is just two years later, everybody's saying: 'This is how it needs to be.'

"This is what I mean when I say that your vision needs to be about introducing change. If there's no change, no one will pay attention. What MindBridge is proving is that, with their big idea, they can change an industry that hasn't changed for decades – an industry that's driven by conservatism, established rules and conventions. Robin was pretty clear about this:

We're not paying too much attention to the conventions, because I think the disruption is going to come from many different industries. I don't think disruption comes if you look at conventions, existing standards or ways of thinking. We chose specifically to think about ourselves as the ones that will have to be disruptive to be successful. So yes, whilst we are going to empathize with our target users, we need to think about this in a different way.

"And that mindset pays off for them. By establishing your vision, you will provide the clarity for many decisions you'll need to make on your journey:

- It clarifies who and what you're for, and who/what you're not for
- It clarifies what's essential to focus your scarce development resources on, and what not
- It clarifies how you go to market in a way that stands out from the rest"

"I clearly get your point, Ton," Rob said. "I realize we underestimate the value of having a clear vision too easily. We talk it down as 'just marketing', but the point is clear that having a compelling big idea is the foundation for creating a remarkable software business. It defines everything."

"Well concluded, Rob," I responded. "But this is just step one. Step two is to put it all into action and use that North Star to make the crucial decisions. That's where the rubber hits the road. You'll see it requires strong leadership to stay on course."

Making your bets and challenge everything that doesn't move the needle

"In my podcast interviews I often ask the question: 'What was the single most important decision that helped you create the impact you deliver today?' The answer more often than not is 'it's not one decision, it's many decisions'. Remarkable things are created when a business creates a compelling vision, live by that vision and stick to it in both good and bad times. This way every decision they make brings them closer to realizing their vision.

"All of that takes leadership because once you get traction there will be many opportunities coming your way that could derail you. That could be customers that just want you to make that 'tiny' shift to fit their (traditional) way of working better. It could be investors that 'seem to know it all', telling you to 'go in this or that direction'. Then there's the never stopping short- versus long-term battle. Let me just peel the onion on this, slice by slice."

Don't let the short-term derail you

"One of the most common traps I see is the pressure for short-term gains, thereby losing the focus on making long-term impact. It's a dangerous one. No matter if you're a start-up or an established vendor, very often prioritizing for short-term gains will give you long-term failure.

"I am not talking about being agile and rapidly delivering new capabilities that are an aid to delivering upon your big idea of solving a critical problem in the market. No, I am talking about sales and short-term profit gains taking over priority.

"Yes, 'the long-term is about a lot of short-terms' (where have I heard that before?), but the problem is often that the objectives are not aligned. No matter what you ask sales, the thing that gets them closer to that next deal will always take priority. Same for the shareholder. I've seen this first-hand in my efforts to deliver roadmaps within a stock-listed company. EBITDA rules – nothing else. The fact is, however, that if top-line grows exponentially, impressive bottom-line growth will follow. That's what we need to keep front and center. And to deliver exponential top-line growth it's key to deliver the shifts in value our customers and prospects expect – they are the measure of what 'excellent' looks like. That drives them to adopt it, commit to buying even more by growing their subscription, or make the risky shift from a competitor to you.

"A widespread issue that illustrates a strong signal on how well you're prepared to stay focused on the essence is how you react to new contracts – especially end of quarter contracts. Too often new deals are closed with organizations that 'almost' fit (but not quite). I have seen development capacity evaporate by +50% just because of such customer contracts. It starts with the celebration by sales. They closed a magnificent € 1,000,000 contract with this lighthouse name, only to discover that one of the clauses states they need 'some' additional features in the next release. What's planned as one release becomes two, three, etc. You get the gist.

"I realize that sometimes customer contracts help you to finance the development of your solution. And that's all OK – as long as the contract extension is 100% focused and in line with delivering upon your big idea. The problem is that too often it's not. If that happens, you either have a sales alignment (or compensation) issue, but more likely a segmentation issue, i.e. it's not crystal clear 'who/what you are for, and who/what you're not for', as I addressed a couple of minutes ago. It all goes back to the first trait we discussed earlier today, remember? Remarkable business software companies realize 'they can't please everyone'.

"So, very often the moment you start responding to contractual commitments is a lagging signal you've lost track of your ideal customer, i.e. the one that would buy your product as is, and pay a premium for it.

"If you're unclear about what defines your ideal customer and the way you stand out in your category, such customer contracts will drive you into the alley of 'average' and ultimately irrelevance. To avoid this, top-management should give a firm 'no!' to contracts that take you 'off track'. Tough to do in the moment, but extremely valuable over the long-run."

"You've just touched upon a sensitive topic, Ton," replied Rob. "This is a discussion I have on a regular basis. And it's a tough call indeed. On the one hand you have the money lurking, and on the other hand you know you have to do a detour and derail your roadmap. I realize now that we're not there with regards to clarifying who we're for, and who we're not for. If I quickly run through the recent cases they were mostly tier 1 banks or tier 4/5 banks, but not the ones that have the typical characteristics that we solve the best in the industry. It's relatively easy to say 'no' to the small ones, but the big ones are tough."

"This is exactly what I mean, Rob," I replied. "I like your quick analysis. This is what it's about to stay focused on the essence. Only then can you retain control over your destiny and create something that delivers a shift in value."

Eliminate randomness

"Talking about that, there is another trap I often see that's very resource hungry: planning your roadmap randomly, i.e. 'from the bottom up'. This doesn't have to be an issue if the vision is crystal clear, including everything that belongs to that, as we just discussed. If that's the case, it will give people at every level guidance on what's a priority and what's not, and as such filter out a lot 'stuff' by itself. However, too often that's either ignored because people don't believe in it, or it's completely absent.

"What you then see is how roadmaps quickly get loaded with 'stuff' that doesn't move the needle. It's merely piling up just by looking in the rear-view mirror, i.e. the ever-growing backlog. It starts with maintenance that needs doing – technological, functional, and compliance, and then moves to upvoted ideas from customers, sales, presales, and product management. These are typically a long, unrelated list of 'interesting ideas', 'hobby horses', 'shiny objects' or requests from your 'key' customers. And the reason why I say 'key' customers with air quotes is that they are typically the ones that acquired your solution five to even ten years ago and have settled with what they have, not the prospective customers you want to be ready for when they come to market in the near future.

"The big challenge with this is that every item seems to make sense in isolation within the scope of the agenda of the issuer, but if you'd challenge them, they shouldn't be in your priority list. Keeping them there results in your capacity filling up to a point where hardly any resources are left to make the investments required to stay ahead in your category. Your roadmap will fill overwhelming with all the 'stuff' everyone believes needs to get done, resulting in weak arguments like 'there's no time for this in the coming release – let's push it to the next release.'

"But this immediately puts pressure on your next release as well. The result: release after release you're pulled out of the magic zone into what I earlier called 'the comfort zone', up to the point where no one cares anymore. So everybody loses here.

"I'm not saying everything should be directed 'top down'; however, providing a framework that sets direction and spurs critical thinking makes a difference. That's why starting right is so important.

"Remember I talked about Aerobotics earlier today on our train ride? When I asked COO Timothy Willis[5] how they deal with this dilemma, he had this piece of advice:

> We always have a laundry list of probably 100 to 200 things that we'd like to do with our software and with our product, but identifying the 10 that will move the needle most is the most critical thing to invest all our resources into.
>
> For instance, with those 10, it doesn't just take a software developer anymore to do something, it's a combination of software development, data science, marketing and sales. What do we actually think will move the revenue needle as well? And what are the 10 biggest improvements that really help doing so.

---

5. https://www.valueinspiration.com/how-ai-is-intelligently-augmenting-farmers-to-exponentially-grow-yields-and-efficiency/

I think that's an area that we know we can always get better at, but it's definitely the advice that I'd give to any software vendor: Start out by trying to identify what really moves the needle and not just what is out there and looks cool at any given point.

"I copy Tim on this approach. And the art is to make everyone account for it. A trick I have used many times in my career is this: work with the contributors to challenge every item on your roadmap to see if it is press-release worthy. These are the items that will very likely move the needle. Then write it directly as it will create the necessary clarity on value, urgency and how it will exceed expectation amongst your ideal customers and prospects. This clarity will not only help with the decision making, it will also help align everyone – from marketing (messaging) and sales (selling points) all the way to your development team (context)."

"Noted!" Rob replied. "I'll challenge the team on this in our upcoming roadmap reviews."

I smiled. "Well, if you do, let me know how it worked out for you."

Go narrow and deep, not wide and shallow

"Related to the randomness or bottom-up decision-making challenge is the urge to always do more, but instead of going 'narrow and deep' on functionality you go 'wide and shallow'.

"A story that inspired me is from Dagmar Schuller,[6] CEO and co-founder of audEERING. audEERING is a company that uses AI to extract information from audio to improve the quality of life and wellbeing of people. This is what she shared:

audEERING is one of the only companies out there that has a very holistic view on the audio signal. We are not only searching for the needle in the haystack, we also search for how did this damn needle come into the haystack in the first place; What was the way? What was the path? And why is it sticking exactly in that haystack, and not in another one.

---

6. https://www.valueinspiration.com/product-innovation-how-blending-ai-with-audio-boosts-motivation-and-impact-for-all-of-us/

And from this holistic approach, we have the possibility to derive on very different correlations and really assess the situation much broader; What is significant in a certain situation? For example: narrowing it down to a certain health state like burnout or depression. You have a certain state, but how did it come to that type of state? What was influencing the state? Do you, for example, feel stressed because your environment that you were exposed to is too loud or too noisy for you? And do you feel less stressed if it's less noisy? Or do you just not care about the noise. You can connect these types of things if you have a holistic view. If you don't have a holistic view, you can just say 'stressed/not stressed,' but it doesn't really tell you why.

"This is what I mean with going 'narrow and deep'. The value opportunity is simply much bigger. Another example comes from Jonah Lopin,[7] CEO of Crayon. I asked him about his view on what creates a remarkable software business and this was his answer:

The key is to focus on solving the complete problem. For example, we set out to enable businesses to understand and act on everything happening outside their four walls, because we believe businesses should be as data-driven about external data – what's happening in their market, with their competitors and customers – as they are about internal data. But it's not enough to provide the data – you need to help customers execute on it.

In the marketing technology world, software helps customers generate tons of sales leads, but never helps them figure out how to close those, how to win those leads in a competitive sales situation. Or the software helps our customers execute on their content marketing, but never helps them understand what their buyers actually care about this quarter that's maybe different from what they cared about last quarter.

That's what we founded our company on. From the beginning we really focused on solving that complete problem for the customer. I

---

7.   https://www.valueinspiration.com/how-ai-helps-increase-win-rates-by-54-by-providing-market-intelligence/

think a failed state for us would have been to say: 'Hey, we just want to go off and do some fancy Machine Learning and AI. And we're just going to do some fancy stuff there,' or 'Hey, we're a data aggregator and we're just going to pull all this data together,' or 'Here's a way to build fancy reports, but we're not going to help you figure out what goes on those reports.'

Instead we focused on solving that complete problem for the customer, which for us is like: How do you understand what's happening in your market? And then, once you understand that: How do use that to drive impact inside your company? The result of that extra effort is that our customers increase their win rate against the competition by more than 50%. That's meaningful impact.

"Do you see where I am going with this, Rob? Remarkable companies understand their customers and go deep. They solve the 'complete problem', as Jonah mentioned. What I see on a day-to-day basis, however, is the opposite. Some people refer to this as the 'Shiny Object Syndrome'. There will always be a flavor of the month – and it's very tempting to jump on it. 'We need a mobile! We need Social! We need Analytics! We need AI! etc.'

"Fact is, hype is created and will always be around, and it's often driven by the wrong angle: it's technology looking for a problem, rather than a problem looking for a solution. It's the urge from vendors to add that 'tick in the box' to their list as in: 'We do AI as well, so we're relevant'. That's where the problem starts. The focus is on adding a project to the roadmap that enables that 'tick', and the result is often a set of features that are far from a solution. Such solutions won't sell, they won't turn customers into fans; in fact, they'll just do the opposite.

"The Gartner Hype Curve was not created out of thin air. The Trough of Disillusion is real. And it gives the industry a bad name. So, challenge yourself and aim to be the one that utilizes the new capabilities in a way that solves some of your customers' most significant problems. Go narrow and 10-inch deep, rather than wide and 1-inch deep. That will give you credits."

"Very recognizable, Ton!" Rob reacted. "This is such a challenge within the industry we're in with my company. It seems there's a flavor of the week, rather than just a flavor of the month. I guess it has to do with the fact our category of solutions is still at the peak of the hype curve, and that the market is still very much searching for what works and what doesn't. But it's clearly a challenge I get on my plate a lot. Every week I have another colleague at my desk bringing up stories about another shiny object they've spotted that we need to consider doing 'as well'. I agree with you – it's about making our bets and always starting from the 'big problem' angle. That requires us to be even clearer about where our value is best placed."

"Spot on," I replied. "And I'd like to add something to that. When I talk about going narrow and deep, it doesn't mean flipping to the other end of the spectrum. It's key to solve the complete problem for the customer, but in order to exceed expectations we have to understand the fine line of where we need to stand out, and where we can be 'average'.

"Let me explain what that means by way of an example from Dan Heath,[8] author of the fascinating books *Made to Stick* and *The Power of Moments*. In one of his interviews he said:

> We've been trained that if we want to create a great experience, logic would hold that all of it's got to be great. It's got to be wall to wall. It's got to be end to end. But in fact, if you pay careful attention to experiences that are really meaningful, really memorable to people, what you'll find is that those experiences are often mostly forgettable and occasionally remarkable. And what happens is we're so busy trying to minimize the problems and the potholes that people experience that we forget to build the peaks that are the remarkable bits.

"What he says here is so true for product development. We're optimizing our products to the N'th degree, to the point where all the extra effort isn't even noticed anymore. The result: we're extremely busy with 'stuff', we always have the feeling we're short of resources, and if we'd have more, we could do an even better job. It's not about that. It's about being good at what we do – just like any of our competitors (at the end it starts with being credible), and be remarkable around the moments that truly matter. And that's indeed about creating 'peaks', and not about 'filling holes'.

"Talking about 'optimizing products to the N'th degree' – that's what my fourth focus point is about. Recognizing dead-ends before it's too late."

---

8. https://podcasts.apple.com/es/podcast/129-best-2018-our-biggest-takeaways-for-business-leaders/id1092751338?i=1000426763482&l=en&mt=2

Recognize dead-ends before it's too late

"There's one more example I'd like to share with you that separates remarkable software businesses from the rest, and that's their ability to stop when they see they are entering a dead-end alley. Let me elaborate a bit on that.

"Too often we start off on a path with our solution that seems the right angle for delivering value at that point in time. However, as the solution evolves in maturity and we add more features, the efforts we put in don't match anymore with the value our customers expect from a solution like this. That's often fueled by the fact technology has evolved so rapidly that the 'old way of doing' things is going out of fashion at a rapid pace.

"These are the signals to be sensitive for because, very often, ignoring them results in silently eating big chunks out of your scarce development resources. Often our guts tell us the moment is there, but somehow our self-talk makes us ignore we have a problem where the only right thing to do is to say 'stop, enough is enough', pull the plug and shift resources to something more strategic, or even to rearchitect the core.

"If I look back at the industry I've been part of all my life, the Enterprise Resource Planning space, you see a lot of examples of this. Numerous ERP vendors around the world have been incrementally evolving their solutions with the shifts in technology; however, they never fundamentally changed the concept of ERP and how transactions are managed. The 'innovation' has pretty much been at the User Interface and deployment level, rather than anything else.

"You see solutions that started in the DOS era, then moved to Windows, then to a web-interface and then got modified to be deployed as a service in the Cloud. Don't get me wrong, in 2001, Cloud was *the* innovation; however, today the opportunities go far beyond 'just the deployment' aspect – and many vendors haven't recognized that yet. And as such, with the incredible evolution of infrastructure, compute power, in-memory techniques, AI and Machine Learning, and so on, a lot of vendors find they have reached the point where their traditional stack is in a dead-end alley. Their solution will soon fail to meet the new expectations, and very often you cannot fix that problem with incremental fixes – it requires a complete overhaul.

"So, it's just waiting for a vendor to stand up and transform how businesses are managed. The vendor that has the guts to step back, pause and challenge the status quo by applying today's technology advancements to decades-old ways of doing things, 'can shake the market to its core,' as Frederic Laluyaux[9] quoted.

"He's the President and CEO of Aera Technology, a company that's enabling the self-driving enterprise. In my interview with him he shared the big idea behind his company that's founded on the opportunity that the traditional vendors in the ERP space fail to see, or act upon:

> *I remember writing this paper. I worked work all night on what is the next big wave post transaction automation – basically, the massive wave of globalization fueled by the relational database and the ERP layer.*

> *The question that I was asking myself is: 'Why do companies grow so deep, so fat, when they grow big? How are decisions being made?' I've been thinking about this for a long, long time, and got really convinced that the next topic would be de-layerization – organizations getting flatter, more nuclear, as opposed to these big, rigid pyramids.*

> *For that you need to enable decisions to be closer to the point of impact. For that you need to enable people to measure in real time the impact of the decisions that they have to take.*

> *What's the trigger is the ability for computer system to manage volume, complexity, real time communication, prediction, and that only became available through the emergence of what I call the internet scale technology. The technology that was made available by the Yahoo's, the LinkedIn's, the Facebook's.*

> *I asked myself several questions a few years back: 'Why do we constrain ourselves with the traditional enterprise software architectures, when you look at what LinkedIn, Facebook or Google are doing at scale, running billions of queries every day with massive algorithms in the background? What's their secret? Why couldn't we take some of that technology and bring it to the enterprise?' So the big idea is cognitive automation and the self-driving enterprise.*

---

9. https://www.valueinspiration.com/product-innovation-the-promise-of-cognitive-technology-to-enable-the-self-driving-enterprise/

"I don't believe this approach is isolated to the ERP industry. It's universal," I said.

"I agree in full with that," Rob said. "I recognize this in our market as well."

"Yes, I can imagine," I continued. "It's something that impacts every vertical – it impacts every domain. Let me share another example in the domain of marketing which Jon Shalowitz,[10] CEO of LiftIgniter, shared with me. They're transforming how digital marketing is done. He formulated their reason for existence this way:

> *The big idea behind LiftIgniter is that for customer interactions and digital customer experiences to exceed expectations, they need to pick up on signals in real time, and related to that, they need to understand your behavior, i.e. 'what you do' in the moment. This is a 180-degree shift with the traditional way of manually tracking and segmenting focusing on 'who you are'. This will give the best prediction of what that user is interested in on that particular moment and will fundamentally change the way we experience websites.*

> *A product like LiftIgniter wouldn't have been possible five, six, seven years ago. It's founded on the advancement in Cloud infrastructure, such as provided by Google, Amazon, or Microsoft. The amount of raw horsepower and the amount of computational work that has to get done is immense, its massive. Even when I joined six months ago, I had no idea until I worked with the team and looked under the counter hood.*

> *We see 150 million unique users a month, we process 20 billion recommendations per month. Every user, every moment of the day, everything they click on, every interaction, every scroll, everything they do on a site to interact with the content, the video, the products, the articles are things that will retrain our model. Not just for that one user, it's for the whole population. Every view is rejiggering or recalculating our model.*

---

10. https://www.valueinspiration.com/product-innovation-how-ai-solves-both-data-privacy-and-customer-experience-challenges-in-real-time/

This would have been impossible five or six years ago. So we're riding the wave and really taking advantage of the technology available today. That's a key differentiator for us.

"What always puzzles me," I continued, "is if these opportunities are so widespread, why don't we see them being addressed more often? It goes back to our early discussion on 'mastering the art of curiosity', however, I still want to make a point about it in relation to 'focusing on the essence'.

"Brian Chesky,[11] co-founder of Airbnb, made a strong argument in his interview with Reid Hoffman, co-founder of LinkedIn. In short, our inability to focus on the essence has to do with the way we communicate with our customers throughout the lifecycle of our solution.

"Brian has a simple method for extracting detailed feedback from users and the magic is simple: he doesn't ask about the product he already built. He asks about the product of their dreams.

We'd ask these questions like, 'What can we do to surprise you? What can we do, not to make this better, but to make you tell everyone about it?' And that answer is different. If I say, 'What can I do to make this better?' They'll say something small. If I were to say, 'Reid, what would it take for me to design something that you would literally tell every single person you've ever encountered?' You start to ask these questions and it really helps you think through this problem.

"The lesson to learn from this is: being customer-focused is good, however, it's your responsibility to ask the right questions. It's about working with your customers to identify the existing and new roadblocks that prevent them from hitting their big objectives and aspirations.

"Kevin Systrom,[12] co-founder of Instagram, added another layer on top of this. In an interview with Tim Ferris he said:

It's important to realize how people are just wired not to be honest, not that they lie. I mean, I guess technically it's a lie. But I don't think it like comes from a bad place, they're wired to avoid conflict.

---

11. https://tim.blog/2018/07/13/the-tim-ferriss-show-transcripts-reid-hoffman-brian-chesky-how-to-scale-to-100m-users/
12. https://tim.blog/2019/04/25/kevin-systrom/

"What this means is that people will always aim to be polite with you, and therefore hide their true feelings about your product. They simply don't want the confrontation.

"Another thing he said was this:

> *The more important your company gets, the higher up you go, the less people are willing to 'be honest'. So you actually have to like dig for it and that's one of the weirdest feelings ever: please tell me something negative [...] and when someone gives you feedback you don't respond in a defensive way. you say 'thank you.' And you encourage the behavior.*

"This allows you to focus on the essence, and reveal new clues early on in the process that you are on the right track, or entering a dead-end alley. The earlier you identify this, the better your opportunity to shift course – even if that means starting over again.

"And that brings me to the third key ingredient that enables remarkable business software companies to focus on the essence: they are resourceful."

Resourcefulness

"The dictionary definition of being resourceful is: 'The ability and creativity to deal skillfully and promptly with new situations and difficulties.'

"That obviously starts with making choices on what functionality is required to create solutions that deliver a shift in value as we just discussed. However, between meeting and exceeding requirements and actually delivering it you can find a wide range of opportunities to be creative.

"Here's where resourcefulness comes in. And becoming resourceful has many faces. Let me go through a couple that I deem most impactful."

Focus on what you do best, buy or partner for the rest

"This might seem an open door, but it isn't. The majority of business software companies believe they should do everything themselves. It's got to do with the 'not invented here' syndrome. That's incredibly resource intensive, especially when you are not 100% clear on what part of the market you aim to own. It has improved considerably over the last few decades. I can remember the time where we were developing our own printer drivers. That's luckily all gone away

– but the notion of 'we need to own every line of code within our solution' is still valid.

"Remarkable companies, on the other hand, focus on the essence – they smartly assign their scarce resources to what drives real value and what's core to their differentiation. Let me illustrate that with another lesson from Jeetu Patel,[13] Chief Product Officer at Box. Beyond his comments on the rapidly changing half-life of products and business models, he also shared his framework for product decisions in a podcast interview with AI at Work:

> You need to be very disciplined about what you pursue versus what you pursue with a partner.
>
> A framework that we typically use is: Anything that is meaningfully core to your business, where you are differentiated based on that capability, you would want to make sure that you're building yourself. Anything that is an essential component, but not core to your differentiation, you might not necessarily want to focus on building yourself but go to someone whose core business it is to do that thing, and partner with them.
>
> We think that this formula works in every step of the value chain. We do the same thing, our suppliers do the same thing, their suppliers do the same thing. What that does is creates a narrow specialization and openness of an ecosystem where the ecosystem just inter-operates with one another. It actually is just a different way to operate in this new economy, compared to the way that it used to be, i.e. a vendor or a company deciding they want to go off and build out the entire stack from top to bottom. And that's just not how the world is going to work in the future. So, you have to be extremely adept at partnering and knowing what's core and what's not core.

"It's the point about 'essential, but not differentiating' that's really valuable. We too often qualify things as 'essential', and as such keep investing in them with our own scarce resources. But the question to raise is: Will that investment help you

---

13. https://podcasts.apple.com/es/podcast/ai-at-box-with-chief-product-officer-jeetu-patel/id1399642701?i=1000430660835&l=en&mt=2

to grow your differentiation, and more importantly, increase the value perception they have on your solution, and their urgency to buy/subscribe to it?"

At that point we entered exit 16 toward Aveiro.

"Where exactly is your hotel situated?" Rob asked.

"It's south of Aveiro, in a suburb called Bairro dos Pescadores. The hotel is called Hotel de Ilhavo," I replied.

"I think I know that place," Rob said. "We're at least going in the right direction with this road. I guess it's about fifteen minutes from here."

"And about what you just explained," he continued. "I realize we have some leverage to gain here as well. I mean, the passion of my development team sometimes gets in the way of themselves. They see the solution, and jump on it. Sometimes I come back after a nice weekend and they call me into their office to showcase what cool features they've added again. All very nice, but what we have to ask ourselves is a) is it truly needed? and b) does it strengthen our differentiation? So having this filter will help to get the focus truly on the essence."

"I have another one to add to your list of filters then," I continued. "The art of elimination."

Instead of optimize: eliminate

"Let me bring back Greg McKeown,[14] author of *Essentialism*. In his podcast with Tim Ferris he gave an anecdote that stuck with me. They discussed 'How to let go of products/ideas/investments that actually hold us back from pursuing the right things.' Here's how Greg responded:

> *My wife will sometimes say to me: 'Is that a storm trooper that you are pursuing?' You used to think this was the thing, but you're pursuing it because of habit, because you caught on to it, because you feel this endowment effect. The false sense that it's my opportunity, it's my thing, it's my goal, and it's not serving me anymore. I think a lot of people have a lot of storm troopers in their life. It's about the stuff that, really, we need to get past and let go, so that we can pursue the right things.*

---

14. https://tim.blog/2019/01/09/greg-mckeown-essentialism/

"Just think about it – what in your portfolio should go? We just keep adding and adding functions, and all of these functions require maintenance and they always have technical depth. In other words, for every line of code you add to your product you are losing a certain percentage of your development force – for ever.

"So the trick here is to really be on your mark on what is actually used and what's not. The worst thing you can end up with is features that are critical to just one customer. We talked about that before as well – this is often coming from these 'on the edge' sales contracts. And the only reason you have that is because you were unclear about who your ideal customer is. See how this trickles through and keeps you 'busy' in the wrong way?"

"Absolutely," responded Rob. "So true, and indeed a silent killer of capacity."

Set boundaries

"Another filter to apply to become resourceful is this one: set boundaries.

"When I ran Global Product Management at Unit4 I used this technique a lot. We created what we called 'investment buckets' and at the start of the year we assigned a strategic investment percentage to each of them. It worked like a charm, because it is simple in concept and keeps you honest about the real priorities.

"We all know software products and platforms require maintenance, and tender love and care. However, you also need to deliver new product development to grow lifetime value of your customers and to ensure you are fit enough to ride the next big wave ahead of you. By assigning buckets you get clarity about the balance of your development investment. That doesn't mean things can't change. They always do. But you'll be assured that if there's a discussion about changing the priorities, you needed to have very good arguments to move resources from one box to another.

"Another benefit of this concept is that it helps in making investment items comparable. This is a challenge CPOs and product owners have to deal with all the time in making the right investment decisions: How do you compare the value of a maintenance item, to adding a new feature that solves a gap in a current function, to extending your solution with a potentially completely new functional area to grow wallet share amongst your customers, to those projects that are your wild bets for the future. It's impossible to compare. It's like comparing apples with oranges.

"Google has used this concept for years and in a very transparent and company-wide way. Tim Ferris asked Eric Schmidt,[15] former Executive Chairman and CEO of Google, this: 'Could you describe or explain what the 70/20/10 model is?' Mr. Schmidt answered as follows:

> *So this was Sergei's idea. And the question was, how do we organize our resources in terms of core things, new things, and experimental things? We had an off-site with the management team, and I still remember Sergei got up on the board, and he did some math. He's a brilliant mathematician. At the end he said: 'The right answer is 70/20/10. 70% on your core business, 20% on adjacent or nearby things, and 10% on wild bets'.*
>
> *He said, 'All of these numbers are right. You need the 70% because you need the revenue growth. You need the 20% because you need to extend your franchise. And you need the 10%, which is crucially important for the things that you will want to do five or ten years from now. And so we would measure 70/20/10, and try to make sure that the urgent was not overwhelming the important.*

"I've heard about this concept before, but must admit I have never implemented it," responded Rob as he drove around a large roundabout. "I think we are reaching a level of maturity now where this is going to be very helpful. There's a healthy customer base by now that's keeping us 'occupied', for lack of a better word. However, we have to ensure we stay relevant for new business as the domain we're acting in is moving so rapidly."

Leverage resources

"That reminds me of another silent resource trap. I am not sure if you have acquired any business yet. Have you?"

"No, not yet," Rob responded.

"Ok, well, if you ever do, keep this one in mind. When I became responsible for managing Unit4's product portfolio back in 2012 it struck me how many products we actually had. I ended up counting over 250 individual products.

[15.] https://tim.blog/2019/04/09/eric-schmidt/

And then I realized just how many resources were actually allocated to 'stuff' that didn't serve the core strategy.

"At a business unit level you wouldn't even recognize it. It was one resource here, half a resource there, one and a half more here because many products were in maintenance mode and the number of resources were cut to the bone. But at a corporate level that all added up to large amounts of FTE that were simply not available anymore for moving the company to the next level.

"The odd thing was, all these product units were, obviously, always scream-ing for more resources. Not big numbers, often in chunks of one or even half an FTE – but again it all adds up, and it doesn't add anything. So, the challenge was, since all acquisitions were done within a certain domain, there was incredible overlap, but no leverage. There were fifteen HR products in the portfolio, twelve payroll products, seventy-five products that did anything with General Ledger, and as such they were basically all doing the same thing in order to move their products forward. I mean, I have seen their roadmaps, and not surprisingly, they all looked alike.

"Obviously it all depends on the goals you have – and if it's keeping existing customers happy, and maximizing profit, then there are always arguments why doing 'this' and 'that' are important. However, it's worth looking into these portfolios to see where there are synergies – and where there are, you should find ways to leverage resources.

"You're going to end up with heavy internal debates, because aligning resources means centralizing control. If you've always had full control over your roadmap and product strategy for your specific product, the last thing you want is 'someone else' taking over – even if that's within your own company. So, the hard part comes in convincing everybody that 'together' means you can move faster. And that starts with having a clear and compelling story – your big idea, the vision. Without that, no one will surrender, not even within your own company boundaries.

"It reminds me of my conversation with Auren Hoffman,[16] CEO of Safe-Graph, a company founded to democratise access to data – in particular to help unlock innovation. When I asked him what he believes is a key element to become a remarkable software company, he said this:

---

[16] https://www.valueinspiration.com/product-innovation-the-power-of-data-fueling-ingenu-ity-as-the-core-gauge-of-innovation/

One thing that companies don't think about enough is: how to get leverage? Therefore most companies are really focused on just throwing people at the problem. If you think of a simple metric like 'revenue per employee', for many companies that number does not go up over time, where actually it should. A lot of companies will talk about their success, stating 'We have grown from 500 to 1,000 people the last two years.' To me, that's a failure. Every time you have to hire someone, it means that you don't have the systems which means you need more humans to grow.

The problem with that is: every time you hire somebody it is going to be harder to communicate internally. Communication is very, very difficult. Even the best companies in the world have some sort of communication problem every time they hire someone. This means the worst companies in the world have an exponential communication problem every time they hire somebody.

So you should do everything possible to avoid this. That means you probably need to hire better people and you need to spend more money around them to enable them to create leverage.

This is one of the core values in our company: We tell everyone when they join our company: you are Warren Buffett. You are a capital allocator. You have money to spend and your goal is to get yourself leverage. If you can get yourself leverage in your own productivity, go do it. If you can get your team productivity up, do it. If you can get the whole company's productivity up by doing something, do it. Your goal is to spend money to get leverage.

"Thought-provoking," Rob replied. "Never thought about it this way. This is not a top-down thing. It works best if everybody 'lives' this in everything they do."

"Agreed," I continued. "Succeeding in this will ultimately make all of you better off. It's a win-win-win situation:

- At the subsidiary level, because they suddenly realize they can get far more traction;
- At a corporate level, since there's maximum leverage of all available resources;

- At the customer level. Remember, a customer that bought your solution five years ago will hold you accountable for keeping it up to standards. If you fail on that level, they might end up not inviting you for their tender next time it comes around.

"The key lesson, therefore, irrespective of how you grow – organically, by acquisition, you name it – is that to become resourceful you have to find ways to align and leverage resources."

Collaborate

"On my quest to identify what helps create remarkable business software companies there's one more angle I found appealing in respect to exceeding customer expectations by being resourceful, and that's collaboration. It's another red thread I picked up from dozens of podcast interviews. Remarkable software businesses don't believe they know it all; in fact, they actively search for alternative insights to help create ideas, to challenge them, and make them better.

"This has nothing to do with outsourcing; to the contrary – often this is about the things they need to do themselves to set themselves apart. It's the outside-in perspective they pay a lot of attention to, because in many cases, even if you are just starting, you are too close to the problem, and product that you are building, to solve it.

"Let me share a view from Anastasia Georgievskaya,[17] co-founder and research scientist at Youth Laboratories:

> The future is in collaboration. This is why you need to be flexible and find a way how you can integrate and collaborate with everyone. Every person can't be a specialist in everything. There are lots of pitfalls that you will have to uncover. There are lots of features and sophisticated problems you need to solve that you didn't realize before, and sometimes you really need to do some fundamental research.
>
> So, we consult a lot. One of the lessons we learned is that many people are receiving it [the Youth Laboratories solution] in a very positive

---

[17.] https://www.valueinspiration.com/how-ai-is-helping-to-increase-confidence-and-life-quality-for-all-of-us/

way. Still there are some people who are very skeptical. They can bring a lot of good advice. What we learned is having critics helps you to find new ways to deliver it, so people optimally understand it."

What I would advise is: always have a look at what's going on around you. Don't hide in your shell. Maybe there are some collaborators nearby who are working on the same problem. You could augment your effort if you collaborate. So be more collaborative and more open-minded. Be open to approaching new problems in different ways.

"Dmitry Matskevich,[18] CEO of Dbrain, added this in relation to what Anastasia said:

It always helps to have a crowd mindset. There are a lot of different people out there. They all live different lives, and are connected to different fields. It's really hard for a team to understand everything and to be able to have exposure to any use case. It really helps us to have some community who can see something different and have a different idea.

"There's one more piece of advice I don't want to keep from you, and that's from Mark Esposito; I talked about him earlier on, remember?"

Rob nodded. "Yes, you spoke about him at dinner at the airport, if I recall correctly."

"Wow, you've got a good memory!" I replied. "Anyway, in his book *Understanding How the Future Unfolds*, the research they did around their DRIVE framework, the V for Volatility taught them some meaningful lessons. When I asked him 'Do you have any advice for software vendors in terms of what they should start doing differently?' he said this:

I think we can all learn from a company like Amazon these days. That platform aggregation service is much more powerful than any individual product. In our book we explored the idea behind it and talk about it as 'combinatorial technologies.'

---

18. https://www.valueinspiration.com/how-ai-provides-new-job-opportunity-for-2b-unbanked-people/

These technologies are combining multiple technology into one. The idea behind the aggregation is that we create much more value. Today, most of the business happens in combination with other businesses. It doesn't happen in isolation. Even the revenue models are rapidly changing.

So the advice I would give them: make products compatible and combinable as much as possible, rather than making products that are protected by intellectual property rights.

This is a lesson that is not easy to learn. You have to give up a lot of what you can consider to be your breakthrough or your technology IPs.

"Food for thought," Rob replied. "It's indeed something that you need to learn to utilize. It's almost a cultural shift. As you said earlier, it's that 'not invented here' thinking that prevents this from happening. But I agree with you, it's always valuable to have someone step in with a fresh pair of eyes, not connected to any politics, and even disconnected from the problem, to spot things that could be your breakthrough moment. So this is indeed something to actively pursue in my company.

"And by the way, we're here. There's your hotel on the right-hand side. Today was fun, and I really look forward to joining you tomorrow and catching some of the vibe of big wave surfing. How about I pick you up at 6.30 a.m. tomorrow? It's about a one-and-a-half-hour drive from here, so we'll be there at 8 a.m. sharp."

"Sounds like a plan!" I responded. "Thanks for your company today, and for getting me this far on my journey. I really appreciate it. See you tomorrow. It's going to be big and memorable!"

We shook hands, I left the car and walked over to my hotel. I was exhausted after a long day travelling, but excited for what was still to come.

Ask yourself

STEP 1: Reflect critically how you score your own ability around this particular trait by rating your organization on a scale of 1 (poor) to 10 (remarkable).

What's your mindset: 'Play to win' (i.e. 'you proactively change while you are at the top of your game') or 'Play not to lose' (i.e. you are holding a reactive posture)?

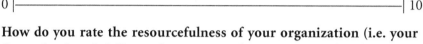

0 |————————————————————————————| 10

How do you rate the resourcefulness of your organization (i.e. your fitness level and ability to free up enough capacity to ride the next big wave ahead of you / stay in the zone where the magic happens)?

0 |————————————————————————————| 10

How do you rate your ability to steer your business by your long-term vision (i.e. every decision is measured against that) instead of short-term tactical focus (i.e. achieving next quarter expectations)?

0 |————————————————————————————| 10

STEP 2: Take ten minutes to reflect on the next actions you could initiate to improve your score.

STEP 3: What's the single action from this list that would give you the biggest impact?

Take it to the next level

- Not only become remarkable, but ensure you'll stay remarkable as well by introducing the 'Remarkable Monday' habit within your organization. Download the three simple steps that will help you create and keep momentum: https://valueinspiration.com/RemarkableMonday
- Join the Remarkable Tribe Program to create accountability with other tech-entrepreneurs like you. Not only will you build traction to shape the business you aspire to be, but you will also obtain new ideas, create new contacts and will be part of a movement that defines what it means to be remarkable as a business software vendor: https://movement.valueinspiration.com

Part 3

The Volume Lever: win more, win bigger

Trait 8
Create momentum

Momentum makes everything easier

I woke up at 5.30 a.m. the following morning, but for some reason it wasn't hard to get out of bed. It was the big day – I was going to experience some of the largest waves on earth, and see some of the world's most courageous surfers in the world ride those waves.

Rob was due to pick me up at 6.30 a.m., so I showered and went down for breakfast. Luckily the kitchen was already open. 'They must have known' I thought. I ate some granola, had a nice strong Portuguese coffee, and before I knew it, Rob was in the lobby.

"Ready to go?" he asked as I checked out.

"Absolutely!" I replied. "I can't wait to experience the forces of Mother Nature for real. And it indeed seems 'big' today. I just checked the Surfline app and the swell is at its peak today, exactly as we hit Nazare. So let's go."

We left the hotel. It was still dark outside. I put my suitcase in the trunk of Robs car, and we drove off.

"Did you have a good night's sleep?" I asked Rob.

"Slept like a baby," he replied. "I actually dreamt about our conversation from yesterday. I got so many ideas from what you shared with me. One thing I realized is that we have to resonate better with our ideal customers. I mean, we grow, and we do nice business, but in the market dynamics we operate in, the potential is much bigger. If we don't take that potential, our competitors will."

"Good thinking," I replied. "John Maxwell once said 'It is never the size of your problem that is the problem. It's a lack of momentum.' That's what you should aim for. It's another key trait of remarkable software companies. Creating momentum is like a flywheel: once in motion, it's very hard to stop. That's when performance increases and when everything feels easier to do.

"You are actually going to see a lot of this today. Momentum is what will define today's winner at the Big Wave contest. The winners are the ones that position themselves best, that have the sharpest eye for where the upcoming wave will peak. With that insight they'll be able to navigate to the right point, paddle in at the right moment, and use the force of the wave to get up and surf.

"So, positioning and timing are everything here. What makes it difficult is the sheer size of the waves. They're monstrous. But that doesn't mean you can just take off and surf every wave at every point. You need the steepest point, where the wall gets vertical. That's where the momentum builds. That's where the force is. That's the flywheel you are looking for. Being slightly off means you have to put way more energy in to get traction and to keep traction.

"And that's the same in business. If you're positioning is 'off' and your timing is 'off' you have to put a lot more energy and money in to get traction. Sure you'll sell here and there, but it drains and it feels like an uphill battle. The moment, however, you position perfectly you'll be able hit the right nerve with your decision makers. They'll get you, you'll resonate, and with that you've found your 'vertical wall' to take off and build momentum. Not with one customer, but with many."

"Nice analogy, Ton," Rob replied. "I can actually picture it vividly. From your experience, what are some of the secrets remarkable software companies apply to create this momentum? I mean, it can't be only positioning and timing?"

"Correct," I replied. "There's more to it. Let me dive into a number of things I see as a common threat from the companies I work with on a day-to-day basis."

At that moment the car accelerated on to the A17 heading for Nazare.

1) Create curiosity

"The first big thing for creating momentum is to create curiosity amongst your ideal customers. This is an art remarkable business software companies master. In their communication they trigger your senses to something you want, even though you might not even realize you need it.

"Let me give you an example from some work I did in the blockchain space. Blockchain is an ideal solution to solve large-scale problems in today's market, like the lack of trust in society, and fighting increasing cybercrime and corruption. However, these are macro issues, not something your prospect will ever be able to solve on their own. So in order to create momentum with a blockchain solution you have to translate these large-scale problems to the aspiration your prospects have for their own business.

"Here's why: we're selfish. The way we, as people, are wired is that we only respond to things that directly impact us. In other words, your prospect doesn't care as much about societal problems as they care about themselves. Anything that doesn't directly impact them might be interesting or touching, but won't inspire firm action. So, going back to the blockchain example, if you want to appeal to potential customer needs, focus on how blockchain allows them to grow their top-line in new and refreshing ways, how it enables them to introduce new business models in ways we've not been able to do before, how it helps them to finally break with the traditional linear growth barriers, or take customer experience to levels we've not thought possible before.

"You want to focus on value scenarios that spark their attention with new or different perspectives. 'Same old, same old' is not going to create curiosity. This is a mistake many vendors make, hence it's a big opportunity to stand out in a positive way.

"When I spoke with Vijay Chittoor,[1] CEO of Blueshift, a platform for intelligent customer engagement, he explained the change and the opportunity beautifully – especially when you start to blend in the power of todays' technologies:

> *By combining power of the AI with the creativity of a marketer we are creating the opportunity for marketers to reclaim the role of the storyteller.*
>
> *With all the data we're leaving behind, marketers and brands now for the first time have a way of understanding us as the dynamic individuals that we've always been. And given the fact every brand is just going to have more and more data, you can easily say the brands that succeed with customers are the ones that put that data to work and deliver the right customer engagement.*

[1.] https://www.valueinspiration.com/product-innovation-how-the-synergy-between-ai-and-marketers-can-result-in-revolutionary-effects-on-the-businesses/

Now here's where it gets interesting. If you increase the relevancy of your communication and drive the right experience, customer curiosity and engagement will go up. Each engagement creates more data, which is the fuel to understand our ideal customers even better. That again helps you to further tune your messaging and become even more relevant in the way you communicate. This leads to more engagement and as such creates true momentum – a flywheel that starts spinning faster and faster, and propels your brand forward.

Once you get that flywheel going, it becomes hard to stop.

"Fact is, you have to do your homework. It's about showcasing empathy and that's not a strength of AI. You literally have to step into your ideal customers' shoes and understand what drives them, what they value, what fears they have, and so forth. Obviously that's different for every organization, but often there are commonalities across sectors. So work with that. I typically use these four viewpoints to establish new and fresh perspectives:

1. Define the big problem they (your ideal customer) aim to solve for their customers. What do they aspire to be? What's their purpose for being in business in the first place?
2. Articulate the top 3–5 business goals they have to deliver upon this aspiration and express how these goals are changing.
3. Understand what your client's evolving challenges are on a macro level. These are external pressures they don't control, but have to address in order to stay relevant. Things like changing business models, entry of new breeds of competition, improving or declining market conditions, regulatory influences, and so forth.
4. Last but not least, identify the top 5 internal roadblocks that stand in the way of your client's success in relation to achieving their aspirations in a world that's changing around them. So, name their 'inabilities to do X, Y and Z'. Focus on the ones that keep them up at night. And think about how your prospect would sell the problem this creates internally.

"These four factors are your magic cocktail to resonate with your ideal customer. It's this mix you have to play with to come up with fresh new perspectives. The better you do that, the more curiosity you'll create. And by better, I mean being articulate in making it highly believable that your solution will create a shift in value from the way they work today, whether that's their own productivity, their company, or divisional top-/bottom-line results, you name it. They need to get that spark that your approach can influence the speed by which they can achieve the aspirations they care about. If that's not clear, it won't ignite their curiosity, hence they won't move."

2) Create urgency

"Another aspect I see as critical with respect to creating momentum is your ability to 'create a sense of urgency'. This is obviously related to creating curiosity, but stands on its own as a capability.

"Throughout my career I've learned there are many ways to do this. It's always fascinating to see the impact it creates when applied the right way. But let me start at the beginning.

"The aspect of 'urgency' is a core component of your value foundation. It goes back to the three fundamental questions we've discussed before: 1) Is what your offer valuable in the eyes of the customer? 2) Is it urgent to them (i.e. is it a key priority)? and 3) Can you exceed their expectations in delivering your solution?

"The fact is, and this might sound funny, but defining it is one thing, executing it, however, is another thing. Every day I see examples of business software companies that would answer all three core questions with 'yes', but still fail to create momentum."

"Tell me why," Rob said as he maneuvered around a slow truck.

"Here's why: because they communicate like everybody else, and as such they fail to stand out."

"I guess that's our dilemma as well," Rob responded. "So, what's the trick? What would you recommend doing differently to change this?"

"Sure," I responded. "If I were to highlight two effective ways to create urgency in marketing or in sales, I'd select these:

Create a gap between what is, and what can be

"This is a very effective technique to drag people in. I might sound like a broken record on this, but it's about the shift in value you create – and as you can imagine, the bigger that shift, the better you'll be able to create desire, and therefore the urgency to take action.

"The better your ability is to pinpoint the one, two or three things where you can create a transformation for your customer, the greater the movement. That starts with understanding a) the most important goals and beliefs that drive your decision-maker's agenda, and b) the biggest roadblocks they face in achieving them. Once you connect your solution to that, that's where the magic happens. I've seen this hundreds of times in my coaching work with sales professionals around their ability to pitch value.

"The first thing you do is to create a common ground with your prospect about the problem, the frustrations that are so typical, and the realization that continuing is actually not an option. This is key to create a level of credibility and trust. From there you become their guide as you take them into the 'what can be' world. You'll show them the path towards the ideal situation. The better you succeed in doing that, the more you'll fuel the urgency. That's where momentum starts.

"The second option I'd select is this one:

Work with fear, uncertainty and/or doubt

"This is the opposite technique. Sometimes the 'carrot' doesn't work, so you'll need to revert to the 'stick'. Creating FUD – Fear, Uncertainty and Doubt – is about that. But be warned, do this in a subtle way. You want to always remain credible. If you move 'across the line' your prospect will notice instantly.

"A way to address this is to do a brainstorm with yourself about the risk of doing nothing for your prospect. Often, they know this in the back of their mind, but it's too far down to make them act. Bringing these risks to their attention helps to make it top of mind and an accelerator for action.

"I'm sure you'll instantly know to name a handful of examples. It's simply translating forward what will happen if the current situation continues. And always try to tie your examples to the core business goals of your ideal customer. That's what matters. If those goals are not met it hurts, and everyone knows it will have consequences. It's avoiding that from happening that creates action.

"Let me give you a couple of examples. A risk of doing nothing could be about negative effects; for example, impact on customers – things like increased churn, lower customer satisfaction ratings. That often translates forward like a snowball, like in impact on revenue, profitability challenges, lowered company valuation, missing exit expectations from your investors, employee retention issues and so on. It could also be that the risk of doing nothing means missing out on something desirable, such as a spike in demand in the market, the difference between being seen as an innovator versus a laggard, and so on.

"At the end, it's all about 'moving the box' like we discussed before. Your prospect thinks about things in their terms, and it's your opportunity and responsibility to take them on a journey to something new and better. It's about planting an idea that shifts people's perspective. This can be something aspirational, something you want to become part of, or the opposite, something that's too ridiculous to be true, but has become so common sense that people don't even realize it anymore. The clearer you are on that, the more urgency you'll inject into the minds of your prospects, the bigger the movement you'll create.

"Let me illustrate this all by sharing a story from one of my clients, David Griffiths,[2] CEO of FiscalTec. He told me this:

> *Our biggest competitor is inertia or lack of awareness. We've got a unique solution that delivers a lot of benefit up front. But CFOs and controllers are very focused around the comfort thought of 'We've got a three-way match. We've got everything covered.'*
>
> *Here's why this is happening: The procure to pay space is dominated by hundreds of different technology vendors across two core areas. Firstly, automating the procurement process, i.e. driving purchase order compliance, POs and three-way matching. The other side is about managing invoices and paying those invoices. A lot of technologies are focused on that type of automation.*
>
> *What we discovered was: There's nothing to oversee all these different technologies to look at fraud and risk. It's three-way matching which sits at the heart of every ERP/accounting system as the cornerstone control, but it hasn't evolved over the last forty years. It hasn't kept up with the times.*

The problem with that is, due to evolution of technology, a lot of organizations are now facing unprecedented levels of risk and fraud. In the UK alone, 97% of all the businesses surveyed had one instance of fraud in the last twelve months. The Associate and Charted Fraud Examiners said, typically around 5% of revenues are lost to fraud, so it's about really, really big numbers.

So for us to create movement it's critical to create a sense of urgency – which is typically not there since CFO's and Controllers have this self-belief they are doing everything they need to do. However, every time we do a risk review, we find things that they are not aware of. It's our obligation to change their perception and create momentum with many of our clients.

"Great example," Rob responded. "It's something I absolutely recognize. There's so much inertia in the market place, and if it's not driven by unawareness, or self-talk, it's skepticism that destroys a lot of progress. People need to open up more, embrace new opportunities. The world would be in a much better place if we did so. But I guess that's easier said than done. We, as a sector, have possibly also created this attitude by over-promising and under-delivering. Many companies have burned themselves and, as a consequence, think twice."

"Good point, Rob," I responded. "This is a valid problem. That's why it's key to be credible and to be able to walk the talk. That goes a long way."

3) Make it easy to move

"Talking about 'walking the talk', this ties well into a third ingredient remarkable software companies do to create momentum: they make it easy to move.

"Let me illustrate this with an example of the opposite. It's an example which is creating a large-scale challenge in the ERP industry: The inability for customers to move from on-premise solutions to the Cloud. It's not easy to move, hence this negatively impacts momentum.

"When I interviewed Vinnie Mirchandani[3] about his book *SAP Nation 3.0* this came up as a serious challenge for the industry at large. It's not only SAP

---

3. https://www.valueinspiration.com/product-innovation-how-the-erp-space-is-transforming-fast-but-slow/

customers who suffer from this, it's a universal issue for any customer using traditional ERP, whether that's from Oracle, Microsoft, Unit4, Sage, you name it. This is how Vinnie illustrated it:

> *Cloud Business Software is twenty years old now. NetSuite was born in '98, Salesforce was born in '99. However, if you do a breakdown by global world region, by industry, by business process, only about 20% is filled. So, the vendor community hasn't delivered enough. And on the other hand, the buyer community has been very slow to adopt it.*

> *I have a category in the book that I call 'by-standers', these are customers who are sticking with on-premise ERP, and are just not moving to any of the cloud solutions. I raised an alarm: 'This is scary, guys. After twenty years, both customers and vendors are just not moving. Something's not right.'*

> *There are a range or reasons for this: on the buyer side the memory of the last implementation is still holding back big numbers of buyers. Secondly, many of them just customized the heck out of their old ERP system and they're worried that they will lose the customizations if the functionality in the new product isn't rich enough. And thirdly: it's the gaps that are still around, so customers think 'I cannot get an entire process, I can only get certain elements of a process, hence I don't move.' Those are the three things that hold people back.*

"Obviously there is no short answer to this problem; however, that doesn't mean 'leaving it like it is,' is the solution. To create momentum, you have to make it easy for customers to move. It's as simple as that. It's about removing the risks and headaches, which are significant. Besides the cost of doing the (re)work, the cost of downtime outweighs all of that. Just think of the disruption coming from those moves, how this impacts our customers' customers, the potential loss of revenue and so forth. It's a responsibility for the industry at large – vendors, system integrators, everybody. So, when I asked Vinnie for his view on how to do this, this was his insight:

> *Too many software vendors view systems integrators as partners. They should be, but to your customer they are an add-on cost, so making*

them efficient is in your best interest. Get your systems integrators to apply Machine Learning and automation to their own business. It's amazing how many systems integrators still sell bodies. Over the last thirty years we've done millions of ERP projects and millions of CRM projects, so why aren't we training our machines to do the parameter configuration. Why aren't we doing automated data conversion, testing and end user training. There's so much automation opportunity. It should be less expensive, and even more importantly, more predictable so we have fewer failed projects. And if the system integrators are not doing it, maybe the software vendors should step up and say: 'I will do it, you don't have to pay for so many bodies.' I think that could be a huge value add. It also becomes a much more attractive offering for any customer that's currently in the by-standers corner.

"I like that thinking," Rob replied. "We could do more on that level as well. As a business software business our business should be about software, not the services that come from that. So the holy grail should be 'Plug & Play'. And why not. I think this would create a very compelling, competitive advantage. All our competitors are doing the opposite. They sell a solution and then come in with an army of people that stay for months and months. No one benefits from that. It actually just brings our margin down."

"Spot on," I responded. "And I realize this works better for one solution over another, but that doesn't mean the aim shouldn't be to make it extremely easy. It has already improved quite a bit when the risk is moved from the customer to the vendor with the transition to the SaaS model, but still you see too many vendors sticking to old on-premise practice doing and thinking.

"But let me share a story that showcases another way it can be done if adopt a different mindset. It's the story behind Senzing, a software vendor that's democratizing the Entity Resolution space, an industry that has traditionally been led by people-intensive deployments, very much alike ERP. When I spoke to Jeff Jonas,[4] their founder and CEO, this is what he told me about their big idea:

---

4. https://www.valueinspiration.com/product-innovation-how-to-obtain-new-competitive-powers-by-using-ai-for-entity-resolution-to-tell-you-whos-who-in-your-data/

I became particularly focused, well really obsessed, with this thing called Entity Resolution, which is technology that figures out when two people are the same. It's a hard problem for folks, and when you can solve that well, you can solve all kinds of problems and create all kinds of competitive advantages. But if you look at these solutions, they primarily require experts to make them operate. They're pretty darn expensive, the good stuff's at least a million.

So, the big idea is to democratize that. Not just to help the big elite organizations understand who-is-who in their data, but what about the small nonprofit who just got duplicates in their Christmas mailing list? What about them?

And here's how: If you can take 10x out of the complexity of getting it going, then why not take 10x out of the price? So, when you change simplicity that much, and you change cost that much, it opens the door to being able to democratize something.

"So when I asked him how simple this really is, he positively surprised me:

Our mantra is: It has to be easy to consume. And that means with so little effort, it is as if it dissolves under your tongue. So, when we came fully out of stealth in June of 2018, we opened up the pipes and let the world just download it. It's very safe for somebody to just give it a go and kick the tires. So, you can download the software for free without even telling us your email address. You just try it on your own data and then call or email us if it's not as easy as we say.

What we see, really 80% of the people that try it tell us it works out of the box, without a single tweak. And by the time the phone rings, or we get an email, it's somebody that says: 'Hey, how much for 100 million records?' And then we say, 'Hey, we publish all the prices on the website, so you didn't even have to call.'

"See the difference? It's not about how 'complex' your product is, it's your mindset. So, if you want to create momentum, the easier you make it for customers to move, the more that will work to your advantage. Simply make it a design principle. Remove all the friction and make it 'dissolve under your tongue' as Jeff stated."

"A lesson learned," Rob replied. "Talking of 'dissolving under the tongue', would you care for a coffee? It's still pretty early and I could use one."

"Me too," I replied.

A minute later Rob parked his car at a cafeteria next to a petrol station.

4) Get customers to talk about you

The cafeteria was already surprisingly busy, and as we walked to the counter, I could smell fresh croissants and coffee.

"You wouldn't expect this at a cafeteria next to a gas station," I said.

"What do you mean?" Rob asked.

"Well, a pretty modern cafeteria where they actually serve fresh croissants, and from what I can see a very good cup of coffee. Normally it's all pre-packaged, fast and impersonal. So I am happily surprised."

"I agree with you," Rob said. "It's rare, but luckily you see it more and more, but mostly in the cities, not on a highway."

At that moment the waiter behind the counter asked us for our order. We ordered an um pingado and an uma meia de leite. Then Rob said, "You should try some of these breads – they're special." He pointed at the bolo de caco and pão de deus. "Let's get one of each," I said. I then paid and was told they'd bring everything to our table when ready.

"What a service," I continued. "Others could learn from this. I now understand why it's already so busy at this time of the day. I mean it's only just 7a.m. on a Saturday morning. But then again, that is what you get when you pay attention to being remarkable. You focus on specific aspects of your business that people care about, and ensure you stand out in exactly that area. Look at us – we've just entered and we're already talking about our experience. It's that powerful. And possibly we'll pass the story onwards to others as well.

"To take it back to our software space: this is yet another aspect of how remarkable software businesses create momentum, they get people to talk about them. Since I just shared the story behind Senzing with you, guess what, the fact they have removed all the friction around Entity Resolution, a domain that used to be complex, expensive, and consequently only in reach of large corporations, is causing people to talk about it. This is literally what Jeff shared with me:

> We've been in business now for over one year, and right now, we're not really marketing. It's kind of interesting; customers and partners that

are interested in our technology are finding us, and the customers that are using our software are telling others about it. So right now, it's kind of all word of mouth and referrals. It's fascinating.

I really had anticipated having to spend a significant amount of money for people to be able to discover us, but I'll tell you, more and more people are just showing up.

"That's a dream to strive for," Rob replied. "And why not? It's a win-win for everybody. For the customer because it's frictionless, and for the business because it's extremely scalable."

At that moment the waiter stopped at our table with our order. We thanked him and left a tip.

Rob cut each bread in half so I could have a taste of both. The first bite made me smile. "Even better than I was hoping for. These guys know their stuff," I said.

"I told you," Rob said, "but must admit that I wasn't expecting it to be this good if I'm honest."

"I agree with you," I replied. "It's remarkable, i.e. worth making a remark about. So powerful. Remember I told you about Bidgely, the company that's transforming the utility/energy industry?"

"Hmm, hmm!" nodded Rob, his mouth full of bolo de caco.

"Well, their customers have actually started to promote them in their own television campaigns. Abhay Gupta, their CEO, shared this when I spoke with him:

What makes us proud is that already a number of our customers are talking about our technology in their TV ads. They're showing our technology to either acquire more customers, do more PR, or educate customers about the tools that the utilities are bringing for their customers.

"It's what happens when you're making the right bets. Your customers will notice and start talking about you. You need that to create momentum. It's about understanding your ideal customers inside out and placing your bets on where you can make the difference for them. And once you do, don't ever stop. Don't think 'you're done'. Your customers want and need you to evolve, and therefore you should. I often see software companies settle on their success and become complacent.

"It reminds me of an interview I listened to with Mayur Gupta,[5] former CMO of Spotify, in Tiffani Bova's 'What's Next?' podcast."

"Another Gupta!" Rob said. "There must be something with that name."

"I guess you are right," I responded, laughing. "But in all seriousness, during his interview he made some very strong arguments:

> *I love what Amazon does and when you read about Jeff Bezos'*
> *mantras. They are challenging themselves every single day to add*
> *incremental value to their most loyal customer. And that to me is*
> *fascinating.*
>
> *They challenge themselves to add value to the customer who's already*
> *loyal and not going anywhere. That's their mindset.*

"Now this may sound obvious, but it strikes me just how many organizations I see that do the exact opposite – they're focused on adding incremental value to their customers *at risk*. When it's almost too late. I agree with Mayur – it's a mindset. And it's one that helps set yourself apart. It all starts with understanding what you are in business for. Here's how Mayur summarized that:

> *In a world where interaction and engagement are absolutely*
> *non-analog, I think that is where those brands have to challenge*
> *themselves. To really go back to the drawing board and ask: 'What*
> *problem are you truly trying to solve?' Are you really in the business of*
> *selling donuts? Or are you in the business of creating an experience*
> *where the donut is perhaps a key component?*

"So, are you in the business of delivering digital banking platforms, ERP, CRM, or payroll, or are you in the business of creating an experience where this solution is a key component?

"Here are some examples: 'Removing the day-to-day chaos' an experience Gusto is embracing with its HR and Payroll suite. Or 'Work smarter and faster than the pace of industry', the experience Uptake is building a business around with its new ERP solution. Or 'Discover new trails to success', the experience Salesforce is actually creating a complete 'Trailblazer' community around.

"The question 'What business are you really in?' helps you go beyond the point

---

5. http://whatsnextpodcast.libsyn.com/the-human-side-of-marketing-and-growth-with-mayur-gupta

of 'what' you deliver and move it to 'why' you deliver it. It helps you define the change you seek to bring to the market the experience you want to leave behind. It forces you to define the big problem you are trying to solve and focus your attention on what truly matters to your ideal customers. What experience do they desire? What would be their ideal world?

"Lots of what you offer will be 'table stakes' – everyone offers it, it's the functionality that gets your foot in the door. And that's fine. However, once you start honing in on what's truly valuable to your customer, solving their biggest (evolving) challenges and/or ambitions, that's when you can carve out your edge, and rise above the surface by exceeding their expectations.

"It will give you the framework to constantly challenge and stretch yourself to keep adding value to your customers who are already loyal, i.e. your fans. And that's a much more fun situation to work in, and while you do, you'll create more fans in the slipstream. That's about creating momentum."

"It's a refreshing way of thinking, Ton," Rob started. "And now it also lands why having fans, not just customers, is going to make a fundamental difference. It all builds on each other. I start to see how, by stacking all the traits of remarkable software businesses on top of each other, you create pure leverage. It becomes like a flywheel – once in motion, it's almost unstoppable. Fascinating...

"But let's go; it's 7.10 a.m. and we still have a forty-five-minute drive to Nazare."

5) Align every aspect of your business

As we merged onto the highway again, Rob said, "You've just suggested a range of different angles with which to drive momentum around the business – and for what I understand, some of it is related to what you do with your product strategy, some is marketing, some is sales. Where do you believe the focus should be?"

"Strong analysis," I responded, "and the answer is 'it depends'. It depends where you are in your lifecycle. If you are just starting out, you obviously have to create a product and that's your prime focus. But if you've been around for a while then it's key to ensure product, marketing and sales are perfectly aligned. It's about building a strong brand. If you do that well, like you just insightfully mentioned, it becomes your flywheel. You'll create leverage that is much, much larger than the sum of its components. And this is indeed what remarkable software companies utilize to grow their momentum.

"Fact is, what I often see is a disconnect. In essence, talking about 'the brand'. Your brand is the word that pops up in people's mind when they see your logo. So, the question is, what do you want that word to be? And are you tuning everything in your company to accomplish this? That's where the need for strong alignment comes in – from product strategy to marketing, to sales, to services and support.

"It all seems very logical, but in practice it can be very hard. So often each department seems to work in their own silo.

- R&D creates the product, often in a vacuum, not working from any brand-narrative. Once the features are there, the goal is accomplished.
- Once finished, it's thrown over the fence, where Marketing does its very best to launch it and promote it. The input is a feature-list, this is 'what it does'. The 'why' – i.e. what burning problem did we see to allocate a significant amount or money in our budget to develop this product or capability – is mostly completely absent.
- Sales then get an artificial target – that they should sell X copies – without any backup on why that number is the target. It's random – therefore could be far too high, leading to all kind of frustrations and too high discounts. Or worse, it's far too low, i.e. we're underplaying potential both in the addressable market and the price we can obtain for the value your solution delivers.
- Service then implements, where the focus is on making it work according to spec, often not taking the overall experience objective into account.

"And let's not forget the things we do inside all these silos that just drive an even bigger gap into our business, rather than making it more cohesive and stronger. Just look at the completely non-aligned incentive structures. Even today I still see situations where R&D is pulling all their energy and focus together around building the strongest Cloud technology to drive growth in SaaS, where at the other end of the spectrum sales bonus schemes are more favorable to continue to sell on-premise license. Or Marketing is creating the perception in the market around fast implementation time and rapid time to value, where the service division is incentivized to grow their service revenue by increasing the number of billable hours.

"All these decisions will likely be taken in good faith, but the end result is non-alignment, and that's where your competition has an opportunity. So to answer your question – everything in your company should be aligned to grow the value you can offer your ideal customers (Product), to grow adoption and wallet share around your offering (Sales), and to build a strong brand around your product that sticks in the minds of your ideal customers and will make them talk about it (Marketing).

"Just to refer back to that interview with Mayur Gupta, he said this about it:

> All three are extremely critical, and it's not either/or; as a matter of fact, they amplify each other. I put them as concentric circles, and the magic happens right at the intersection of growing the brand, growing the user base and growing the user value.
>
> You have to think beyond the mechanics and the science of bringing them and keeping them and giving them carrots. You have to build that emotional and cultural connection where they feel that you are part of their life.

"That's where and why alignment create the leverage you need. Another company that's really strong on alignment is Google. Remember I told you about Eric Schmidt[6] last night? This is what he shared in that same interview with Tim Ferris when he talked about one of his coaches, Bill Campbell:

> He was a principal person who had high integrity. He expected it from others and he thought that a successful life was one we live consistent with those principles, and having a purpose that you cared about.
>
> His job as a coach was to get everyone to feel that they had achieved that, while collectively getting the team to have that feeling as well.
>
> I will tell you that there's nothing more fun than having a very fast-moving team, where everyone's rowing in the same direction. That feeling of power, that feeling of excitement and [that] feeling of energy.

"And to illustrate this is not just important when you are at the scale of Google, here's another story from Plum, the company I also talked about earlier. In my conversation with Caitlin MacGregor, their CEO, we specifically addressed the importance of alignment. When I asked her 'What was the toughest decision

---

6. https://tim.blog/2019/04/09/eric-schmidt/

that you had to make, in order to get where you are today?', this is what she said:

> *Making the decision to pivot and create our own product from scratch instead of licensing was a really big move that we had to make early on. Our needs as an organization evolved, and that meant some people that helped us get off the ground simply weren't the right fit to get us the rest of the way.*
>
> *However, having gone past the five-year mark has definitely made me appreciate the importance of organizational alignment as you grow. Creating that alignment demands work, effort, and tough decisions.*
>
> *But now I can say that there is a lot of power in setting the bar high when it comes to the people on our team, and the alignment we share. We've really found our sweet spot and I want to make sure I keep that in place.*
>
> *But it takes work to get there. It's the commitment and belief that we can go even further together. That ability requires a social contract. We've figured it out. And it's amazing. As we scale, alignment is the one thing I don't want to lose sight of.*

"Thought-provoking," Rob responded. "But it goes back to the principle of building one single team as a total business, rather than groups of strong individuals that run 'their own business' inside your business. Food for thought, and definitely something to assess my own business on in the coming period."

Ask yourself

STEP 1: Reflect critically how you score your own ability around this particular trait by rating your organization on a scale of 1 (poor) to 10 (remarkable).

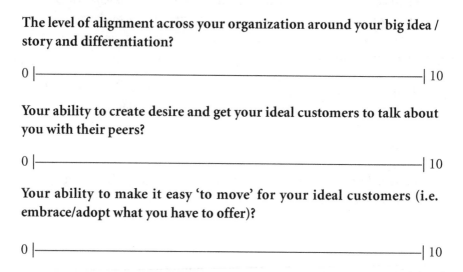

The level of alignment across your organization around your big idea / story and differentiation?

0 |————————————————————————————| 10

Your ability to create desire and get your ideal customers to talk about you with their peers?

0 |————————————————————————————| 10

Your ability to make it easy 'to move' for your ideal customers (i.e. embrace/adopt what you have to offer)?

0 |————————————————————————————| 10

STEP 2: Take ten minutes to reflect on the next actions you could initiate to improve your score.

STEP 3: What's the single action from this list that would give you the biggest impact?

Take it to the next level

- Not only become remarkable, but ensure you'll stay remarkable as well by introducing the 'Remarkable Monday' habit within your organization. Download the three simple steps that will help you create and keep momentum: https://valueinspiration.com/RemarkableMonday
- Join the Remarkable Tribe Program to create accountability with other tech-entrepreneurs like you. Not only will you build traction to shape the business you aspire to be, but you will also obtain new ideas, create new contacts and will be part of a movement that defines what it means to be remarkable as a business software vendor: https://movement.valueinspiration.com

Trait 9
Sell the idea, not the product

The power of the big idea

As we merged onto the A8 I saw the first signs for Nazare appearing.

"Less than half an hour to go," Rob said. "We're nicely on time."

I checked the WSL app for the latest news on the Big Wave event. It still mentioned 8 a.m. as the start of the first heat.

The sun was rising, there were hardly any clouds in the sky, and the wind seemed calm. The conditions were perfect.

Then Rob started: "We just discussed the different ways remarkable software companies create momentum around their solutions, but beyond that, are there any other secrets to their ability to outperform other companies in sales?"

"Sure thing," I replied. "Creating momentum is one thing – and for that you need a product people desire to have. We covered all of that. You can have the best product in the world, but if your messaging fails, it all goes flat. That's why another critical trait of a remarkable business software company is this one: they sell the idea, not the product.

"Let me tell you about Amy Williams,[1] CEO of Good-Loop, an advertising platform that's built around an ingenious idea to connect people, brands and good causes in a more meaningful, and consequently more effective, way. Every time someone watches an ad through her platform, they unlock a free charity donation, funded by the advertiser. When I asked her about the catalyst for her breakthrough moment, this is what she said:

[1.] https://www.valueinspiration.com/product-innovation-how-doing-good-and-making-a-big-bottom-line-impact-go-perfectly-hand-in-hand/

Let me start at the beginning: I left my job in the ad industry, which was scary, but I felt this drive to build my own thing. I didn't know what it was going to be, but I knew I wanted to build something I was proud of. I went travelling and ended up in Argentina in this awesome little comedor – which is kind of like a soup kitchen for young kids. Working with these kids in the outskirts of Buenos Aires, the team are making a real impact, feeding over thirty kids every week on a super tight budgets.

That really fueled me because it made me see you don't need a huge amount of money to do a lot of good in the world. Coming from an industry where, on average, a brand will spend about £10 million per campaign on video content, this is where it clicked: I wanted to be the force that uses that money to fund more meaningful change and make the world a better place.

Having an idea is one thing, but until you find a solution to a big problem, you're not going to get customers excited. The breakthrough came when I started to reframe it around ad-blocking and the public perception of the ad industry. I realized that making advertising more impactful and more meaningful could actually solve a lot of the problems that the industry was suffering from – proof that social impact can be a competitive advantage!

"It goes all the way back to the very start. Remember when we started our journey yesterday in Valencia, when I explained the magic behind creating your own massive wave by being very clear about two things: First, your big idea about the change you want to bring to the world, and second, defining very specifically the audience that will benefit from this the most, and how.

"This 'package' becomes your lifeline. Your big idea is the critical connection between you and your sweet-spot market. So sharing that big idea becomes your force. The massive push in your back. And the power of that should not be underestimated, here's why."

By owning the idea, you own the audience

"Let's start with the first advantage: by owning the idea, you own the audience.

"This is about the fact that big ideas change perspectives. By owning the audience, you can convince them what to pay attention to, and with that you define the market place.

"By owning the idea you'll reveal problems or opportunities your audience is sometimes not even aware of. You'll be able to turn something really complex into something really simple, and with that trigger something valuable and desirable.

"Selling the idea, not the product has helped create numerous remarkable business software companies. Just look at vendors like Drift. They're not selling a chatbot or a conversational marketing platform. They're selling you the idea that 'the traditional way of marketing is over'. They sell you on the idea of the 'old way' (before Drift) and the 'new way' (after Drift).

"I told you earlier on this trip about my conversation with Mike Schneider,[2] CEO of First. They don't sell you yet another CRM product to become more efficient managing your clients. No, instead, in their suite-spot market, real estate, they own the idea of 'never lose another client'. That's their promise, and they live up to it. It's highly valuable to their ideal customers who are losing out on 60% of the opportunities coming from people they actually know that either want to sell their property, or buy a new one. It's not about the product, it's about the idea.

"Slack does precisely the same. They don't sell you a social collaboration tool. They make you imagine 'what you can accomplish together.' Their big idea is the foundation for them to create the momentum we talked about earlier this morning. They, like many other remarkable software businesses, use it to create this big gap between 'what is' and 'what can be'. As one of the founders, Stewart Butterfield from Slack, once said:

> *What we are selling is not the software product because there are just not many buyers for this software product. That's why what we're selling is organizational transformation. The software just happens to be the part we're able to build and ship.*

---

2. https://www.valueinspiration.com/product-innovation-how-human-ai-combos-creates-disruptive-competitive-advantage-in-real-estate-sales/

227

"See what I mean? Their big idea is about the change they bring to the world – it's a piece of a larger puzzle that's very valuable and urgent to their ideal customers. Their customers are not interested per se in 'the product' in isolation. However, by owning the idea of 'accomplishing more together in a world of transformation' they own their audience, positively influence them, as such create desire and then ride an enormous wave as a consequence.

"Here's another example: Evernote. I've been using the product for years now and still can spell out the big idea behind the company that sold me the catchphrase: 'remember everything'. Again, they don't sell you a tool to collect notes, instead they sell you on their big idea. That's so powerful, and yet so simple."

It unlocks the money

"The second very important benefit of selling the idea, not the product, is related to this: it unlocks the money. In other words, if people believe in the idea and the fact it unlocks unique value, they will be prepared to pay a premium. The word 'discount' is not coming up at all. This works with prospects, with customers, with everything.

"Simply look at it the other way around. Let's imagine you are aiming to get seed funding for your business. You connect with the Venture Capital (VC) world. Correct?"

"Correct," Rob replied.

"Well," I continued, "to obtain funding, especially for the first round, you'll have to convince VCs about one thing: the big idea behind your business. They need to be convinced about the potential behind this idea and that it will create a shift of change in the market that's monetizable. Without that belief, any further discussion is not happening. It's the first paragraph they look for in your memorandum, and the first slide they expect in your pitch deck. For them it's all about the money.

"The funny thing is: while we all know that, why do we use this approach on VCs, but often forget to use it in our go-to market. If it can convince a VC to fund capital, it can convince a prospect to invest as well. Both want a shift in value in return, and as such, it's not about your product, it's about the idea behind your product. They need to be triggered by this idea and be convinced that the way you solve it enables them to solve some of their biggest problems, and achieve some of their biggest ambitions. If that's not clear then they'll politely say 'thanks, but no thanks.'

"The best ideas communicate change, positive change. That's valuable. The bigger that perceived value, the larger the amount of money it will unlock – whether that's funding, or the price of your next deal. People expect a value exchange, and if they can find that in your big idea, they are prepared to pay a premium."

"You have a point there," Rob said.

"Thanks," I replied. "But I am not finished yet. Since this is about unlocking money, let's talk about that for a while: the price tag on our software. Do you have a formal pricelist?"

"Yes, we do," Rob replied.

"What's that price based on?" I asked.

"Well, it's in line with our biggest competitors. We managed to get their pricelist, studied it, and based our own price on that – just a bit lower so we have an advantage in the negotiation round."

"That's what I feared," I continued. "Let me repeat a quote from marketing guru Seth Godin[3]:

> *When you are the cheapest you are not promising change. You're just*
> *selling the same, but cheaper.*

"Just think about that. Don't get me wrong, I am not criticizing you here. I've been there, and made the same mistake in my career. I was responsible for pricing strategy in my previous job, and it taught me a lot. As they say: it's been a love/hate relationship. We were selling the commodity of commodities: back-office software. This type of software is seen as a cost of doing business. As our CEO always said: 'There's software you want, and there's software you need'. ERP / Finance / HR etc. are in the latter category, and I can tell you, that doesn't help.

"However, that doesn't mean the price needs to be low. We were competing against the big guns of the world – SAP, Oracle, Microsoft Dynamics, Workday, you name it. And doing business in over twenty-six countries around the world our position was sometimes 'market leader' and sometimes 'market entrant'. Now here's the odd thing: no matter where we were selling, the argument we always had was: 'We need to gain market share, so we need to lower our price'. Or 'We are the market leader, our competition is undercutting our price, so to get the business we need to lower our price.'

[3.]   https://www.amazon.com/This-Marketing-Cant-Until-Learn/dp/0525540830

"No matter what happened, a lot of people thought we needed to be cheaper in order to sell something. It drove me nuts. That said, there was one thing that kept me sane – some parts of the business proved that we could sell at twice the price of our nearest competitor, that we could keep list price, or even sell above that.

"People told me that local government was the toughest to sell to. They even had their own published rules about how much something was 'allowed to cost' per year. Their budget was cut every single year by central government. They simply had no money, but were always expected to do more and more.

"To me, that's a value signal of the best kind. They are not a sad bunch; they just have a business pain that's screaming to be solved. If you can convince them about the shift in value your solution will bring, I guarantee they will be happy to pay a premium. But it means you have to sell change. You have to make them believe in the big idea behind your solution, how this drives significant value, and how your approach will exceed expectations. Once you do that, you're able to not only sell at double the price of your competitors, you'll also start to win more. That's where you'll gain momentum.

"Let me share another story with you. Remember I told you about Frederic Laluyaux,[4] CEO of Area Technology, who are enabling 'the self-driving enterprise'? He gave an intriguing anecdote about the power of the big idea to unlock the money:

> We launched a concept in June 2017, and I remember saying, 'This is it. This is a concept that can carry us for the next 10 years. This is the story.' I didn't know whether people would react by saying 'this is completely crazy', or 'this is something that we get.'

> So, with a certain apprehension, we presented our vision to a combination of industry analysts and potential customers and we quickly realized that we were onto something big. Two things really surprised me.

> The first is that we discovered that what we were pushing was actually a C-Level conversation. As it touches on changing how work is done, it is an exec topic.

---

4. https://www.valueinspiration.com/product-innovation-the-promise-of-cognitive-technology-to-enable-the-self-driving-enterprise/

The second surprise was that, while we thought we were way ahead of the curve here, most executives who we talked to were not surprised by what we had to present. Their reaction was mostly 'where the heck have you been?' as opposed to 'this is too advanced for us'.

"That's the power of communicating your big idea. I can guarantee you, if they had been selling the product and all its hyped features, they would not have discussions at the executive level. Change the conversation to the big idea, and the concept behind it changes too. Because that's what triggers executives – the big picture value conversation about creating competitive advantage, getting ahead of the pack, solving some of their largest issues, and removing some of their largest roadblocks that stand between failure and success."

"I get your point," Rob said. "If the value is there, price is not the issue. And the real value is not coming from features as such, it's coming from the belief in the change our customers are able to make to secure their future. That's what we're actually selling."

"You got it," I replied. "But there's more."

Ideas that are repeated change the world

"The third benefit is the potential to create larger-than-life impact. I subscribe to the daily inspirations from Simon Sinek and here's one that stuck with me:

Simple ideas are easier to understand.

Ideas that are easier to understand are repeated.

Ideas that are repeated change the world.

"There's so much truth here. Big ideas catch you, but those that are simple and memorable often gets shared. They are remarkable, i.e. worth making a remark about. They will get repeated by your own employees, because it makes them proud. That will help align your organization, and that builds momentum. Better though, it will get repeated by your customers, and that will help you create a movement. That's where reach kicks in in a way that hardly any company can afford to pay for themselves through their marketing effort. It can help your business take off and scale beyond any prediction in your business plan.

"It's the sole concept behind TED. If you're invited to speak on one of the

TED stages around the world, it's a confirmation you've got 'an idea worth spreading.'

"It's why Susanne Baars[5] got invited for TEDxINSEAD and TEDxAmsterdamED – to share her moonshot idea about saving millions of lives by creating universal access to life-saving information. Right now she's building the world's largest community for rare diseases and cancer. Connecting patients, loved ones and passionate scientists to find cures faster.

"It's why Nadine Hachach-Haram[6] was invited to the TED stage – to share her big idea on how augmented reality could change the future of surgery. As Hachach-Haram says: 'Through simple, everyday devices that we take for granted, we can really do miraculous things.' This simple but powerful idea got understood and repeated a lot. It's changing the world as we speak."

It triggers a conversation

"The reason why having a simple, big idea is so powerful was nicely illustrated by Jay Baer, author of the book *Talk Triggers*[7] He said that word of mouth is directly responsible for 19% of all purchases, and influences as much as 90%. Every human on earth relies on word of mouth to make buying decisions. Yet even today, fewer than 1% of companies have an actual strategy for generating these crucial customer conversations.

"The reality is that every movement starts with a story. Big ideas have the power to unite like-minded people. This builds a bond, it helps grow a community, and that in itself builds trust and gives people a reason to keep coming back. The community will start to collaborate, add value to each other, and this grows the value of the total, and it takes part of the pressure off your shoulders. It's a win-win for everybody.

"Salesforce is an excellent example of a company that smartly uses this. They're not just selling you on the idea to become a trailblazer. They actually encourage you to become part of a tribe of trailblazers – as they say: 'a community of 2.3 million like-minded people, partners, and developers all brought together and driven by a common goal: blazing a trail for, and right alongside, their customers.'"

---

5. https://www.youtube.com/watch?v=xFv1svnd4wo

6. https://www.ted.com/talks/nadine_hachach_haram_how_augmented_reality_could_change_the_future_of_surgery?language=en

7. https://www.amazon.com/Talk-Triggers-Complete-Creating-Customers/dp/0525537279

"Fascinating," Rob said. "I've never thought about it that way. We're always so engrained in our day-to-day work. We think what we do is normal. We sometimes don't see the impact we can make. But if I quickly reflect on some of our banking customers, I can only say we have created meaningful transformation. We're helping them thrive again in a world that's transforming so rapidly. That story is worth sharing. And we don't pay enough attention to that."

At that moment Rob took the exit off the A8, heading towards Nazare.

He continued: "Now that you have me excited about articulating the big idea behind my company, have you got any suggestions on what to pay attention to?"

"Sure thing," I replied. "Let me give you my top five."

It's not about you

"The first thing is to realize it's not about you. As Tina Sharkey[8], co-founder and CEO of Brandless, wisely said:

A brand is not what you say about yourself. It's really what a friend tells a friend.

"If a friend (your customer) tells a friend (your prospect) about your product, they communicate the essence of the value you create for them that's worth making a remark about. They communicate the big idea behind your company. They communicate the reason why they'd buy it again.

"It's as simple as that. It all starts with the very simple mindset, that your marketing is not about you, but about your ideal customers. Too often we position ourselves as the hero in our marketing efforts. Just open any website and read the essence of the communication. Often you see things like 'Our vision is to become the leader in X, Y and Z.', 'We've been growing double digit for years', and 'Our product is the only real-time ABC', 'We're the #1 Cloud ERP', and so on.

"So many companies are selfish. Born as an idea about themselves, they raise money talking about themselves, they sell products talking about themselves. Most brands aren't good at telling stories beyond themselves. They believe their product is their customer's only goal. The reality is so different."

---

8. https://podcasts.apple.com/es/podcast/building-storybrand-donald-miller-clarify-your-message/id1092751338?i=1000425490410&l=en&mt=2

It's all about what matters to them

"Interbrand[9] publishes annual reports about the secrets to growth for the world's most famous brands. A conclusion that resonated with me was this:

> *The brands generating the most stable growth over the past ten years are those with the highest overall scores on Relevance and Responsiveness. What's more, the top ten fastest-growing brands over the last five years are those where Relevance and Responsiveness are their top-performing dimensions.*

"I am particularly intrigued by 'Relevance'. Aiming for relevance forces us to think like our customers. It forces us to show empathy for their wants, their needs, their beliefs, what they see, and what they care about. This enables us to be sensitive to their biggest challenges; to dig deep to understand the things that keep them awake at night, and why that is the case. It forces us to understand their frustrations. If your big idea is about that, you are on to something."

Stop being the hero: be the guide

"At the end it's about a change in mindset. I've come to learn that remarkable business software companies master the art of 'selling without selling'. Let me illustrate this with a quote:

> *The big shift is to stop thinking of prospects, stop talking about people you are marketing to or at, and instead say: 'Where are my students?'*

"This comes from Seth Godin[10] in one of his interviews with Tim Ferris. He sums it up really nicely: instead of being the hero yourself, aim to make your customer the hero. That means your role changes to be the Sherpa, the guide, or if you will, the teacher. Doing so will help you make the shift to communicate in a way that invite people to enrol on a journey.

[9.] www.interbrand.com/wp-content/uploads/2018/10/Interbrand_Best_Global_Brands_ 2018.pdf

[10.] itunes.apple.com/es/podcast/the-tim-ferriss- show/id863897795?l=en&mt=2&i= 1000423013324

"And that's the essence: it's not about selling, it's about enrolling. Instead of selling to your prospects, you are preparing them to *buy* from you by educating them about the alternative ways you solve their challenges. You paint a picture of what can be and show a simple path how to get there. This requires a different attitude – one of helping, guiding, and caring. But story by story, you'll grow their trust. And trust over time equals power."

It's about change

"The second key thing to take into account is this: it's about selling change.

"Let me share another quote, this time from Nancy Duarte[11], a writer, speaker and CEO of Duarte Design. In an interview with Tiffani Bova she said this:

> If you communicate an idea in a way that resonates, change will happen / you're not selling a product, you are selling change.

"If your big idea is about change, it becomes extremely powerful. Just reflect on products or brands you admire. Products you've become a fan of. What you'll recognize is that most of these products dominate a specific category. They outsell their peers, not by a factor of percentages, but typically take the more substantial part of the cake. Products you've become a fan of are also not sold at a discount. They come at a premium, and you're happy to pay that premium. The difference is very often: they sell change.

"Irrespective of the product or service you sell, it's not about the features, it's about the result the features create – the change. Ultimately customers buy change. They have an aspiration of an end-state, and something stands in their way to achieve that. As such what they are looking for is a solution that helps them get rid of the problem and get them to the aspired state in the most remarkable way, and, if possible, far beyond it. It's the change where the value is created."

[11.]   http://whatsnextpodcast.libsyn.com/website/storytelling-in-business-with-nancy-duarte

The benefit of the benefit

"The typical mistake too many business software companies make, and honestly, I've been guilty of this as well, is that they'll brag about the features and the benefits of those features, but forget to connect the dots. In other words, they don't facilitate in making their prospects envision how the accumulated benefit of their solution helps them achieve their larger aspirations. They forget to translate the benefit forward. They forget to communicate the benefit of the benefit.

"The way I always approach it is to gain a common ground on the definition of the problem to solve. But that's not where it stops, because all too often what the customers think is the problem, is really not the problem. So, the art is really to make the connection to the core business goals of the company, and ideally their long-term ambitions/vision. This is where problem, impact and urgency come together. Once you switch to that model, you start selling change. Success will follow.

"Let me give you an example from the blockchain world. Blockchain is still relatively new, and a lot of companies are focused on educating the public about the basics of what it is. They spend a lot of time in explaining public blockchain, private blockchain, their security mechanisms, transaction speed, and so on. However, instead of explaining the 'what', i.e. the features, blockchain vendors would create far more momentum if they described 'what could be' thanks to the technology.

"Vendors like Provenance[12] get that right. They sell the big idea, and the change it results in. The idea they communicate is 'Every product has a story'. Their solution empowers shoppers around the world to choose their product based on telling its authentic 'story', i.e. what's its origin, how has it been produced, what has happened with the product from its inception to its end-result, etc. So, it's not about its features or the fact they use blockchain to facilitate making this a reality. It's about selling a shift for retailers and brands to instil 100% trust and transparency. This is transformational, it's positive change. That's competitive advantage."

"I am starting to get the idea, Ton," Rob said. "Lots of stuff to think through in the coming weeks. We're far too feature-oriented, and I clearly see how that's not working to our full advantage. It doesn't give us a seat at the table with the

---

[12.] https://www.provenance.org/

right people as our ideal customers, and besides that, it doesn't give us a strong position of negotiation. So lots of room for improvement!"

At that point we approached a roundabout.

"Nazare, here we are!" Rob said with a smile.

"I guess we best follow the crowd," I responded. "As expected, we are not the only ones on our way to the event, but what I see here is surprising. Gosh, what traffic at this time of the day. It's not even 8 a.m.!"

It's about changing perception

"Where was I?" I continued. "Ah yes, the third ingredient to pay attention to. And it's closely related to the second one: changing perception. While that might sound similar, it's radically different, and highly important to sell the idea, not the product. Here's why. Remember that your prospect is running its business with full focus – day in, day out. They are the specialist. They know every detail about it.

"You, on the other hand, have a much broader picture. First of all, you are not 'one of them' – you are an outsider running a completely different business. Secondly, you work with 'the sector' and as such you see many companies like your ideal customer, but still they are all different. That gives you a significant advantage because you can see things they've become completely blinded to.

"It's very much what we're going to experience today. You possibly have an established picture of what surfing is all about – we all have. But to see the art of what's possible with really big waves will change your perception for ever, and likely will put everything you knew about surfing in a completely different light. The same is true in business. If you master the art of changing perception, you're on track to be remarkable in the eyes of your ideal customer, and as such become highly successful. It will define the essence of your brand in the eyes of the customer."

The difference in value between something you 'need' and something you 'want'

"I've seen time after time that positioning your product in one or another category can result in a major difference in terms of your chances to win and, very importantly, the rates you can charge. Let's take ERP products as an example again. It's back-office, it's actually a cost of doing business, you need it but you don't want it. That's the perception. However, that doesn't mean you have to settle with that – if you find a way to position it in such a way that it ties to the aspirations of your prospect, the value perception changes completely, and so do your odds to win.

"I've seen this time after time in my previous company. The moment we switched from selling our ERP for efficiency reasons to the core engine to drive business change, our differentiation win-rates went up, as well as deal value.

"Here's another example: I've recently completed a value proposition project for the market leader in Mobile App Security. The traditional perspective on this type of technology is 'it's a cost of doing business'. You need to avoid hackers from attacking your assets and stealing your IP or confidential data. That's all true if you think about 'what' it does.

"However, that doesn't mean you have to position it this way. If you move the box towards, for example, 'winning the battle for customer loyalty', suddenly it has board-level attention and it becomes something you 'want' instead if something you 'need'. It totally changes the value perception, and urgency, and as such opens new doors.

"But let me give you an example from a company that's actually disrupting our own space – the business software industry: Engineer.ai. It's a good example of how 'we' have become complacent to running our own business. And they're opening our eyes, by changing our perspective. Their big idea is this: 'Make software as easy as ordering pizza.'

"Their whole premise is that while many people have brilliant ideas, very few actually implement them. It's too cumbersome, they don't have the technical know-how, or the resources. This is the problem Engineer.ai takes away. Their promise: 'Together we bring your idea to life. Twice as fast. 1/3 the cost. Enterprise grade.'

"Sachin Dev Duggal,[13] CEO of Engineer.ai, told me this:

> *One of the things that I'm driven by every day is the ability for technology to transform people's lives. We're in a world today where a lot of folks feel somewhat disenfranchised by the technology promise:*

---

13. https://www.valueinspiration.com/product-innovation-how-ai-helps-bring-your-idea-to-life/

something that was meant to help them grow, help them make more money, help them have more time at home. And instead, in many cases it's the opposite.

We took a thesis view that over the next decade most companies would become software companies, whether they like it or not, or whether they realize it or not. Existing businesses as well as hundreds of millions of new businesses that are being started, are trying to figure out how to stay relevant in an ever so pure digital economy.

Building software is hard. It's the hardest thing you're going to do in your life, potentially even more than your university degree. We think, however, that there's a really strong opportunity to transform how software is built.

We're moving from a world where software means working with a cottage industry where everything is slow and requires traditional know-how. It's inefficient, it's super risky. And so, there's often a trade-off that we see in our customers between the fear of being irrelevant, then they come up with an idea, and then it's basically the fear of failure.

It's like the sine wave that they keep oscillating between those two. And until they cross the line of fear, they're not really building or moving ahead. That's the problem we're solving. We're allowing anybody with an idea to be able to build it, whether they're at the edge at a big company, a small business owner, or they're an entrepreneur with an idea.

"Do you see what I mean, Rob? What they are doing is effectively moving their ideal customers' perception from 'software development is hard and costly' to 'now you can start building software in a way that's as easy as ordering pizza.' Makes you think, right?"

"It sure does!" Rob said.

"That's what I thought," I replied. "There are two things happening here:

1. First, it's about opening your ideal customers' eyes to see that their the aspirations can be achieved in a radically different and better way.

2. Second, it's about opening their eyes to the opportunity of achieving things the never thought possible before. It's about painting a vivid picture of the shifts in progress and shifts in value that can be achieved in ways they hadn't thought about before.

"Remarkable business software companies use these two concepts to build their advantage and set themselves apart. They use their outsiders' position and sector knowledge to change the perspectives of their prospects. And that's valuable. It goes back to the power behind the big idea – if you own the idea, you own the audience. That's what this is about. Doing that in a credible way builds trust, and hence you become their Sherpa, their guide."

"I see what you mean, Ton," Rob replied as he navigated his car through some very narrow streets. "And I can tell you, we're not doing this at all. It's like our customers – we run our business on a day-to-day basis, almost in automatic mode. We sell 'what' we have, not 'why' we have developed it in the first place – and that's where the mismatch is."

"You're not alone on this, Rob," I continued. "It's so common. Virtually all business software company focuses on the 'fit' of their product within their market. They are doing 'the expected'. Product market fit is the foundation to be relevant in your market. It gets you a foot in the door. It's the reason to be invited into the procurement process of your customer."

"Agreed," Rob replied.

"However, time after time companies that become remarkable in their space have something extra: they align brand with product in a very effective way. So instead of focusing on just product-market-fit, they create product-brand-fit. Here's why that matters: Let's look at the definition of a brand: 'An associative memory in the brain of the consumer, who connects – or associates – the brand with a set of brand attributes, benefits, impressions or emotions.'

"To me the definition of 'brand' is simply 'the promise'. It describes what you stand for as a company, the most basic connection between the problem and the solution. And this is what makes the connection so strong. Strong brands, whether they have the best products in the market or not, create the perception in the minds of their customer that they need this product because of that 'promise'. This is what Engineer.ai does effectively. They have a unique ability to change perception, own the idea, and own the audience. This is why people stand in line at the moment of launch, this is why they are prepared to pay a premium, and this is why they talk about your product to their peers and friends."

It's about the problem

"And that brings me to the fourth ingredient to pay attention to in articulating your big idea: Start with the problem.

"This might sound like an open door, but trust me, it isn't. We somehow always forget this – and not only with our messaging. Let me ask you a simple question: What do you do?"

"What do I do?" Rob repeated.

"Yes," I answered.

"Well, I run a software company that develops digital banking platforms."

"Exactly what I expected you to say," I replied. "Imagine it wasn't me asking this, but a complete stranger. Although there's nothing technically wrong with what you answered, the conversation would 99% sure go flat, directly after you'd provided this answer. Hardly anyone would say 'Oh interesting, tell me more!'

"Imagine If you'd have answered it like this: 'If I'd ask you the top three companies you'd love to engage with, banks are probably not on that list, right? Many banks today are facing a loyalty crisis with their customers and I'm running a software company that solves this.'

"Do you see the difference? It's conversational. It's recognizable. It's effortless to comprehend. Moreover, it invites more. The difference is: I started with the problem.

"People are always looking for the problem – that's how we are wired. Without the problem there's no context, and as such all information goes to waste. Remarkable business software companies get this. It's a fundamental element in their communication – no matter if you see it on their website, or if you speak to them informally. They use every opportunity to spread their big idea.

"There are various techniques to do this. In this particular example I addressed an 'experience' issue that's very recognizable. Another way to do this is to create a 'common' enemy. Don't mistake this for your competitors. I see that a lot. In the ERP space Oracle is known for bashing SAP, for example. I wouldn't waste my energy there – bad for your credibility. Instead address frustrating frictions by 'naming the cause'. In storytelling this is called 'the villain'.

"Drift, for example, is making 'forms' the enemy. Forms on your website drag the process, they're frustrating, they waste time.

"Salesforce got very strong momentum in early 2000 by formulating the villain as '(on-premise) software'. Their key message was: 'No Software'. It got them a lot of traction to transform the market with CRM as a service.

"The effect comes in many forms: they can stay away from the feature-function war that's typically going on. Instead they optimally position themselves simply by focusing their communication on their big idea in a way that's memorable and credible. With this they change perception around a real problem in the market, showcase clear differentiation and own their audience. Here's where they win."

At that moment we approached the dunes, and we were directed to park the car in the sandy skirts alongside the road. Rob navigated to a spot as close as possible to the beach and parked up.

It's about making it memorable and shareable

The sun was already up and we could feel its power already. However, given it was early February, it was still relatively chilly. As such, we unpacked some extra clothes from the trunk of Rob's car.

"I must not forget my camera and my big lens," I said.

Rob locked the car and we started following the crowd towards the beach.

"Listen," I said, and stopped for a moment. "You can already hear the waves crashing, and we're still a couple of hundred meters away from the beach. It's going to be a memorable day!"

"I hope so," Rob replied, smiling. "It's the first time I have actually experienced an event like this, and your passion for it has had its effect on me already. My expectations are high."

"You're not going to be disappointed," I said. "You'll remember this day for a long time.

"Talking about that, let me quickly share the last ingredient I have come to value in relation to communicating your big idea, which is: It's about making it memorable and shareable."

Deliver stories that people remember

"You don't just want to deliver stories; you want to deliver stories your audience will remember.

"That's a different ball game. And for this your big idea needs to be communicated in the most simplistic and memorable way. Once you achieve that, your ideas become shareable.

"Mike Ganino,[14] executive producer for TEDxCambridge, gave some helpful advice in relation to this in his podcast with Dr. Diane Hamilton. He said:

> *Think about the one thing you want your audience to walk away with. You want a simple idea. So what do you need to strip out to make it clean and clear?*

> *The second thing is: People remember stories. They remember experiences. So what can you do or add so that people can repeat it? Architect your message around 'what is the experience you want people to have when they need you? What stories are they going to be able to repeat? What are they going to be able to say?*

Ensure nothing gets lost in translation

The key aspect is creating 'clarity'. KJ Blattenbauer[15] expressed this in a different way in a FireNation podcast interview:

> *Successful brands know how they want to position themselves, exactly how to clearly communicate their value proposition to their target audience, no one else, their target audience. And they're able to do so in clear and concise terms so nothing is lost in translation.*

"The last five words are critical here: nothing is lost in translation.

"We want to make a connection with our ideal customer, but instead we always seem create more distance. We use jargon and big empty words that our customers don't understand or simply tag as 'superficial' and 'hyped'. Especially in the IT industry, we're masters at that: Real-time, Transform, Agility, Adaptive, Intelligent, Single Source, etc.

"And then the acronyms: GRC, EPM, CPM, GIS, BIM – if there's a category, there's an acronym or another piece of jargon for it. It's a typical example of

---

talking inside-out. This is the business we're in, this is how Gartner, IDC or Forrester label what we do. Fact is, our customers are in a different business. For them, this is all 'noise'.

"Somehow we're trying to be too clever, use words we'd never use in a normal conversation. We often aim to sound 'smart' or 'modern', where actually the opposite is true. We tend to speak 'at' our target audience, not 'with' our target audience. The result: it creates an artificial distance that's more harm than help."

Murder your darlings

"Our communication can be perfectly clear and clean, and written in a way where nothing gets lost in translation, still we have the tendency to tell too much. In communication the old saying 'less is more' is not an understatement.

"And it's not just in marketing communication. Product owners, marketers, sales, we all make it an art to just throw everything in. We think 'more is better.' More features, more products, more messages, more options. The result: our prospects get confused, and more often than not, decide to do nothing at all.

"So, as Nancy Duarte[16] once blogged:

> *We have to murder our darlings. If you want your most important*
> *ideas to shine, you'll want to learn to make those severe cuts and let go*
> *of seemingly brilliant or well-written ideas . . .*

"I agree with that advice. It works. I've coached hundreds of business software professionals in order to help them create their perfect pitch. The pitch battle at the very end of each workshop proves time after time that the ones that master simplicity gain a clear advantage over their 'competition'. As such 'murder your darlings' is always high on the list of key take-aways in the final reflection session.

- If we don't make the choices, our prospects won't either
- If we don't focus our new features on the essence, we won't exceed the expectations of our customers
- If we don't get clear about the benefits beyond the features, our prospects won't call us

---

[16.] https://www.linkedin.com/pulse/how-write-great-talk-murder-your-darlings-nancy-duarte/

- If we don't get clear about our big idea and differentiation, our prospects won't pay the premium

"So the key take-away is to refine your idea to become clear and sticky.

"Your customer should be able to read and understand your big idea and the value you offer immediately. This means it should be written in their language. It should describe your value and benefits the way your customer would describe them.

"Even if you are selling to the most seasoned expert, that doesn't mean you need to confuse. Make it easy to understand. By focusing on the essence we can capture someone's attention, resonate in the right way, create curiosity, make it memorable and shareable. With that we create momentum."

Meanwhile Rob and I were approaching the beach. As we walked along a narrow sand-path in the shade of some big pine trees we suddenly reached the peak of the dunes and we could finally see the surf. It was huge ... big sets were coming in that were easily 10–12 meters high. It promised to be a magical day.

Ask yourself

STEP 1: Reflect critically how you score your own ability around this particular trait by rating your organization on a scale of 1 (poor) to 10 (remarkable).

Where's the bulk of your focus: sell your product or selling the big idea behind it?

0 |————————————————————————| 10

What's your ability to create a shift in (value) perspective amongst your ideal customers, i.e. spark their attention with new or different perspectives?

0 |————————————————————————| 10

What's your ability to own your/a big idea within your category – something compelling, clear, sticky and sharable?

0 |————————————————————————| 10

STEP 2: Take ten minutes to reflect on the next actions you could initiate to improve your score.

STEP 3: What's the single action from this list that would give you the biggest impact?

Take it to the next level

- Not only become remarkable, but ensure you'll stay remarkable as well by introducing the 'Remarkable Monday' habit within your organization. Download the three simple steps that will help you create and keep momentum: https://valueinspiration.com/RemarkableMonday
- Join the Remarkable Tribe Program to create accountability with other tech-entrepreneurs like you. Not only will you build traction to shape the business you aspire to be, but you will also obtain new ideas, create new contacts and will be part of a movement that defines what it means to be remarkable as a business software vendor: https://movement.valueinspiration.com

Trait 10
Surprise and hit the right nerve

As we walked up the beach Rob said, "I was expecting a lot, but this is truly surprising. You have an impression of what you think it will be like, but now that I am here, it's beyond expectation. Nature at its best!"

"I agree," I responded. "Same here. I knew it was going to be a unique experience, and that's exactly why I made the effort to be here and see it with my own eyes. To hear it, to feel it, to smell it and to see the best of the best.

"It's what we've been talking about since yesterday afternoon – this is where it all comes together. If I make the connection to our software business again – it's the moment of your launch, or the moment of the pitch for this important deal that can make your quarter or year. Everything comes together – and if you nail it, you win.

"And to win you need to bring something extra. You actually touched upon it a moment ago: you need to surprise, and do the unusual. It's yet another trait remarkable software companies have. And it's key to winning people over.

"You know, hard facts are important, but surprise and emotion even more. We both know prospects are being bombarded with messages every single day – one vendor claiming to be even more impressive than the other. Fact is, virtually all companies in your category sound the same, addressing the same 'problems', claiming the same benefits, having the same features, and backing their claims up with ample numbers of customers that prove their credibility. That's why so many vendors find it so difficult to stand out. Only once companies start to blend in arguments and examples that are unusual do they make a connection that makes them rise above the surface. That's where things start to resonate and stick. That's where underdogs win the war against the established.

"Surprises are a very effective and fun way to set your business apart from the competition. And virtually everybody forgets to do it. Nine out of ten websites I explore fail to surprise. Nine out of ten sales pitches I see fail to surprise.

"I've done dozens of sales pitch battle events over the years, and I can guarantee that the ones that incorporate an aspect of surprise virtually always win hands-down. It's that powerful.

"Steve Jobs was a master at doing this. Everyone remembers how he introduced the iPhone back in 2007. Everyone remembers how he revealed the MacBook Air from the envelope. That surprised, and sent a very strong message that tells the whole story about the differentiation of his product in one single move. That sticks.

"Ideally, you want prospects and customers to be talking about you long after you have left the building. You want to plant an idea that sticks with them and is worth remarking about. If you use it in sales, it will set you apart from the others they've seen. Very often your prospects will place you high on their buying list, if not directly in 'Pole Position'. That will help improve both your sales win rates and your average deal value.

"One other thing: Surprise is not about facts. In fact, it's the opposite. I once heard someone say this:

> Not everything that's countable counts, and not everything that counts is countable.

"Just think about that. Surprises are about that. You say or do something that communicates the essence of what you try to get across in a remarkable way. That's not countable, but counts more than you think."

In the meantime we'd arrived at the sea. You could feel the ground shaking as the massive sets came in and broke on the reef. A number of surfers passed us with their boards, walked into the water and hopped on a jet ski that was already waiting for them. A fascinating experience to see the jet skis find their ideal line through those mountainous waves to get the athletes safely into the take-off area, maneuvering between the immense breaking sets they encountered on their way.

"Do you ever watch TED Talks, Rob?" I asked.

"Sometimes. Why?" he responded.

"Have you ever seen software icon Bill Gates[1] talk about fighting malaria?"

"No," Rob replied.

[1.] https://www.ted.com/talks/bill_gates_unplugged?language=en#t-333740

"Well, you should," I continued. "It's another perfect example of surprising an audience with a very simple message that no one will ever forget.

"He wanted to make the point that we have to unite in order to win the fight against malaria in third world countries. And this requires people in first world countries to do something. What he figured was, you only get action from friction, when people really feel the reality, and that doing nothing is not an option. But how do you do that if this is happening all so 'far way' and is simply not 'our' problem. What he did was the unusual.

"When he came on stage, a jar was already waiting for him on a table. A third of the way through his talk he walked over to the jar and explained that he'd brought some mosquitos from his last trip to Africa. He opened it 'so that they could fly freely, just like they do out there'. You can imagine the reaction. Whether they were truly infected mosquitos or not doesn't matter – the message was clear. It surprised everyone. In fact, the TED Talk went viral. That's how powerful it is to do the unusual, and surprise. You make your message stick and you ignite action.

"As Seth Godin once said in one of his TED Talks: 'Surprise – the riskiest thing to do is to be safe'."

Empathize

"Surprises come in many forms," I continued, "but there are a number of things to keep in mind.

"One thing is – it sounds too obvious to be true – but in order to resonate you need to ensure you align with your audience. You need to empathize with them.

"It goes back to thinking outside-in, stepping into the shoes of your ideal customer, asking the right questions and listening intensively. With that you'll truly understand the struggles they go through every single day in order to make a difference, to achieve their objectives and aspirations. The way you choose to surprise needs to 'speak their language' in order to be understood and felt.

"Jeffrey Shaw,[2] author of *LINGO*, once said on the Fire Nation podcast:

> *The ultimate compliment we can get for our marketing / sales efforts is when the recipient of your message says 'you totally get me – it's like you are in my head'.*

---

2. https://www.eofire.com/podcast/jeffreyshaw2/

"In essence it's about making the perfect connection. That's where remarkable software businesses separate themselves from the rest. I picked up a Gartner[3] quote that confirms this: 'Over 90% of tech company content continue to be egocentric, focused on them (products, capabilities, company) instead of the customer (and the benefits that their solutions enable).'

"That's where the issue lies: as long as you keep talking about 'us' and 'we' you'll fail to create that empathic connection. But let's define empathy first:

> *The ability to sense other people's emotions, coupled with the ability to imagine what someone else might be thinking or feeling.*

"This to me implies it's not a one-off thing. It's a journey. And business-to-business is all about that. I hardly ever see businesses buy software based on impulse. It's a process that can conclude in a matter of days, but often it's longer. That's where empathy becomes a very important instrument in your communication mix. A company that was created on that premise was CliClap, an AI-powered autonomous lead generation and qualification solution. Yonatan Snir,[4] it's co-founder and CEO, said this to me:

> *We have a lot of traffic on the website that's not converting today, and many tools and many new tactics are being used to try and fix that. But eventually, we see that only friction converts.*
>
> *The benchmarks stated today by Forrester, Marketing Sherpa and other research, talk about 2 to 4% converting to leads, and only a half percent is converted into opportunities.*
>
> *The reason for that is that in B2B you give the same experience to everyone. The fact is, it's not a one size fits all. A lot of people are being missed out, because they're not used to getting this kind of experience in today's world. The marketing tactics that we've been using for so long, are not adjusted to how we want to consume content and get informed. So we're being pushed too much to fill out forms in order to get our data, way before we're ready to move to the next step.*

[3.] https://blogs.gartner.com/todd-berkowitz/20171218_ten-fearless-predictions-for-b2b-sales-and-marketing-i/

[4.] https://www.valueinspiration.com/product-innovation-how-ai-can-help-marketers-generate-more-leads-with-higher-quality-and-less-effort/

So, the idea is to try and empathize with each visitor and understand for each visitor when, and what's the next best thing. And when it's ready, ready to stick and move to the next level of engagement, we enable that. Not too soon, not too late.

"So what CliClap is doing is spoon-feeding potential buyers with exactly the right content to guide them through the journey. It's all based on behavior. They are in charge, they decide when the moment is right to say 'yes, now is the time.' The effect of this approach is that you're forced to optimize your approach in order to resonate ad optimally empathize with your audience – once you get this right it becomes a flywheel."

"Thanks for that insight," Rob said. "I realize we fall into that trap as well. But the odd thing is, we know our audience inside out since we've worked with them day in, day out for years. Still, I realize now that we manage to build an artificial wall through our communication where we fail to empathize with them in the right way."

"It all starts with the realization, Rob," I replied. "It's never too late to change course, and turn the ship. And talking about that, the first heat is about to start, so let's walk up the dunes to the judge's area, that way we'll have a great view of the action to come."

"Great idea," Rob said. "And let's get a cup of coffee as well – I could use something to warm up."

Be clear you are not for everybody

As we walked along the shoreline we heard a loud horn indicating the first heat was on. Six big wave surfers started to paddle out to optimally position themselves to catch the first wave of the day.

And as we started climbing onto the rocks on the left part of the beach we could see a big set coming in. An enormous wedge, so typical for Nazare, was building up to at least 12–13 meters, and at the moment it was about to break we could see the first take-off. It's only when you see that happening that you realize the proportions. The size of the wave literally dwarfed the surfer, who took off to the right, thereby escaping the crash of the tip of the wave, and was then chased by a wall of white water three or four times the height of the surfer himself. The heat was on – literally.

"Wow!" Rob said, staring at the scene. His mouth hung open in amazement.

"One word – spectacular!" he said. "Now I see what you mean. It's in a league of its own. I can imagine if you master this, there's nothing like it."

"Exactly," I replied. "I hoped you were going to react like this. And if not, no hard feelings. Then it's simply not for you. And that's not a problem. This is exactly how you want your ideal customers to react as well when they see you 'in action'. Do you remember our train ride yesterday afternoon, when I talked about forcing yourself to define what big waves you can ride in your market, where you can be the elite?"

"Sure thing," Rob replied.

"Well," I continued, "as I told you, it's about clarifying two things. First, your big idea about the change you want to bring to the world, and in relation to that, defining very specifically who's the audience that will benefit from this the most, i.e. your ideal customer.

"You want to be super specific – you want your ideal customers to say 'That's what I want!' They become your fans. There will obviously be a group that couldn't care less. And that's not an issue; you can't please everyone. The moment you do that, you're like everyone else, and you'll fight the downwards spiral of high loss rates, high discounts and low satisfaction. That's what you want to avoid at all times.

"Nick Hughes,[5] CEO of Founders Live, shared an interesting view in respect to this in an interview on the Delivering Extra podcast. On the question 'How to be successful as a company?' he answered this:

> *You should end up turning people off.*

"I concur with him, and here's why: If you communicate in generic terms, it won't resonate – with anybody. You'll sound just like all 'the others'. It won't turn people off, but it won't turn people on either. Here's some further insight from Nick:

> *If you are trying to be the twenty things for everybody, you're not going to go anywhere because you're too spread out and you're trying to solve everyone's problem. And that is impossible.*

> *The more detailed, direct and pinpointed you are in what you stand for, what problem you're solving and the solution you're bringing to*

the table, you're going to be attractive to a certain segment, which ends up meaning you'll get traction, you'll actually get users and customers and you'll grow.

The counter effect of this is that you'll turn people and/or companies away, and that's great because you want to be deflecting companies or customers that aren't really meant to be your customers. So, the more clear you are with your message, the more that's going to happen, quicker. That creates momentum and that creates growth.

"So, what you should be aiming for is being so specific that you'll enable your ideal customers to say 'that's for me!' and all the others (the ones you don't want anyway) 'not for me'. Here's an example:

"It's better to say 'We help business software companies double the success rate of their international implementation projects' than 'We help professional services organizations of any size become more efficient'.

"It's better to say 'We enable humanitarian charities in Africa to make nine out of ten farmers self-sustainable' than 'We enable not for profit organizations around the globe make more informed decisions'.

"To resonate and hit the right nerve you need to be extremely clear who you're for. Aim to answer very specifically what defines the organizations where you can solve their most pressing challenge in a way you'll exceed expectations beyond what the alternative options offer. If you articulate that well, your ideal customers will find you, and that's where momentum starts."

Trigger emotions

We walked to a kiosk in the jury area to buy a warm drink. The position of the sun was still low and as such it felt quite cold behind the dunes. As we arrived at the kiosk, we realized we were not the only ones.

"A good example of what you are looking for in business," I said. "People lining up to get your product!"

"Ha ha," Rob laughed. "That's the dream to have people queuing up in front of our door to get a subscription for our software."

"It's a good thing to strive for though," I replied. "They might not actually be knocking on your door, but they could come in masses to your periodic customer events, just to ensure they don't miss out on what you have to offer.

"It's an art remarkable software businesses understand very well. They understand people don't desire products. They desire the feelings that products give them. It's about the emotion it triggers. That defines the action. Just like what's happening here. We're all waiting in line picturing the warm and joyful feeling we get from drinking a good cup of coffee.

"It's exactly this understanding that enables remarkable software companies to find new ways to surprise and hit the right nerve, again and again. No matter what product or module you add to your suite, be ensured you keep the emotion in focus, i.e. the feeling your product should give your ideal customers when they use it. This starts with product design and should translate all the way through marketing and sales. It raises expectations, but hey, that's a good challenge to have.

"Triggering emotions is extremely powerful to trigger a reaction. And I don't mean emotions in the sense of making people cry. To the contrary. Emotions go much broader. This can be addressing fear, frustrations, anxiety, joy, fun, accomplishment, aspiration, you name it. Take this moment: we're cold, it's still early and that triggers us to put in the effort to find a place that sells coffee. We're even prepared to wait for five or even ten minutes.

"The odd things is, in our marketing communication and sales process emotion is often forgotten. Whether on purpose or not, we tend to make everything dry, dull and very factual. What we forget is that even the most fact-hungry decision makers are people too. Decisions are often made with the heart, and that's where emotion comes in – big time.

"I mentioned Salesforce before as being an excellent example of a company that sells their big idea. In their communication they have a very natural way of playing to the emotions of their ideal customers. For example, they address the natural aspiration people have to become successful. That's why they are stressing to 'become a trailblazer.' They smartly use that in every aspect of their go-to-market – at the highest level, all the way down to the product level. It creates a bond, people have a natural desire to be surrounded with successful people and businesses, and as such it resonates.

"Another company that's using emotion in their core marketing communication is Collective[I], which I've highlighted yesterday during our flight. They are opening the eyes of their ideal customers with statements like:

> '70% of sales management's time is spent on administrative, internally focused tasks'

> 'Only 46% of forecasted deals close'

'Up to 52% of sales professionals miss quota, leading 25% of them to lose their jobs every year, despite over 1 trillion USD invested in their success.'

"Very often buyers are not actively aware – so the only way to get their attention and compel them to take action is to trigger their emotion. Doing this accomplishes two things: it highlights universal pain points, and it converts these challenges into a big opportunity. Transformative solutions are what Chief Sales Officers, Chief Marketing Officers and Revenue Operations leaders – the key decision makers of their solution – crave. Hence, it triggers action – and that's where Collective[i] smartly tells its story about how they facilitate 'The science of buying, and The art of selling.'"

"I told you earlier this morning about how First.io is owning their audience with the big idea 'Never lose another customer'. The way they have phrased this is 100% optimized to trigger an emotion. This simple short phrase stands out and hits the right nerve with their ideal customers, and hence it triggers action."

"Powerful indeed," Rob replied as he ordered two cappuccinos at the counter. "It makes me think again about all the opportunity we have in our business to trigger the emotions of our key decision makers. There are so many I realize now. It just needs us to always start with the customer and the problem in mind. The rest will follow from there."

"Well said, Rob," I replied. "You're formulating the right conclusion."

Create desire by communicating an experience

We walked back with our coffee and tried to find a good spot in the sun to follow the action on the water. At that moment another big set came in and we saw another surfer launch with perfect timing from the tip of the wedge.

"Isn't this amazing," Rob said. "We're standing here in the dunes, elevated a good 10 meters above sea level, and these guys are actually taking off at the same height. We almost have to look up, rather than down. The sheer size of the waves is unimaginable, and you have to physically be here to experiencing it."

"That's what I have been talking about all the time," I said. "It's what turned me into a fan: that experience of everything coming together as a perfect cocktail. The unimaginable power of nature together with the art to conquer that power is creating memorable surf moments. Sure, I can see this online as well, but to experience it for real is what makes it memorable. And that's so powerful.

"And that concept works everywhere, whether it's leisure like today, or business. If you create memorable experiences you can get everyone and everything in motion. Remarkable software businesses understand this and use it to surprise their customers and hit the right nerve.

"Remember we talked about 'What business are you in, no, what business are you really in?' yesterday when we left Valencia?"

"Yep," Rob answered.

"That what this goes back to. You are not in the business to sell digital banking platforms. You are in the business to enable tier 2 and tier 3 banks help *their* customers to be one step ahead in life. In essence that is all about selling an experience. It's the outcome your customers are looking for to create competitive advantage and to stay relevant in their industry.

"Gusto, a company I've mentioned before, uses this concept across the full spectrum of their communication, and in a way that's very natural and credible. Their solution lets companies manage all their HR and payroll tasks in one place, online. Gusto succeeded when they created their value proposition in that it both makes the company's uniqueness plain, and it states their value in a way that is simple, credible, and selling an emotion.

"Their value proposition starts with the simple rallying cry:

> *'It's time to tame the chaos of payroll, benefits, and HR. Get it all done with Gusto.'*

"Not only does it directly address the customer (in familiar language) and talk about troubling problems the platform solves, it also clearly summarizes what benefits their service affords users and tells the story of how it can lead an organization from chaotic to manageable. They're selling the experience, not the features.

"An aspect that strengthens selling the experience is the fact they master the art of simplicity in their communication. Nothing gets lost in translation. No jargon, no hyped words. It's all about the customer, empathizing with them, and triggering the right emotions. I mean, if you talk about payroll, what do you think of?"

"Well, if you ask me, it's not exactly something I'd like to do, let alone build a company around," Rob said, laughing.

"Correct," I responded. "Still, Gusto did exactly that, and they make good business with it, simply because they solve a problem, and know how to connect with their market. Let me give you an example of what's on their website. Their promise: Payroll made easy.

The three top benefits:
1. Make payroll a breeze (85% of customers say Gusto is easier to use than their previous payroll provider)
2. Get it right (3 out of 4 customers say Gusto makes compliance easier)
3. Find your zen (77% of customers say that Gusto takes tedious tasks off their plates)

"I mean, just think about that: no features, but instead a simple and elegant message that communicates the experience instead. Their decision makers know what payroll is all about. They expect you have what it takes to deliver table stakes. Gusto understands this perfectly – therefore hones in on selling the idea and the experience. They are addressing the emotion, and talk *with* people, not *at* them. What's extra powerful is that for every benefit they add concrete proof points that tell me one thing: these guys get it. If I was a payroll clerk, I'd call them."

"Me too!" Rob replied. "I'll make a note of this, see if they have a Portuguese localization. Sound like a fun and fresh company to do business with."

"Here you go!" I said. "It touched you as well – and instantly gave you a perception of 'fun' and 'fresh' on top. And all that for a payroll provider. It just demonstrates how powerful it is to surprise by communicating an experience.

"I told you earlier about inPowered, the AI company that's transforming the digital advertising space. They're creating strong desire amongst digital marketers with one simple headline: 'We Deliver Attention. Not Clicks.' They then back up their claim with the line 'A single platform to get your content read or watched across all native channels.' Again, that simple line creates desire because it communicates a desired end stage, the experience of true 'attention'.

"Before I forget, an alternative way to communicate an experience is to build on familiarity. One way to achieve that is by using metaphors. Metaphors are ideal to provide clarity or identify hidden similarities between two ideas. In the business software space a lot of focus is on reimagining the way we can do things. A lot of the inspiration for that comes from other industries, domains, or even things, and as such provides new fresh perspectives to create the shifts in value your customers are looking for. The same works to create surprises in your communication.

"To tie it back to Steve Jobs revealing the MacBook Air: the envelope Steve used to reveal the MacBook Air told the full story: 'If it fits in a letter-sized envelope its very thin and very light. Job done.' That's the metaphor you are looking for to build a mental picture of the value you are trying to get across.

"What you see here as well is: less is more. Literally. It reminds me of an interview with Jesse Cole,[6] author of the book *Find your Yellow Tux*. This guy really understands selling an experience. He manages two summer league amateur baseball teams, so nothing premier league, but gets their 4,000 seats sold out every single game, a year in advance. He shared this:

Whoever says the most things in the least amount of words – wins.

"It's spells out the power of simplicity and memorability. And to do this well you have to take a step back, reflect, and commit to what you want to own in the minds of your customers. What's the single thing that people need to remember when they visit your site? Read your nurturing campaign emails? See you on stage? Or speak to you in person during a prospective meeting? What's that single experience or thought you can surprise them with? That's both hard and, in many cases, scary as it forces you to take a position (that will likely qualify people out). But at the end that's what matters most to resonate with the right audience and create desire."

Create a sense of urgency

As I sipped my coffee, I checked the scoring of the athletes on my WSL app.

"The scoring is one that's conceptually interesting," I said. "The best two scores count, however, the best score gets multiplied. And that can throw the ranking per heat upside down in a second. The current best surfer has 18.7 points, and the surfer positioned sixth has just 3.3 points, so technically everyone can still win as there are still seven minutes on the clock. It creates a sense of urgency that's extremely strong amongst all the contenders. They all know they can still surprise everyone by doing the unexpected.

---

6.   https://itunes.apple.com/es/podcast/building-storybrand-donald-miller-clarify-your-message/id1092751338?l=en&mt=2&i=1000423225650

"Creating a sense of urgency is an essential ingredient to perform in business as well. If you understand well how to create a sense of urgency you'll make things a lot easier for yourself and the business you run. I see too many companies do that in a way I'd not recommend: luring customers to sign by giving a large discount. That's too easy. It demonstrates weakness."

Action comes from tension, desire and fear

"Remarkable software business create urgency around the value they create. They know action comes from tension, desire and fear. One thing they often do is connect the dots, i.e. bring together all the points we just discussed:

- They empathize by doing their homework on what's going on in the world of their ideal customer.
- They pinpoint the most important challenge on the agenda of their ideal prospect – the one that, if they solve it, generates most value.
- They then translate their key points, painting a vivid picture of the value they deliver, and the experience it will provide.
- They layer their arguments and don't stop by only mentioning the core challenge. Instead they create positive tension.

Creating positive tension with your prospects

"This last point is more critical than you might think. Let me explain: Parry Malm,[7] co-founder and CEO of Phrasee, is a big promotor of using positive ethics in marketing.[8] Their advice: swap pressure for positivity. Here's why: Ethical marketing is not only the right thing to do, it can also drive commercial benefits.

"The research uncovered that going the negative way makes people feel angry (48%), inadequate (39%), sad (38%), or anxious (38%). 56% agree that brands using negative emotions are, in part, responsible for harming people's mental health. 63% agree that brands using high-pressure selling tactics are responsible for getting people into financial difficulty. 27% agree that anxiety-

---

[7.] https://www.valueinspiration.com/product-innovation-how-ai-can-make-you-more-money-in-marketing/

[8.] https://phrasee.co/emotions-matter/

inducing marketing has made them buy things they have later regretted. All in all 76% agree that they are turned off by brands that use high-pressure selling tactics.

"Creating tension is critical to create action. Without tension people don't move and businesses don't make decisions. Tension comes merely from two things: The threatening of safety and a change of status. That's where the opportunity lies for marketing to create the right type of tension: positive tension. That drives genuine action, and that's what you are aiming for. You can do it in a cynical and negative way, using fear tactics to pressure people, or in a positive way by talking about the positive things you bring to market, with the ultimate goal of creating enduring relationships with your customers."

Translate things forward

"Another aspect of creating positive tension is to focus on the 'benefit of the benefit', or the 'consequence of the consequence' if you will. It's a key aspect to create urgency.

It helps you to build a bridge and connect your solution to the higher-level goals, ideally the vision of your ideal customer. Every well-respected business has a North Star, a direction in which they eagerly want to aim for together. So, what stands in between achieving that and where they are today is a series of roadblocks. It's the task of every software vendor to help remove those road-blocks – whether small or big. It can very well be that by removing a minor roadblock, you unlock the route to accelerate progress towards their North Star. Making your customer aware of that will increase their desire, raise the urgency to fix it, and as such put your project higher on the priority list.

"Let me illustrate this. Let's take contractors as a category. Organizations in this category have 'excellence' high on their priority list. It helps them to grow their brand value. So this is often how they position themselves to their customers. Excellence is what drives them and what they want to be known for. As such, this is what they invest in.

"Now imagine you offer a solution for Field Service Maintenance. The obvious route would be to communicate 'increased efficiency and resource utilization' as key benefits of your solution. At the end that's what it does. However, why not translate that forward and focus on the benefit of the benefit, i.e. the impact your solution has on the brand perception of your clients. With your solution they will be able to fix every issue at the first attempt, it will allow them to get an engineer to the location faster, within the hour. To go beyond that, they will be able to remove potential issues pro-actively. Guess what this does with the brand value of your customers? That's gold. So where increasing utilization and improving efficiency would get them interested, increasing their brand value would get them to act. That's what it is all about.

"Following this process allows you to craft and tell a compelling story, build-ing tension between 'what is' and 'what can be', and progress their story to end on a 'high'. This can only lead to a reaction which is 'I want this' or 'Not for me' – but nothing in between. And that's good. Either you progress on a value sell, or you say goodbye as early as possible in the process.

"As said before, you'll become successful if you understand you can't please everyone. It's not important that everyone in the world knows about you. It's about focusing your time, money and energy on making the connection so that the right people know about and want your solution. That's about under-standing who your ideal customers are, what they aspire (desire), what keeps them up at night (challenge), and why doing nothing is not an option (fear of missing out/fear of loss).

"That opens up a host of opportunities to create urgency around. For example, there are factors that are completely outside your customers' control that they should be taking action on. Shifts in the economy and customer demand can all affect them. And if they feel as though their competitor might take a chunk of their market, they're more likely to act.

"Just be aware you shouldn't go overboard with this. There's a fine line between hitting their emotions and your credibility. Nevertheless, incorpor-ating arguments on why doing nothing is not an option are a great way to show your customers the true value of your services. Being concrete is another key aspect in this. So go deep on understanding what's hurting the business at this moment (or what could be in the near future) and aim to connect your value story to the vision or cause of your prospect – this adds meaning, relevance, and often helps to hit the right 'nerve', simply because that's what they deeply care about. Once they see and feel the connection – they'll act, with urgency.

"A last point on this. Ensure you understand the difference between cause and effect. I continue to see so many vendors communicate the fact they offer a fantastic user-experience, i.e. remove the pain of bad usability. Or they offer built-in flexibility, i.e. remove the pain of rigidity in business systems. And while that's all good, and in many cases valid technically, it's not what drives urgency. It's about what you get, not why you should desire it. What you should do is challenge this from a customer viewpoint.

"Let me give you an example from my previous job. I have corrected many slides of colleagues that communicated a poor user interface as a critical pain point in the market segment that we addressed. Although I understand the thinking, it can't be. The user interface can never be the pain point; it can only result in a pain point. A poor user interface can indeed result in making unnecessary errors that impact the customer experience. It can result in an inability to deal with demand peaks, which can lead to missing deadlines or inferior quality. It can result in poor user adoption, which could then result in delays in data entry – and if that's the foundation of your service, invoicing this could result in cash flow challenges, revenue leakage, and eventually profitability crisis.

"These consequences are what keeps people awake at night; here's where things start to resonate. So the trick is to embrace the viewpoint of your ideal customer and then aim to reveal how the cause (the user interface, the poor flexibility, etc.) negatively impacts their business by translating things forward. It's that impact that's recognizable at the customer end. This is what they are fighting every single day. This is your opportunity to be the guide and help them become the hero. The better you make your customer feel the effect of doing nothing, the bigger the urgency you'll create."

Making connections is more important than getting attention

"All in all, this is about making a connection with your ideal customer. As Dharmendra Katiya once said:

Making connections is more important than getting attention.

"There's a lot of value in this. So often we focus on reach, spending large portions of our marketing budgets on online ads to interrupt people who we believe could potentially be our customers. Yes, it's attention – but is it the attention we want? Too often it's attention without making a connection."

Getting attention is easy – making a connection is hard

"As I said a couple of minutes ago, making a connection is about empathy. Put yourself in the shoes of your ideal customer and really try to understand what they believe, what they need and want, what they care about and what they see. It's about looking through their lens, not yours. This is hard.

"Just look at what you communicate on your own website through the eyes of your ideal customer. If you think about their number one 'want' – does it 'connect'? If the answer is 'No, not really' then think about the companies you admire yourself and see how they make the connection with you. There's a lot to learn from that."

"That's a valid point, Ton," Rob said. "Another thing to add to my list. This is worth critically reviewing our own material upon."

It's about triggering emotions

"Connections are made when we trigger people's emotions. When we hit exactly the right nerve. As Jeffrey Shaw rightfully said, the best compliment you can get is when a prospect tells you 'it feels like you read my mind. This is exactly what I/we want.'

You will see that 'the want' is not a feature. They don't want your slick UI, your role-based dashboards, your smart algorithm or your open APIs. They don't even want your secure Cloud or the fact you are the cheapest. To really connect you'll see you get traction when you address what they really care about – and that's about 'safety', 'strength', 'impact', 'status', 'peace of mind', 'freedom', 'creativity', 'power', 'reliability', and so on."

Dig deep

"And even this is possibly still far too wide to make the real connection. Let me give an example around 'impact'. As you can imagine, the bootstrapping owner likely has a different set of 'wants' than the CEO of a venture-backed or publicly traded software company. I'm not just talking about hashtags or Euros, but what scale of impact. Is it worldwide or regional impact? Is it an internal or external impact? Do they aim to have a big exit, pocket some FU money and move on to the next opportunity, or is their drive independency and their mission to create a lasting impact in the market?

"You could go on and on – but the lesson to learn is that to make a meaningful connection you have to dig deep. An investment of time that's very well spent – because making the connection drives action, whether that's a firm 'This is for me!' or 'Not for me'. It's getting that level of clarity about what it is all about."

Rob nodded and said, "So simple, so obvious, and yet so under-utilized … I've come to realize in the last two days that everything would be so much easier if we took a couple of steps back – look at the big picture, define what we stand for and get clear about the change we seek to make for our ideal customers. This drives everything. It will boost energy rather than drain it. It will allow us to pull things off that make us proud. That's valuable. I actually can't wait to get back to the office on Monday! What time is it, by the way?"

"9.30 a.m.," I replied.

"Then I need to get going. Remember I told you yesterday that I have an appointment in Lisbon at 11 a.m.?"

"Then we better get moving, Rob," I replied.

We jumped up and started walking back to Rob's car.

Ask yourself

STEP 1: Reflect critically how you score your own ability around this particular trait by rating your organization on a scale of 1 (poor) to 10 (remarkable).

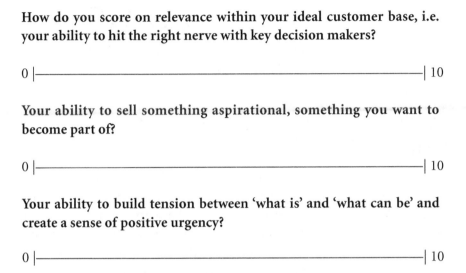

How do you score on relevance within your ideal customer base, i.e. your ability to hit the right nerve with key decision makers?

0 |————————————————————————————————| 10

Your ability to sell something aspirational, something you want to become part of?

0 |————————————————————————————————| 10

Your ability to build tension between 'what is' and 'what can be' and create a sense of positive urgency?

0 |————————————————————————————————| 10

STEP 2: Take ten minutes to reflect on the next actions you could initiate to improve your score.

STEP 3: What's the single action from this list that would give you the biggest impact?

Take it to the next level

- Not only become remarkable, but ensure you'll stay remarkable as well by introducing the 'Remarkable Monday' habit within your organization. Download the three simple steps that will help you create and keep momentum: https://valueinspiration.com/RemarkableMonday
- Join the Remarkable Tribe Program to create accountability with other tech-entrepreneurs like you. Not only will you build traction to shape the business you aspire to be, but you will also obtain new ideas, create new contacts and will be part of a movement that defines what it means to be remarkable as a business software vendor: https://movement.valueinspiration.com

Becoming the business you always aspired to be: Remarkable and Impactful

A software business that makes you proud – really proud

"I've really appreciated getting to know you, Ton," Rob said as we walked down the dunes towards the beach. "You've inspired me in so many ways about the opportunity to make a far bigger impact with the venture than we envisioned when we started. Your outside-in perspective made me realize we are undermining the potential for our customers, and that of our own business. I am so full of energy to start part two of our journey when I get back into the office Monday."

"I am glad to hear that, Rob. I'm glad I could provide that spark to ignite this in you. It's the reason why I started my business in the first place; helping people like you shape the business you've always aspired to be: Remarkable and Impactful.

"It's all about mindset. The people I work with, 'tech-entrepreneurs-on-a-mission' is how I refer to them, all have something in common. They're going above and beyond to shape their business into something that makes them proud – really proud.

"Just think about that. What would make you really proud of your venture? What would that feel like? Would it be when:

- You heard an anecdote from one of your customers who had come to you expressing how valuable you have become for them?
- That they cannot imagine what their business would be like without you?
- Would it be the evidence of momentum you are experiencing that you're solving something that's truly broken – a problem that, once you are *done*,

will have made a significant contribution towards making the world a better place?

- When you read the story about the recognition you are getting from the market for the impact you create?
- When Gartner name you *a vendor to watch?*
- When you've become a magnet for the best talent in the market?
- When virtually every customer turns into a fan and spreads the word for you faster than you can spread it yourself?

"When I asked Parry Malm,[1] CEO of Phrasee, he summed it up really well:

> *The thing I'm most proud of is the team we've built here. A product is just a product, right? I don't wake up each morning and go 'Oh, my God, I can't wait to create more subject lines.' What I think is really cool, though, is we've created a new industry, we've created new job categories, we've created something from absolutely nothing.*
>
> *The average age of our team is about 30, two-thirds of them are female. We are a very a-typical technology company. And I'm really proud of that. We're just showing that you don't have to do what's been done before. The world is a wide place and just because some fancy expert or corporate suit says you're supposed to do something, it doesn't mean you have to do it like that.*

"What's that story about your software business you'd like to share with everyone because it makes you genuinely proud?

"That is the foundation to becoming remarkable."

On a mission to deliver impact your customers will talk about

This leads to another thing these tech-entrepreneurs have in common: It's not about them, it's about their customers. They don't exist to make themselves or their owners rich. To the contrary: they exist to uniquely solve the most valuable and critical problems that are keeping their ideal customers behind.

[1.] https://www.valueinspiration.com/product-innovation-how-ai-can-make-you-more-money-in-marketing/

"They are starting with the simple question: 'Who/what do we want our customers to become?' They realize that by crafting a mission around the change they seek to make for their customers, all the rest – the revenue, the profit – will follow. It puts everything in motion.

"They know it's 'change' that makes customers buy – nothing else. Their investment will always be about getting from *here* to somewhere more desirable. That's what they are prepared to pay a premium for.

"Setting a clear mission around this 'change' provides them with the North Star that provides the clarity to make the right decisions and the energy to go the extra mile to deliver the change in such a way it will create a shift in value.

"This keeps them honest to challenge themselves day-in day-out whether they are investing enough time, effort and money into the initiatives that get them closer towards delivering their promise. It forces them to think in clear outcomes. It forces them to go deep on the inner aspirations of their ideal customer, and what's stopping these same customers from achieving that in a world that evolves in front of their eyes.

"It drives their curiosity to challenge the status quo and continuously raise key questions like:

- Why is this happening?
- Why are we doing it like that?
- What's 'broken'?
- What problems is this creating?
- What value is being destroyed as a consequence?
- Who are suffering most from this?
- Which of those problems would be most valuable and urgent to solve?
- How can we do this in a way that exceeds expectations?

"That's where the foundation is created to deliver impact customers will talk about.

Receiving remarkable value by providing remarkable value

"This is what it is essentially all about: Delivering impact your customers will talk about.

"The key question is: when would your customers start talking about the impact you make on them? The rule of thumb: when you're creating something that makes them more valuable; more valuable to their customers, to their investors, to their shareholders, to their employees. When it provides them with a position of advantage. Something that makes them proud. This is what remarkable software companies understand extremely well. So well, in fact, that sometimes that position of advantage gets so big that it becomes anti-viral, i.e. customers treat it as their best kept secret. Remember the story on First.io?"

"Totally!" Rob replied.

"The lesson to learn from this is what this does to your position. By *providing* remarkable value you'll receive remarkable value. It turns the powers to your side. Instead of selling, remarkable business software companies turn prospects and customers into buyers. Their ideal customers qualify themselves in because it's clear to them that you a) solve a challenge that allows them to achieve an aspiration high on their agenda (i.e. the value and urgency are clear) and, b) you are demonstrating a shift in value (i.e. you exceed expectations compared to their alternatives). This make them *want* to change.

"As Seth Godin stated in one of his blogs:[2]

> *People don't change (unless they want to). Humans are unique in their*
> *ability to willingly change. We can change our attitude, our*
> *appearance and our skillset. But only when we want to. The hard part,*
> *then, isn't the changing it. It's the wanting it.*

"This is what remarkable business software companies master. They create positive tension and make people *want* their solution ... badly. And this gives them total pricing control as well. They could 10x their price and still make their customers realize it's a bargain and say 'I'd love to buy that. Thank you!'

---

2. https://seths.blog/2019/07/people-dont-change/

"They know it's not about making a dollar, it's about making a difference. It's about creating value, not merely extracting it. As Sachin Dev Duggal,[3] CEO of Engineer.ai, stated:

> It's about finding a way to make it lucrative for everyone. We win if the whole thing wins. Value first, the rest follows from there.

"Olin Hyde,[4] CEO of LeadCrunch, formulated it like this:

> I want to leave the world better than I found it. I want to look back at my life and see that it mattered and that I had an impact. And that's not going to be measured with dollars, that's going to be measured by people.

> I would argue some of the most successful companies in the world have built their businesses entirely based on delivering more value to the customer than what they're charging. They're building something customers can't live without.

Being remarkable makes everything easier

"Fascinating thought, right? Building something your customers can't live without Once this happens, you won't just have a lot of customers. You'll have customers that become your biggest fans. And once a customer turns into a fan . . .

... they will tell others about you
... they become more invested in your success – so the conversation becomes two-way
... they will tell you things they'd generally hide – that will give powerful insights and potentially another pivot point
... they will see more good than bad in your solution
... they will come back for more

[3.] https://www.valueinspiration.com/product-innovation-how-ai-helps-bring-your-idea-to-life/

[4.] https://www.valueinspiration.com/product-innovation-how-you-can-create-your-unfair-competitive-advantage-by-applying-ai-to-lead-targeting/

... they will eagerly try new things out – be the first to take the risk when you release your next big thing

... they will stand up for you when you need help

"It makes everything you do easier, more fun and more rewarding.

"It will give you a boost in confidence.

"It will create space, momentum and freedom to do more good.

"It will make you proud.

"Just take LeadCrunch, the business Olin Hyde leads. Taking a different approach to solve the problem of lead targeting, as well as the way to charge for it, exceeds the expectation of every one of their customers. They now openly state the solution gives them 'an unfair competitive advantage'.

"This makes everything easier for LeadCrunch, thereby experiencing many of the effects described above. The result: impressive growth of 20% per month, and besides that: defensible differentiation that has become the flywheel behind their business to grow even faster and bigger.

"That's the Remarkable Effect.

"When you are clear about the change you seek to make; who it's for and who it's *not* for; and then give them more value than you take – you'll be rewarded for it generously. The more specific and clear you get, the bigger the rewards; or better: the effect. It's the clarity that does the magic. It becomes your compass, your North Star.

"Think about marketing: the moment our ideal customers say 'that's (for) me!' we make a connection that drives action. That's what we want. And even if people say 'that's not for me' that's still good. How many people do you have in your pipeline that haven't come to that conclusion yet, Rob?"

"To be honest, too many, I am afraid," Rob replied.

"That's what I mean," I continued. "That's an incredible waste of time, energy, and money.

"And that brings me to the bigger revelation: the clarity (around your segmentation and positioning) makes everything easier. It will not only be far easier to connect with your ideal customers; it will also be less costly. Here's why: Your ideal customers will find you. What you communicate resonates, is valuable to them, and urgent, i.e. a priority on their agenda. That creates desire.

"It doesn't only help in marketing, however.

"Think about Sales. Your clarity helps prospects qualify in or out (both good) at the earliest stage in the process, and from there it drives both win-rates and deal-value up. Your ideal customers will be prepared to pay a premium instead of asking for the big discount because 'you're all alike'.

"Think about Services. Your clarity drives the most significant chance to turn customers into fans. The fit is clear. They are using your product the way it was meant to be, and this means the cost of service goes down. Besides that, fans spread the word for you, which goes back to your gain in marketing.

"Think about Product Development. Your clarity helps you become extremely resourceful. It makes it easier to decide what goes into the roadmap and what not. Every hour of development investment aids the big idea and makes the value proposition stronger.

"Think about Alignment. Your clarity turns all noses in the same direction. It's clear 'who you are for', and 'who you are not for'. It's clear what's the change you seek to make and what this means for your ideal customers. This allows everyone to stay curious and contribute. This drives accountability and momentum.

"This creates a flywheel that, once in motion, is hard to stop. It will help you become the business software company you've always aspired to run: Remarkable and Impactful."

Crazy ... until it's not

"No one says this is easy. Sure, it's takes hard work and perseverance. It might even feel crazy at first. But it's not impossible. It actually doesn't have to be harder than what you are doing today. It's often even easier just because of the clarity that's created. That's where everything clicks and connects.

"It's very much about starting off on the right mindset. The mindset to do something remarkable. As they say, the devil is in the detail. It's the small things that often make the biggest difference. So, start there. Pick one area of your solution where you deliver the biggest value potential for your ideal customers, and exceed their expectations exactly there.

"Realize that in today's market the riskiest thing to do is to be safe. As such, remarkable business software companies are *playing to win* (and with that I mean: win the heart of their customer, over and over again.) instead of *playing not to lose*. They believe you can't achieve extraordinary results with an ordinary mindset. They say *'we're growing, let's change something'* – thereby playing to the top of their strength. They go by the mantra of giving more than what was asked, and doing more than what was expected. That's how they turn something average into something remarkable.

"I recently heard the phrase: 'The greatest danger for most of us is not that our aim is too high and we miss it, but that it is too low and we reach it.' It's this realization that I see driving many remarkable software companies. They often start off on something that seems crazy ... until it's not.

"They come with the mindset we can change anything – but we are responsible for ourselves, no one else is. Asking 'how did you do this?' is often answered with the simple 'we just started'. It reminds me of Amy Williams,[5] CEO of Good-Loop. This is what she shared with me:

> *I think so many people have ideas, and so few people start. Actually just starting it you're already ten times further ahead than most people who talk about ideas in the pub, and then the ideas never leave the pub. So many entrepreneurs have so many brilliant ideas now, through networking, through investors, through events, and the key thing that threads us all together is the ability to just start, even though it's not perfect. And even though you are still so far away from the vision you have: don't wait for this perfect. Don't wait till the right moment. Don't wait for the stars to align. Just start.*

"Another example that springs to mind is from Vikram Modgil,[6] founder of TheGoodAI.org. TheGoodAI is about getting the ball rolling around the globe to create applications that are well thought through around human centricity, fairness, interpretability, and explainability, privacy and security. This is all about making more people aware, becoming engaged, and taking action. He said:

> *People are beginning to embrace AI, and I noticed that there are some unnecessary, or unconscious biases that come into our businesses. They creep in and if you're not conscious, if you're not alert, they can impact lives. That is something that should not happen.*
>
> *So with that thought, and knowledge and understanding, I wanted to contribute back and I started looking for forums where I could get involved. Unfortunately, I couldn't find anything, which was exactly what I wanted this to become. So I thought: 'Okay, normally everybody is hesitant on starting something like this on their own,*

---

5.   https://www.valueinspiration.com/product-innovation-how-doing-good-and-making-a-big-bottom-line-impact-go-perfectly-hand-in-hand/

6.   https://www.valueinspiration.com/why-increasing-trust-and-removing-bias-is-essential-to-increase-the-impact-of-ai/

> *because it takes a lot of money, a lot of time, a lot of people.' This is what I wanted to challenge. I wanted to start something which was focused on helping one person at a time. And even if two people showed up, that would be a success.*

> *I believe we have to promote action-oriented behaviors. It's more valuable to start something, than do nothing. Start doing something very small and basic. It doesn't need to be grand, it doesn't require a lot of people or money to start something and make an impact.*

"It's the power of 'the start'. As they say 'Rome wasn't built in a day' – it's the same with creating remarkable impact. There will never be an ideal moment. So, starting already puts you in a far better position than any of your peers.

"If something is remarkable, i.e. worth making a remark about, it typically meets three key criteria: It's valuable, it's urgent (i.e. high priority), and expectations are exceeded.

"The trinity of the three aspects creates energy. It's perceived as unusual. And the thing with unusual things is there's no manual; it requires you to offer something in a way that's not been done like that before. And since there's no guarantee you will succeed, it often stops people from doing what they so strongly believe in.

"But not the companies that aim to be remarkable. They go with the question: What has to be true? As Joe Gerber, MD of IDEO CoLab, stated:

> *It's an optimistic question. It's about 'What are the conditions in which this would work? And how do you start to prove to yourself that they either are happening, or not.'*

> *It's not about ignoring the risks, but it's about an optimistic view of what needs to happen in order for this thing to work and how do we work towards that.*

"It's also not about the question 'can it be done?', but far more about the question 'do we have the guts?'

"Just imagine what can be achieved if we can overcome that essence of that very question: 'Do we have the guts?' When everybody is saying 'this is crazy', 'you are crazy' – and you prove them wrong. It's the belief that it's better to invest in something that's going to create a shift in value, rather than be busy with something that's about incremental value at best.

"Dagmar Schuller, CEO and co-founder of audEERING, summed it up nicely when I interviewed her:

Follow your dreams and follow your intentions. Nothing is just black and white. Innovation is a process of failure and a process of learning from experience. But especially it is a process of fighting for what you think you can achieve, and not getting disturbed or somehow demotivated because people just always tell you, that's not what you can do.

With Einstein it wasn't the case that everybody immediately said: 'Okay, of course, relativity theory, you're going to come up with it.' It's not happening that way.

If you really want to innovate, you just have to keep your path. But you have to be flexible enough to allow yourself to look left and right whether you are missing something.

And if you fall down, get up again and move forward.

"And here's another one from Tulika Tripathi, CEO of Snaphunt. This is what she said:

I didn't want to be the person who said: 'I also had this idea a few years ago, but I didn't do it.' So I've done it, because it needed to be made.

Beyond that, I believe you should not settle for second best. You should aim high and then see how to shop around for what's the best way to achieve things beyond what you thought was possible.

"That's the mindset of a remarkable business software company."

"Wow. I am sold, Ton," Rob stated as we stopped by his car. "It was so valuable spending this time with you over the past twenty-four hours. It changed my mindset, and made me realize that what stands between being average and creating remarkable impact is just me – no one else.

"You've opened my eyes to what I need to do to take my business to the next level and deliver upon the true promise our customers are hoping for. I am already envisioning what this will look like in a year from now: We'll be a different company all together – one to be proud to work with and for.

"So *muito obrigado!*' as we say in Portuguese … and one suggestion for you, Ton: you should write a book about this."

What's stopping you?

You and your team likely have developed a solid product already. You know it has great potential. You have the drive and the passion within you – so the only thing that stops your from unleashing the remarkable effect inside your software business is you.

Remember – as Bernadette Jiwa put it beautifully in her book 'Meaningful': 'Success is not what you make – but the difference that it makes in people's life'.

I wrote this book with the purpose to guide you to do exactly that. Yes, it's a journey – and possibly one that never stops simply because everything evolves. This is exactly why the opportunity is so compelling. The moment you embrace the key traits of a remarkable software company everything becomes easier, more rewarding and so much more fun.

So what's stopping you from delivering the change you seek to make? Your ideal customers need it.

Know you are not alone. That's why I established the Remarkable Tribe Program – a community of tech-entrepreneurs-on-a-mission just like you, strengthening each other to shape the software business they've always aspired to run: Remarkable and Impactful.

The program provides you the structure, cadence and support to close the gap on each of the ten traits discussed in this book. It will help you turn ideas into tangible action, i.e., stop dreaming and start doing.

Good luck on making some big waves!

About the Author

Ton Dobbe was born in one of the flattest countries in Europe – The Netherlands and raised as the son of a tulip farmer.

He learned the essence of entrepreneurship from working all his spare time with his father in the famous colored tulip and hyacinth fields. However, he aspired something bigger. So, in 1991, he made the switch to the business software industry. In years that followed, he evolved to being globally responsible for product marketing, product management, analyst relationship, and ultimately chief evangelist for an international enterprise software firm.

Throughout his career, he saw first-hand what remarkable impact can be delivered when product marketing is applied the right way – everything becomes easier. The second life-lesson he learned was about leverage, i.e., creating a 1+1=3 effect. This happens when we align every aspect of our software business (From product development to marketing to sales to services, and support) around the change you seek to make in our market.

Being immersed in business software for so long, he came to believe this there's a need to redefine what we think of as success beyond the metric of size. Here's why: There are thousands of business software companies that are creating significant impact, and doing the most remarkable things. However, they aren't necessarily the ones that are getting the most venture capital funding or growing the fastest.

So he made it his mission to change this. That's why he founded Value Inspiration in September 2017 – to help tech-entrepreneurs-on-a-mission unleash the remarkable effect inside their business and get the recognition they deserve.

By helping as many as possible tech-entrepreneurs achieve this, he believes he can deliver his most significant contribution in making our world a better place.

This encouraged him, amongst others, to start hosting a weekly podcast, with the sole purpose of sharing remarkable stories of the value we can unlock when technology and people blend in the right way. This effort has transpired in now being a globally recognized influencer in marketing, innovation, and disruptive technologies such as AI.

To discuss ways to work with Ton, or to have him speak at your event, visit: https://valueinspiration.com/contact or connect through Linkedin: https://www.linkedin.com/in/tondobbe/

To obtain more ideas and inspiration check out:

The Podcast: https://valueinspiration.com/category/podcast/

The Blog: https://valueinspiration.com/blog

The Tribe: https://movement.valueinspiration.com

Acknowledgements

This book has been a journey – literally. It's an accumulation of experiences, learnings, aha-moments over many years.

I never aspired to write a book. I never thought I actually could do it in the first place. It's fascinating how you can surprise yourself by just starting and then committing. But I am not going to take the credits for that – there are many people in my life that have contributed in their own special way.

First my parents. Without you, obviously, this journey wouldn't have been possible. And although you were not the ones encouraging me to write my book, you taught me that nothing happens by itself, and if you want to succeed in life you have to step up and do the work. So thanks mom and dad for planting that seed when I was young and being there always for me and my family.

To the three people that have been of the biggest importance in my life: My wife Joly and my two boys, Dion and Pascal. I love you – I can't thank you enough for your unconditional support and always being there in your own special way. And Joly, you are my biggest motivator. I admire you for your relentless energy to go beyond yourself to make what we have achieved possible - thereby always putting yourself last in order to take care of us. That's not gone unnoticed. You bring out the remarkable effect in all of three of us.

A big thanks to Chris Ouwinga, who saw something in me in 1990 when I was still a student. Thanks for paving the path to start my career at Unit4, and for being my boss for close to 15 years. Thanks for the opportunity you gave me to learn so much, the freedom to add value to the company in the best possible way, and how you enabled me and my family to start a new chapter of our life in Spain.

Special thanks to Ab van Marion. You've been a mentor to me. Thanks for the special memories from all our travel together and the business sense you've taught me. Will never forget that.

To Predrag Jakovljevic (PJ) for your honest feedback back in 2005 – it sparked a pivotal moment in my career that led to the discoveries and experiences that formed me.

To Judith Rothrock, for being my coach in so many aspects of what Product Marketing is really all about. You showed me the value and made it meaningful to me.

To Susanne Baars, not only for being an inspirator on my podcast, but more for convincing me to write this book. You make the difference.

To Sophie Bennett for being my coach while writing this book. Without your guidance I'd been steerless. Kudo's to you for bringing the best in me in this process.

And last but not least: A big thank you to all the tech-entrepreneurs-on-a-mission who have been a guest on my podcast so far. Thanks for putting in the effort and showing up to share the big ideas behind your company and the lessons you've learned in making the change you seek to make. Without you this book could not exist. Together we know more and together we can achieve more. That inspires me week after week to show up and go the extra mile to help you all create the Remarkable Effect.

Praise for
The Remarkable Effect

"Execution is important, but what if everyone in your market is executing? How do you differentiate? Read this book if you strive to build something truly great – something that truly stands out."

Jonah Lopin, CEO Crayon

"Ton Dobbe's latest book helps to foundationally and strategically improve the way you do business. He takes you on a journey of discovery to find ultimate performance solutions. Ton shares how to make your organization not only impactful but remarkable!"

Dr. Diane Hamilton, CEO of Tonerra and author of Cracking the Curiosity Code

"Great technology and product features are not enough to win today. Brand, storytelling, and category definition is what helps you win today. I believe this book is important because it will educate entrepreneurs on the importance of selling an idea (starting with the why), and not a product."

Tomas Ratia, CEO of Frase.io

"*The Remarkable Effect* bridges the strategic marketing gap and serves two core purposes that can really help technology companies win in competitive market places where today's access to data is easy but deal conversion remains challenging. First, it removes the blinders that stymie executives at both start-ups and aging companies who mean well, but are trapped in myopic 'we breathe our own exhaust' thinking. Second, it provides an earnest and proven checklist of activities to undertake to determine optimum market positioning/actions. Written in a fun, 'let me tell you a story' narrative, *The Remarkable Effect* is a productive read chock full of sound advice. I highly recommend it!"

Judith Rothrock, President of JRocket Marketing

"Ton's three prong unified approach to re-imagining the value proposition, for creating brands that are 'remarkable,' kept me up all night reading his recipe for success in tomorrow's marketplace. Any start-up innovator, with a world-changing insight on solving a Big and Urgent Problem, that is not following these principles is doing a disservice to their perspective customers (and their stakeholders), who are desperately in need of battling for survival in our era of accelerated Creative Destruction."

"After reading your book a world-changing insight flashed before my eyes - I started and could not stop thinking about how my company is helping empower our clients and their stakeholders to play an active role in creating a human-machine combo that is amplifying their intelligence."

Efrem Hoffman, CEO RunningAlpha

CPSIA information can be obtained
at www.ICGtesting.com
Printed in the USA
BVHW041458110220
572028BV00010B/699

9 781789 630978